DECLINE AND DISCONTENT

DECLINE AND DISCONTENT

Communism and the West Today

Paul Hollander

Transaction Publishers
New Brunswick (U.S.A.) and London (U.K.)

Library of Congress Catalog Number: 91-2192
ISBN: 0-88738-434-X
Printed in the United States of America

Library of Congress Cataloging-in-Publication Data

Hollander, Paul, 1932–
    Decline and discontent : communism and the West today / Paul
Hollander.
        p.   cm.
    Includes bibliographical references and index.
    ISBN 0-88738-434-X
    1. Communism—1945– 2. Intellectual life—History—20th century.
3. Political alienation. 4. Ideology. I. Title.
HX44.H55   1991
335.43′09′04—dc20   91-2192
                                                            CIP

Contents

Acknowledgments

I wish to express my thanks to Irving Louis Horowitz whose encouragement played a major part in my putting this volume together. I am also thankful for the continued support of the Earhart Foundation which has generously provided funding for my research expenses. The essay on the Institute for Policy Studies was part of a project on social criticism in the United States in recent times which was supported by the Ethics and Public Policy Center in 1986–87.

Permission to reprint copyrighted material is gratefully acknowledged to the following publications and publishers:

"Hungarian Paradoxes" was published in *Commentary*, in January 1988 under the title "My Hungary and Theirs."

"Politics and Social Problems" is reprinted from A. Jones et al., eds. *Soviet Social Problems*. Boulder: Westview Publishers, 1991.

"Postmortem on Soviet Propaganda?" is a thoroughly revised version of an article entitled "Ideological Noise" published in *Encounter*, December 1989.

"A New Look at the Russian Revolution" is an expanded version of a review of Richard Pipes' *The Russian Revolution* published in the *Wall Street Journal* on 17 October 1990.

A shorter version of "The God That Failed Revisited" was originally published in *The New Criterion* in October 1990 under the title "Losing Faith."

"A Guide to the Deformation of the Sixties" is a longer version of a review of David Horowitz's and Peter Collier's, *Destructive Gener-*

viii **Decline and Discontent**

ation: Second Thoughts About the 60s published in *First Things*, April 1990.

"From Iconoclasm to Conventional Wisdom" is reprinted from *Academic Questions*, Fall 1989.

"George Kennan: Critic of Western Decadence" is reprinted from *Crisis*, September 1989 where it appeared under the title "George Kennan's Long Exile."

"An End to the Pilgrimage?" is the updated preface to the third edition of *Political Pilgrims* published by the University Press of America in 1990.

A somewhat different version of "Resisting the Lessons of History" appeared in the Fall 1990 *Orbis* under the title "The Berlin Wall Collapses, the Adversary Culture Endures."

"Intellectuals in the East and West" is a revised and expanded version of an article which appeared in *Society* in Spring 1990.

The following are published here for the first time:

"Social Problems in Hungary" originated in a paper delivered in April 1988 at a conference at Penn State University on Reform in Hungary.

"Nature of Discontent with Communist System" originated in a paper presented in September 1988 in Washington, D.C. at a conference on Eastern Europe organized by the Washington Institute.

"Institute for Policy Studies: Case Study in Radical Social Criticism" was written during 1987–88.

"Self-Esteem, Role Models and Educational Achievement" was written in 1990.

"Sidney Hook: Critic of the Critics" was delivered at his memorial service in September 1989 in South Wardsboro, Vt.

"New Antiwar Movement, Old Social Criticism" originated in a presentation at a conference on the Gulf War in Washington, D.C. in January 1991 organized by the Standing Committee on Law and National Security of the American Bar Association.

Introduction
The Decline of Communism and the Malaise in the West

I don't support the idea of reburying the remains of people who are guilty of crimes against the Soviet people. I say the dead should be left where they are, including those buried at the Kremlin Wall. But their tombstones should be marked with the words: "Guilty of bloody crimes against the nation and humanity."
—Reader's letter in *Ogonyok*, 1990

. . . we are called to recognize that what some historians have called discovery in reality was an invasion and colonization with legalized occupation, genocide, economic exploitation and a deep level of institutional racism and moral decadence . . . Therefore the Governing Board of the National Council of Churches of Christ in the USA [d]eclares 1992 to be a year of reflection and repentance . . .
—Resolution of the National Council of Churches of Christ in the USA, 1990

There are . . . all around us, signs of social, cultural and moral disintegration. They exist in both the capitalist and socialist camps.
—Barrington Moore Jr., *Authority and Inequality Under Capitalism and Socialism*

This third volume of my shorter writings reflects long-standing preoccupations. They include communist systems, the peculiarities of Western intellectuals, the problems of cultural and social cohesion in

Western societies and the hostility American society inspires among various elite groups at home and abroad. These writings also attest to a new found interest in matters Hungarian; they include two essays about present day Hungary, my native country. This expansion of my interest in Hungarian social conditions has been stimulated by the momentous political changes that have unfolded in Hungary (and the rest of Eastern Europe) in the last few years. Annual visits to Hungary during the second half of the 1980s further nurtured my interest.

Another new topic in this collection represents the revival of an old interest untouched since graduate school (when I wrote a seminar paper on it), namely the disaffection communist systems and movements ultimately inspire in both fellow-travelling intellectuals and the "ordinary people" obliged to live under them. The surfacing of this interest was also prompted by the events of the last few years. Two essays in the first part of the book address different aspects of this subject ("The Nature of Discontent with Communist Systems" and "The God That Failed Revisited").

Of the 17 pieces in the volume (excluding this introduction) 11 have been published before and are reprinted here, several of them with substantial revisions. I did not attempt to bring everything "up to date"; this would have been an impossible task given the state of flux and rate of change in Eastern Europe and the Soviet Union.

The writings in this volume readily divide into two sets of topics. Those addressing developments and conditions in communist (or by now postcommunist) states are grouped in the first part under the heading "The Failure of Communism" which are obvious enough. The second part offers essays that chronicle and probe the symptoms of cultural decline and social conflict in the West, (primarily the United States), the hostility Western values and institutions continue to inspire, the abundant vestiges of the adversarial outlook that survived both the 70s and the 80s—in short what I here call "the malaise in the West." More generally this "malaise" refers to discontents the sources of which are not always clear and are less easily defined than those which caused the collapse of communist systems. In Western societies, foremost the United States, a wide range of highly personal discontents have taken social-political forms and found public expression since the 1960s. Perhaps because this phenomenon is more puzzling and controversial, more of these writings are addressed to it. The volume concludes with an essay that compares and seeks to explain the part played by intellectuals in Western and communist systems respectively in influencing public discourse and the political agenda.

It is an unexpected irony of history that the rapid and unexpected decomposition of communist states gathered force at a time (in the late 1980s) when numerous American analysts and pundits were developing scenarios depicting and predicting the decline of the United States and basking in the public acclaim of those endorsing both their project and the process itself they sought to explain. By contrast, the rapid disintegration of communist states had not been envisioned, least of all by those who were habitually (and often gleefully) preoccupied with the moral and material defects of the United States and capitalism. The predisposition to perceive the West and the United States in particular as decadent was far more readily and eagerly entertained than similar processes in communist systems. While the decline of communism has become a reality, the decline of the West remains a fantasy—wishful for some, fearful for others.

The essays in this volume address, in different ways, these two phenomena of recent times; the historic collapse of communist systems on the one hand and the "malaise in the West" on the other, a phenomenon associated with what I had earlier called "the survival of the adversary culture"[1] in the American context. The nature of this relationship—between the moral failure and political decay of communist systems and the anticipated decline and rejection of Western societies—is a matter of that defies easy definition especially since it is possible to loathe Western societies without admiring any specific communist system.[2]

While there was a time when it appeared that the aversion to Western societies among Westerners was at least in part nurtured by the apparent success and ascendant power of communist systems, the opposite does not seem to hold true: the disintegration and increasingly manifest weaknesses of the remaining communist systems do not seem to undermine the intensely critical, indeed alienated disposition of numerous Western intellectuals and their followers. To be sure this is not an assessment all would accept; Dennis Wrong, for example, strenuously argued, (both in a review of my book dealing with the persistence of these attitudes and in correspondence occasioned by the review) that my concern with the "radical remnants" was "excessive" and "As for 'left domination of major and especially elite universities'" he failed to notice any such thing. He concluded that I was "flogging a dead horse . . . even deader since [I] wrote [the] book . . . "[3] alluding presumably to the changes in Eastern Europe. He thus seemed to share the widespread assumption that the decomposition and discrediting of communist states dealt a decisive blow to residual leftist sympathies and beliefs in the West. By contrast, as I see it, the decline of "existing socialist systems" does indeed present a problem to Western leftists, but it has not led, in most cases, to any sweeping or thoroughgoing reassessment on their part.

The relevance of the decay of communism for political estrangement in the West, and especially the United States, is further explored in the essays entitled "The God That Failed Revisited", "An End to the Pilgrimage?" and "Resisting the Lessons of History."

The relationship between communist and Western societies has been subject to various interpretations and conjectures over time. Not long ago communist systems were seen as deadly enemies of Western societies and values and their seeming strength was juxtaposed to the spreading weakness of the West—its alleged decadence. Throughout the Cold War years the opposite belief was also voiced: if the West stayed strong, communist states will eventually lose steam and grow weaker. Some believed that, for better or worse, the two systems would ultimately converge, as would all modern industrial societies. Among critics of American society and foreign policy it was also popular to maintain that the conflict between the superpowers had no realistic basis; much of it amounted to "mirror imaging" or mutual projection of their shortcomings upon one another.[4] The so-called revisionist historians were inclined to blame the United States for the Cold War and most global tensions. It was also frequently argued that rulers in each system used the other to deflect attention from their domestic social problems and deficiencies. There was however consensus that East and West were interdependent, events and trends in one sphere had an impact on the other.

Western critics of communist systems and those sympathetic toward them (seeking to "understand" them) had one thing in common:

neither anticipated the rapid unravelling that took place in the last few years and culminating in the historic changes of 1989. I was among those who did not expect and found difficult even to conceive of the disintegration of communist systems, especially that of the Soviet Union. It is a great pleasure to acknowledge here such a constricted vision and limited powers of prediction in view of the fact that the wholly unexpected development represents a great gain for hundreds of millions of people and ultimately for mankind as a whole.

The benefits of this unravelling are manifold. There is the restoration of political freedom and self-determination for the former Soviet bloc nations in Eastern Europe; there is the great expansion of political freedom in the Soviet Union itself; there is diminished Soviet assistance to highly repressive systems around the world (such as Cuba and Ethiopia) and probably also less help to assorted anti-Western terrorist groups. More generally "the Soviet model" for industrially underdeveloped nations around the world is now largely a thing of the past. There is also hope, in the postcommunist systems, for improved standards of living and a more productive and efficient economy, but that is less imminent and less easily attainable. At last it is also possible that those around the world who were inspired by the ideas of Marxism-Leninism—the vast majority residing outside communist or formerly communist countries—will finally give up these pursuits and thereby spare themselves and those under their sway a great deal of the disappointment and suffering that the attempted realization of these ideas invariably entailed. This too will be a long process as these ideals will not be lightly abandoned, not without a great deal of reluctance, indeed tenuous resistance.

Understanding these events is no easy matter not even, or especially, for those who have been professionally engaged in the study of communist systems. Social scientists in general should be chastened by this latest historic example of how difficult it is to foresee major political transformations.

As several of the writings included in this volume make clear the social and economic problems and difficulties of these systems have been long-standing and were reasonably well known especially among specialists—but these problems were thought to be compatible with the survival, even stability of communist states. The latter seemed highly successful in maintaining themselves in power without popular consent, indeed in spite of the massive disaffection and resentment of their peoples. Communist governments greatly improved ways of staying in power that rested on a combination of coercion, propaganda, control over the economy, a suitably docile population, and an endlessly proclaimed sense of legitimacy.

The Soviet Union played a crucial role in spreading or propping up similar systems and in offering what used to be called fraternal aid not only to its East European dependencies but even to far-flung allies and outposts like Cuba, Nicaragua, North Korea, and Vietnam as well as several similarly inclined governments in Africa.

The unravelling examined here can certainly be traced to a greatly diminished Soviet ability to maintain this empire through a combination of military, economic, and political ties and pressures. But we know little about the specific stages and assessments through which Soviet leaders reached the conclusion that it no longer mattered if the countries of Eastern Europe achieved self-determination, or that they were incapable of keeping these countries in the Soviet orbit, or that the pluralization of Soviet political and public life itself was permissible, or could no longer be obstructed, or that the Soviet economy had to be rescued through privatization.

The rapid decline of communism and the associated changes in what used to be the Soviet sphere provided many surprises. The most unexpected development was the sudden demoralization and irresoluteness of formerly ruthless and calculating leaders, apparently resigned to the loss or curtailment of their power. But equally striking was the emergence of autonomous social movements and organizations in both Eastern Europe and the Soviet Union out of the ranks of what were thought to be docile, atomized, and intimidated masses. Nor was the determination and intensity expected with which the newly liberated activists and critics in these countries embarked on ferreting out, exposing, and discrediting the vast amount of falsehood that officialdom so diligently constructed over decades. Even in the Soviet Union the campaign of delegitimation has exceeded the wildest expectations (of even those who had few illusions about the popular support the authorities enjoyed), as Soviet authors began to expose the vast gaps separating theory from practice, promise from reality. Conversing with an American journalist, a Soviet history teacher (from the high school Mrs. Gorbachev had attended) observed: "Everybody has to believe in something. . . . In your country you believe in God. In ours we had some kind of faith in a bright future. Now we have lost this belief and found nothing to replace it."[5]

From these changes in outlook and the opportunity for free expression we can now learn more about the purges and other misdeeds of the Soviet authorities from Soviet sources than from American "revisionist" historians who even in recent years have sought to minimize the murderous and repressive features of the system under Stalin.[6] It is not hard to understand why Soviet readers prefer such Western studies of Soviet history as have been written by Robert Conquest and Richard Pipes (sometimes dismissed by their Western colleagues as "cold warriors" or obsessed anticommunists) than those originating with Western closet Leninists and Marxists, admirers of rapid industrialization from a distance, and believers in forces of history no more accountable moral judgment than earthquakes.

New revelations also came from the East regarding the specifics of social and economic problems. As some of the following essays will show, contrary to Western preconceptions these phenomena—crime, corruption, pollution, family decay, alcoholism—have been widespread and deeply rooted in communist societies. It is also clear by now that perhaps the most resounding failure of these systems has been the creation of the "new Soviet man" or "new socialist man." Indeed alienation itself, for a long time defined as the exclusive malaise of capitalist societies, has not only emerged but its existence is publicly acknowledged and widely discussed. At a roundtable discussion on "alienation under socialism" it was noted

> It is a secret to no one that alienation has penetrated into all spheres of socialist society, into the economy, politics and culture, and has affected practically all vital centers and social institutions. It has imposed and continues to impose an indelible stamp on interpersonal relations and on everyday realities . . .[7]

How far the Soviet Union has gone in abandoning its legitimating ideology and fantasies of creating a new man may be gauged by recalling some of the official aspirations conveyed in the 1961 Program of the Soviet Communist Party and juxtaposing them with recent comments of Solzhenitsyn published in *Komsomolskaya Pravda*. It may be recalled that the time when this Program was written was officially defined as the period of transition to communism, when "the moral principles of society become increasingly important; the sphere of action of the moral factor expands and the importance of the administrative control of human relations diminishes accordingly." The emerging "new man . . . will combine harmoniously spiritual wealth, moral purity and a perfect physique."

The "moral code of the builder of communism," that is to say, of the then living Soviet people was supposed comprise these principles:

Conscientious labor for the good of society. . . .
Concern . . . for the preservation of public wealth.
A high sense of public duty. . . .
Collectivism and comradely mutual assistance. . . .
Humane relations and mutual respect between individuals—man is to man a friend, a comrade and a brother.
Honesty and truthfulness, moral purity and modesty. . . .
An uncompromising attitude to injustice, parasitism, dishonesty, careerism and money-grubbing.[8]

In the fall of 1990 Solzhenistsyn wrote in *Komsomolskaya Pravda*:

The death knell has sounded for Communism. . . . Who of us does not know our troubles, covered as they are with mendacious statistics? Having been dragging in search of the blind and malicious Marxist-Leninist utopia for 70 years, we put a full third of our population upon the executioner's block during the incompetently conducted, self-annihilating "patriotic war". . . . We have driven away the very instinct for growing wheat for our bread. . . . We have spoiled . . . our cities, poisoned our rivers. . . . We have exhausted our women by forcing them to do laborious work. . . . Lawlessness reigns over all depths of the country. And we cling only to one thing: not to be deprived of stupefying drunkenness. . . . We have no resources for the provinces, neither economic nor spiritual. We have no resources for the Empire. . . . Let it fall from our shoulders. . . .

For three-fourths of this century we got so poor and tired and lost all hope that many are now helpless and resigned. . . . For half century no one has found any reward for work. . . .

All this nomenklatura bureaucracy, millions of the parasites with their grand salaries, privileges and special shops—we must put an end to feeding them. . .
No road for the people for the most urgent things will ever be open . . . unless the Communist-Leninist party . . . is completely separated from any influence on economic and state life, completely gives up control over us or any aspect of our lives.[9]

It is safe to say that the transition to communism will be even longer than the least optimistic of Marxist-Leninist ideologues had anticipated.

II

As the Soviet Union continues its slide into decay and other communist states are being transformed into multiparty systems all those in the West who looked to these states with some degree of hope and approval and sympathized with the Soviet Union—if only as a counterweight to what they saw as the imperialism of the United States— are under pressure to undertake a reassessment of some kind. As Robert Heilbroner put it: "the collapse of the planned economies has forced us to rethink the meaning of socialism. As a semireligious vision of a transformed humanity, it has been dealt devastating blows in the twentieth century. As a blueprint for a rationally planned society, it is in tatters."[10]

As will be shown below, the "rethinking" suggested and undertaken by Heilbroner has not been widely followed by most supporters of socialist systems and socialist ideals. More typically they have undertaken arduous efforts to salvage the ideals by dissociating them from the practices of the now defunct or collapsing systems. As the existing socialist alternatives to democratic capitalism, or Western democracy fade, the pursuit of such alternatives is becoming increasingly theoretical and imaginary. Those who are no longer openly supportive of any existing socialist system remain nonetheless attached to an anti-Western, anti-capitalist posture.

Some readers may take exception to my linking the critiques of the United States or American society to the broader rejection of Western social systems and cultural values. I have linked these attitudes because they strike me as inseparable. The United States has come to represent, in the eyes of the social critics discussed here, the most malign attributes of Western culture and capitalism in its most unrestrained, predatory form; it is seen as the standard-bearer of all the false values, flawed institutional practices, corruptions and injustices they find intolerable in the modern world. Because of its economic and military power, the United States is (correctly) perceived as the linchpin of Western societies. For all these reasons anti-Western, anticapitalist and anti-American attitudes form a triad difficult to separate.]

[The views expressed in a letter to the editor of the *New York Times* are typical of the mindset of those who refuse to find any vindication for American and Western values and forms of social organization in the collapse of communism: "Before rushing to celebrate the victory and vindication of the 'American experiment,' American should take a closer look at their own society." That society, the writer noted, was one in which "millions are consigned to the hopelessness of poverty, homelessness, drugs and crime. The idealistic mood in those countries [of Eastern Europe] would be appalled at the high level of toleration of outrageous suffering in this 'free and democratic' nation."[11]

The entrenched nature of such anti-Western attitudes are in sharp contrast to the disposition of citizens under communist systems who became immunized through experience against what Jean-François Revel once called "the totalitarian temptation." The remarks of the Czech journalist who visited Nicaragua during the 1990 elections are illuminating:

> In Czechoslovakia, where I live, the kind of sloganeering and rhetoric I heard— not from the Sandinistas but their *internacionalista* supporters—was, until recently, background noise of our lives. The difference is that at home nobody believed in such stuff, not the captive audience and not the speakers either. Or at least I am too young to remember such a time. For that you have to go back to the late forties and early fifties. I had to come all the way to Managua to find out what it was like. . . . In Managua, just a couple of months after my country awoke from the totalitarian nightmare, I got a whiff of the atmosphere of its beginning, as exhaled by the Sandinistas of the Western world.[12]

Several ways of dealing with the collapse of Nicaragua and other communist systems emerged among adversarial groups and individuals. One was to use these developments as new ways to discredit the United States and capitalism. They resourcefully revived and reinvigorated the moral equivalence thesis adding a new twist; it now gives credit to the Soviet Union for progress and contrasts this to the stubborn attachment of the United States to its old and bad ways. For instance in the words of the executive director of the Traprock Peace Center in Massachusetts (associated with the American Friends Service Committee) "Democracy now seems to be making triumphal advances everywhere except in the United States."[13]

More often we are reminded that the evils of communism are irrelevant to the evils and corruption of capitalism which continue to dominate the United States and much of the world; or that the problems communist systems now face barely differ from those of capitalist countries. Another proposition often put forward is that communist systems now unravelling had nothing to do with Marxism hence their collapse does not discredit the theory; that a renewal of Marxism is not only possible but imminent now that the systems that brought discredit upon it no longer exist.

Other critics of capitalism and the United States (or Western culture) act as if nothing had happened in the last few years; they resolutely avert their eyes from these historic transformations preferring to focus their attention on domestic matters. The latter may include advocating repentance for the misdeeds of Columbus (as did the National Council of Churches of Christ, an old hand at wallowing in collective guilt), boycotting Salvadorian coffee beans, "deconstructing" literature (or the legal system), championing reverse discrimination, and revising the curriculum of schools and colleges in pursuit of a clearly articulated political and social-critical agenda.

While the decline and newly confirmed unpopularity of communist systems reduced their appeals for those previously supportive of them, a lingering sympathy survived. As Dennis Wrong observed, "The uncertain feeling from some on the left [regarding the disintegration of communism–P.H.] . . . reflects . . . a feeling that communism, for all its faults and failures, was at least an economic system utterly different from capitalism.[14] Among the "good causes" left, the Marxist-Leninist guerrillas in El Salvador retained the support of their American friends (including preeminently the churches) who continue to champion them. This support in all probability contributed in 1990 to the halving of American aid to the government of that country, in addition to congressional revulsion over the killing of Jesuit priests a year earlier.

Also symptomatic of such lingering sympathies has been the difficulty two emigré Cuban film makers experienced in getting National Public Television to show their documentary ("Nobody Listened") about human rights abuses in Cuba. While there is no indication that

Public Television officials were ever concerned with the "controversial" or one-sided nature of documentaries about human rights abuses in Guatemala or South Africa, they decided that a documentary about Cuban repression was controversial and hence could only be shown if paired, for balance, with a sycophantic presentation of Castro and Cuba entitled "The Uncompromising Revolution" made by Saul Landau[15] perhaps the most dedicated and durable apologist for Castro and his regime in the United States.

Throughout the late 1980s South Africa continued to hold the attention of adversarial groups especially on campuses as demands for divestment and boycotts were put forward with monotonous regularity regardless of their actual contribution to either the political liberation or material welfare of the black population in South Africa. Protest against the policies of the South African authorities was often combined with a rejection of corporate power and more generally capitalism. Upon closer inspection it was often hard to separate these protests from a more general antiestablishmentarianism. The attitude of a student protestor who in 1987 acknowledged that to him "South Africa is just a convenient issue that helps to expose the system . . . of corporate capitalism" reverberated in the remark of a New York real estate broker who in 1990 during the Mandela visit admitted that "it is not that South Africa per se interests me . . . I am just interested in so-called good causes.[16] It is one of the few predictions here made that if the African National Congress were to succeed in gaining power South Africa would become the new magnet for political pilgrims and tourists in the West.

III

It is possible and important to separate the hostile social criticism emanating in an uninterrupted stream from the adversary culture from a reasoned stocktaking of the problems of the West and the United States in particular. Certainly the decomposition of the communist states does not mean that all is well in the United States. While capitalism remains a highly productive and viable economic system, and while political pluralism is quite sturdy and most citizens in Western countries have no desire for any fundamental social-political transformation, there is a variety of phenomena in the West and especially in the United States that are problematic. Despite the moral and material superiority of Western over communist systems there are phenomena in the West that bring to mind words like decay and decadence.

Several approaches to this topic may be charted. The most popular notions of decadence in the United States focus on economic matters such as budget deficits, declining gross national product and competitiveness in international markets, loss of workmanship, and what is often described as the "crumbling infrastructure."

The second approach stresses moral decay associated with disintegration of the family, the growth of welfare dependency, drug addiction, violent crime, homelessness, the jostling of interest groups for advantages unconcerned with public good. Many would agree with a student who wrote in the *Harvard Crimson* that "Historians tell us that not one single empire in world history was ever destroyed by invading armies or economic forces but rather were decayed and rotted from the inside out, causing the society . . . to collapse in anarchy."[17]

Not infrequently the first and second approaches are combined as in the lament of Richard Goodwin according to whom America

is being destroyed, not only by its public leadership, but by all those able to influence the course of events. . . . We must all share responsibility for the incredible waste and extravagance, the rampant greed and disregard for longterm consequence. . . . The rot at the foundation is visible and spreading. We continue to accumulate an already unmanageable debt; our industries have become less productive and competitive. . . . More than 40 million citizens are now below the . . . poverty level . . . [there is] the accelerating cycle of waste and decline. . . . In a little more than a decade we have betrayed the hope of centuries . . . [the latter presumably a reference to the Reagan presidencies–P.H.][18]

A third view of decadence favored here (not necessarily to the exclusion of others) focuses on the persistence of estrangement or alienation, embittered social criticism, loss of collective self-esteem among elite groups, a spreading aversion to risk-taking, decline of educational and intellectual standards, the growth of "taboo topics" in teaching and academic research, and the newly intensifying hostility to Western culture that combines with the attributions of racism, sexism, ethnocentrism, and other evils supposedly peculiar to American society.

It would be hard to find anything more revealing of the depth and intensity of the estrangement here discussed than the hostility of the highly educated, of the cultural elite, toward their own culture, a development which coincided during the 1970s and 80s with the progressive politicization of academic life. During these years an extraordinary venom toward Western cultural traditions and products has surfaced—whether in the framework of the theories of "deconstruction," or in the educational programs advocating "multicultural" or "Afrocentric" studies or "cultural diversity," in the sneering at "Eurocentrism." Each of these terms has become a codeword for finding new ways to denigrate Western values and ideas. Nothing is further from these educational innovations than the spirit of genuine diversity as all these programs attack Western culture in singularly stereotyped and standardized ways. An American student of literature wrote:

> Ours is a strange time, but it has in it . . . few things stranger than the violence and even hatred with which the old literature was deconstructed by those who earn their living teaching and writing about it . . . at the moment, in 1990, the most popular subjects of criticism and undergraduate and graduate courses are still those that demonstrate how meaningless, or paradoxically, how wicked and antiprogressive, the old literature has been . . . how badly it has treated those who are not white, how regularly it has voiced an aristocratic jackbooted ethos or propagandized for a brutally materialistic capitalism. . . . Literature has been seen as a . . . place at which to get at and discredit capitalist ideology, to advance Third World, minority, and feminist causes.[19]

While one may argue as to how consequential in the larger scheme of things are trends in literary criticism and the policies of English departments, the attitudes they reveal provide a good measure of the hostility the prevailing social order and its established values inspire. The impassioned attacks on Western culture or civilization and the authors and works associated with them reflect an alienation far more profound than one that is inspired by observable social injustices and transient political causes. These attitudes bespeak a genuine radicalism that addresses fundamentals, that does indeed seek to go to the roots of Western social order and thought. Not even classical music has been immune from these attacks. Under the guise of "cultural diversity" the battle against making any distinction has been joined, (or rather revived from the 1960s) and classical music was among its many targets; it was after all, "elitist" and for the most part, created by dead white males of Europe. Edward Rothstein, the music critic wrote: "The aim is to eliminate any distinction between or within musics other than on grounds of their origin. Each culture has its music; and so each culture has an equal right to attention and money for the presentation of its music. . . . The objective is . . . to achieve 'equity'. . . . In the view of the 'multiculturalists' music . . . functions as a reinforcement of group identity." He also noted that "an animus against the West" combined with "political energies born of resentment and alienation"[20] drive the so-called multiculturalist impulse which has little to do either with culture or diversity.

Eugene Genovese has noted the determination among these culture critics to show "that Christianity and Western civilization indulged in horrors that no other religions and civilizations would . . . have dreamed of. . . . Christianity and the West stand condemned as the great enemy of the world's peoples, whose traditions ostensibly have been more freedom-loving and less ethnocentric." He pointed out that

> those who are today attacking the canon [i.e., traditional humanistic curriculum] have no interest in reforming it to include the great black, female and other voices . . . excluded from it . . . they are not so much attacking Western Civilization courses as Western civilization. . . . It appears that anything that comes with a cri de coeur for the poor, the oppressed, and the downtrodden passes muster and may expect to be greeted with hosannas, and never mind how absurd the arguments and how blundering the scholarship.[21]

The last point is resoundingly confirmed by the respectful treatment accorded on the part of academic intellectuals and educational experts to such curricular innovations as "Afrocentric" studies and more generally the spreading movement to introduce "multicultural" education in public school systems. It is the largely uncritical acceptance of ideas that in other contexts would be critically scrutinized, resisted, and finally rejected that is significant for a discussion of decadence in our cultural life.

It is also relevant for the trends here noted that while on most major campuses campaigns are under way to expose and attack "stereotypes," anti-white, anti-male, anti-European attitudes and stereotypes proliferate and are deeply embedded in the new "multicultural" programs. For example it was noted that the report (*The Curriculum of Inclusion: Report of the Task Force on Minorities*, 1989) produced in New York State in support of a new, "multicultural" curriculum is consistently Europhobic. It repeatedly expresses negative judgments on "European Americans" and on everything Western and European. All people with white skin are referred to as "Anglo-Saxons" and "WASPS." Europe, says the Report, is uniquely responsible for producing aggressive individuals who "were ready to discover, invade and conquer foreign land because of greed, racism and national egoism." All white people are held collectively guilty for the historical crimes of slavery and racism. There is no mention of "Anglo-Saxons" who opposed slavery and racism.[22]

These efforts to denigrate Western culture and glorify the non-Western have an invidious, compensatory strain that reminds the historically aware reader of the corresponding, discredited policies of Nazi Germany and the Soviet Union (under Stalin) that were designed to bolster national pride by an appeal to a largely imaginary past and its largely imaginary glories. Thus it came about that children in the Soviet Union were taught that virtually every important scientific discovery was made by a Russian, and German children learned about the uniquely distinctive and innately superior qualities of Germans. In a similar spirit "particularists [who champion the new ethnic studies in the United States—P.H.] reject any accommodation among groups, any interactions that blur the lines between them. The brand of history that they espouse is one in which everyone is either a descendant of victims or oppressors. By doing so, ancient hatreds are fanned and recreated in each new generation."[23] Shelby Steele also observed,

> This elevation of difference undermines the communal impulse by making each group foreign and inaccessible to others . . . in the process each group mythologizes and mystifies its difference, puts it beyond the full comprehension of outsiders. Difference becomes an inaccessible preciousness toward which outsiders are expected to be simply and uncomprehendingly reverential.[24]

A recent report on what was called "inspirational Black history" revealed that

> reaching for ways to inspire black students, a growing number of educators are trying to tell them about their own ancestors, bringing tales of African kings and little known black inventors, scientists and artists into the classroom. . . .
>
> [In] one school system using an Afrocentric approach [in Indianapolis] . . . Pat A. Brown told a high school class that African people were "the first to show genius in art and architecture." . . . [she] also said Africans had sailed to the

Americas 2000 years before "anyone even heard of Columbus." "And," she said, "it was a black man who had drawn up the plans for Bell's telephone."

"I can go on and on to tell you that Africans . . . did more than most." Ms. Brown concluded. . . . Addressing a class . . . recently Ms. Brown pointed out that Africa was three times the size of the United States and said that black Egyptians had developed the first system of writing.[25]

Ms. Brown now in charge of these innovations in the Indianapolis school system is a former elementary school teacher who reportedly buttressed her arguments about the genius of Africans with her own slides of her trip to Egypt that testified to the existence of modern hotels.

According to a text popular among advocates of Afrocentric studies entitled *What They Never Told You in History Class*, "Moses, Jesus, Buddha, Mohammed and Vishnu were Africans; . . . the first Indians, Chinese, Hebrews, Greeks, Romans, Britains and Americans were Africans; . . . the first mathematicians, scientists, astronomers and physicians were Africans."[26]

Given the contrast between these portrayals of a distant past rich in accomplishments and the lack of similar, observable accomplishments of African nations in more recent times, black students in the United States can only conclude (and they are clearly encouraged to do so in these programs) that present day problems are the result of white cunning, aggression, and conspiracy, and that past accomplishments were deliberately obliterated as in the case of the (supposedly) black Egyptians whose noses were chiseled off (from ancient statues) by white racist archeologists "so that future generations would not see the typically African facial characteristics."[27] This message of white mischief also underlies the arguments for preferential policies in the United States and elsewhere postulating that the difficulties and disadvantages of the intended beneficiaries of these policies are caused entirely by the ill-will of their oppressors. But as Thomas Sowell noted, "A sense of group grievance is seldom a prelude to just treatment of others. More often it heralds a 'Now it's our turn' attitude. No one felt or promoted a sense of being historically aggrieved more than Adolf Hitler."[28]

We have come full circle from the times when the public and students in particular were ceaselessly warned about the dangers and evils of ethnocentrism, to the sanctioning, praising, and encouraging of a new, virulent ethnocentrism on the part of formerly oppressed groups. The new exaltation of such ethnic pride is currently defined as a celebration of ethnic diversity.

These programs of study are more than outlets for minority resentment or demagogic scapegoating. They are invariably legitimated by the claim that exposing minorities and especially blacks to the past achievements of their group will enhance individual self-esteem which in turn will improve academic performance.

The academic policies and programs here discussed are also supported by vintage sixties notions of "relevance" (without necessarily using that word) which usually denotes whatever students find interesting and part of their life. It is an idea difficult to reconcile with education as a process of broadening interest, opening new horizons, adding new knowledge, and making students aware of matters outside the narrow limits of their personal life and experience. A supporter of such minority studies wrote: "Along with demographic we need intellectual affirmative action . . . minority students' performance is generally improved in proportion to a course's inclusion of minority texts or concerns. Nor is this purely an ethnic matter: precisely the same breakdown would occur along gender of class lines."[29] Is geology or physics a minority concern? Are women expected to excel in women's studies and the offspring of workers in the study of working-class life? That is exactly the idea: students will do better when they study themselves or their group—however defined—along ethnic, gender or class lines. It is also averred—compounding the anti-intellectual thrust of this school of thought—that students will do especially well when taught by members of their subgroup.

I argue in one of the essays below ("Self-esteem and Education") that there is little evidence to show *either* that individual self-esteem can be raised by these methods *or* that higher self-esteem necessarily translates into better academic performance, especially since self-esteem is often based on nonacademic, nonintellectual criteria. As Diane Ravitch wrote "knowing about the travails and triumphs of one's forebears does not necessarily translate into either self-esteem or personal accomplishment."[30] More likely than either of these outcomes the educational policies sketched above have a good chance of creating or increasing a self-righteous resentment and legitimating reluctance to take responsibility for one's life in a world allegedly controlled by malevolent and powerful conspiratorial forces.

The contrast between the advocacy of this new, approved ethnocentrism and the past repudiation of ethnocentrism is paralleled by the contrast between past avowals of nondiscrimination and the current institutionalized endorsement of preferential policies, or reverse discrimination also known as affirmative action that evolved over the past quarter century. There is also an all too plausible connection between the rise and entrenchment of these policies and the notion of decline or decadence.

In the first place, it may be argued that when elite groups of a society (intellectuals, educators, politicians, lawyers) embrace a policy that is, to say the least, questionable, yet cannot be subjected to public criticism or evaluation, the larger society is poorly served. When the adoption of these policies proceeds without meaningful debate and when the elites in question refuse to confront information that casts serious doubt on the efficacy of these policies social justice and rationality are also threatened.

These programs (of preferential treatment) may also be seen as symptomatic of decay since they weaken academic and intellectual standards by lowering requirements for selected groups. These policies also weaken the fabric of society and its political legitimacy as they create new grievances among those at whose expense preferential treatment is dispensed (for example, students with higher scores who are refused admission to a particular college, workers with more seniority who do not get promoted) and may contribute to the demoralization of the work force. These policies certainly increase levels of intergroup hostility.

Thomas Sowell summed up the problematic features of preferential policies:

1. Preferential policies, even when explicitly . . . defined as "temporary," have tended not only to persist but expand in scope, either embracing more groups or spreading to wider realms of the same groups, or both. . . .
2. The benefits [of preferential treatment] have usually gone disproportionately to those members already more fortunate.
3. Group polarization has tended to increase in the wake of preferential programs . . . in ways ranging from political backlash to mob violence . . .

4. Fraudulent claims of belonging to the designated beneficiary groups have been widespread.[31]

It is also noteworthy that while there has for decades existed a veritable industry called "evaluation research" devoted to assessing the results of various federally funded programs there have been no efforts made to find out about the intended and unintended consequences of the wide variety of affirmative action programs.[32]

The suspension of common sense and the deterioration of reasoned public discourse is also reflected in the generally unchallenged belief (bolstered by both legislation and court rulings) that the preferential policies are justified by the persistence of discrimination *as revealed in statistical disparities*. Sowell wrote:

> Statistical disparities between groups are often the sole evidence cited as proof of discrimination. Implicit in this approach is the assumption that disparities in excess of those attributable to random chance can be regarded as *prima facie* evidence of adverse actions by individuals, institutions, or "society" against the group for whom compensatory preferences are sought. . . . To know how one group's employment, education or other pattern differs statistically from another's is usually easy. What is difficult to know are the many variables determining the interest, skill and performance of those individuals from various groups who are being considered for particular jobs, roles. . . . What is virtually impossible to know are the patterns that would exist in a non-discriminatory world.[33]

Sowell concludes that it is arbitrary and unfounded to assume that groups would be evenly "represented" (in various hierarchies, institutions, positions of power) in the absence of discrimination—yet this is precisely the assumption American legislators, judges, educators, and intellectuals have adopted and has become conventional wisdom rarely challenged by those who do not wish to risk being accused of racist bigotry.

The irrationality of the attitudes and policies here examined is further reflected, in Sowell's view, In "the determined refusal to examine the characteristics of a group nominated for preferences" and in "the setting of numerical 'goals' *without the slightest mention* of the size of the pool of qualified people from whom these goals are to be met."[34]

Although routinely denied, these policies and practices have had considerable bearing on standards. "The sense of entitlement—independent of skills or performance" is one result. The growth of disincentives for both the preferred and those not preferred is another. Preferential admission in various educational institutions in turn often leads to "affirmative grading" that evolves out of the desire to reduce attrition among groups admitted under lowered admission standards. Tom Hayden proposed legislation in California to assure not only the admission of minority groups in prescribed proportions but also their retention and graduation![35] Finally, there is the built-in contradiction between admitting students under lowered standards and the goal of raising the level of their performance later on. Again as Sowell put it, "Forcing students to meet higher standards . . . will be . . . all the more difficult if the students know that these standards are unnecessary for them to reach whatever educational or employment goals they have, or even to be promoted to the next grade."[36]

The relationship between such attempts to remedy racism and the undermining of standards was also forcefully demonstrated at a conference entitled "From the Eurocentric University to the Multicultural University" held in Oakland, California in 1989. One of the speakers, Charles Willie (professor of education at Harvard), "began by saying that calls for increased excellence in American colleges and universities discriminate against minorities since the criterion of excellence works to exclude minorities from the university. No matter whether these tests are biased or not, Willie argued, they should still be eliminated because they 'terrorize' minority students."[37] These sentiments evidently came to inform the admissions policies of the University of California at Berkeley (among others) providing further proof of the palpable connection between preferential policies and lowered standards. Thus in

1987 out of 3242 applications for admission to the freshmen class, only 16 Blacks and 32 Hispanics satisfied the set of academic requirements normally required . . . [nonetheless] the 1987 freshmen class [in the words of a Berkeley university representative] . . . is wonderfully diverse [and] . . . closely reflects the actual distribution of California high school graduates: 2% American Indian, 25% Asian, 12% black, 17% Hispanic, 40% white . . . [38]

Obviously such ethnic proportionality was achieved by lowering the standards of admission for blacks and Hispanics who could otherwise not been represented in the percentage proportions described above.

It bears repeating that the problems of race, discrimination, and the remedies devised to eliminate them not only have led to unintended consequences for members of the preferred groups but also for American society as a whole and especially for prevailing educational standards and intellectual discourse. The rhetoric about race, race relations, and affirmative action has produced an unprecedented amount of public piety and unctuousness and has institutionalized a new type of hypocrisy that has made it virtually impossible to discuss these matters honestly in public. Stanley Crouch, another courageous black intellectual observed that "not only black America but this nation itself [was sent] into an intellectual tailspin on the subjects of race . . . culture . . . heritage. Where there was not outright foolishness, there was a mongering of the maudlin and a base opportunism."[39] Among the unforeseen results of this climate of opinion and the lack of forthrightness it entails has been the lack of effective programs that might help those who truly need it. As Willard Gaylin wrote:

> The black community . . . has been as badly served by its friends as by its enemies. If the black family was falling apart, rather than examine what this hemorrhage might mean to the future . . . there were those in the intellectual community prepared to romanticize the patterns of absent fathers and teenage mothers as "alternative family structures"; and in the same way the concept of "black speech" romanticized the lack of education that enslaved large segments of the black population.[40]

Another by-product of these developments has been the transformation, indeed the loss of meaning of the concept of racism. While it used to denote an a priori hostility or disrespect toward those belonging to particular racial or ethnic groups regardless of their individual character or performance, it has become a term of political abuse, a means of ultimate denigration designed to silence and intimidate those who disagree with preferential policies or express criticism *on any ground* of individuals belonging to the protected minorities. Thus it has become routine to accuse of racism anybody who would fail to hire, admit, or promote on any ground, or acquit (when accused in court) members of these minorities, or who may find fault with their performance on any ground, in any role-civic, familial, occupational, or intellectual.

Correspondingly, tests or examinations where minorities do not perform well are reflexively dismissed as racist or culturally biased. Likewise, "any suggestion that members of a formerly despised and mistreated group may be capable of wrongdoing is punished with utmost severity."[41]

Nowhere are the new conceptions of race and racism more pronounced than on the campuses and nowhere have they been given more unqualified support. An academic observer of these trends wrote:

> American universities are aflame with race fever. Official committees on "racism and cultural diversity," departmental commissioners of moral sanitation, and free-lance vigilantes are in a state of high alert for signs (real or alleged) of "racism." Their Argus-eyes maintain unrelaxing surveillance of statistical charts documenting failure to meet racial quotas in hiring and enrollment, of verbal insults by "white" students against "people of color," and of classroom remarks by professors imprudent enough either to risk generalization about a group *or* to declare that generalizations about groups tell us nothing about individuals.[42]

Omitted from this listing of those professionally concerned with these matters have been the "affirmative action officers" (whose livelihood depends on finding discrimination) employed at all sizable colleges and universities, (and at other institutions as well); nor was mention made of "consultants on oppression/liberation issues" a new calling that apparently also emerged of late in response to new demands.[43]

It is likely that the surging preoccupation with racism originates not so much in the actual increase of what can legitimately be called racism[44] but in a displacement of the social-critical impulse and energy from areas where it can no longer be deployed with good effect. Edward Alexander noted that "with a little job retraining, yesterday's economic determinist becomes today's race (and 'gender') determinist."[45] In other words, racism has become *the* key critique of contemporary American society and culture, perhaps in part because those accused of it so readily acquiesce in these charges, because members of elite groups and the educated classes have become imbued with a sense of guilt for the sins of their ancestors. Indeed the less guilty people or institutions are of any discernible racism the more eagerly they accept these charges, as do the administrators and faculties of superliberal elite colleges which have gone to great length to dispense preferential treatment only to be accused of racism at every turn.

Clustered around the critiques of racism—and in some ways modelled on it—are attributions and critiques of sexism, heterosexism, classism, elitism, and homophobia.

It is of interest to note in the evolution of these critiques a trend toward concern with matters less clearly political, more of life-style or sexual preference, and a concern with details of more intimate personal interaction. In such respects much of the new social criticism is quite unlike the social critiques of the past, which were anchored in more clear cut and rigorous institutional analysis and focused on matters unambiguously political or economic. To be sure, attempts to expand the notion of "political" (as in the "politics of housework" and "the political economy of . . . " innumerable matters) have been with us since the 1960s, resulting from the effort to link the personal to the political and to hold the social system responsible for an unusually wide range of personal afflictions and grievances. The arresting features of the latest critiques is their vagueness and the opportunities this vagueness provides for institutionalized hysteria and witch-hunting. These elusive and often hard to document charges culminate in the attributions of "insensitivity" (and "harassment") which are open to the most varied interpretations and can mean almost anything an individual wants them to mean. The peculiarity of this charge is brought into sharper focus if one tries to imagine it being used by any seasoned social critic or representative of a political or revolutionary movement. It is a concept that more clearly belongs to the relationship of parents and children, patients and therapists, or lovers; it is also one that highlights the narcissistic, self-indulgent quality of some of these critiques. The complaint about insensitivity conjures up touchy, thin-skinned individuals ready to take offense when their unique needs and vulnerabilities—not readily revealed to casual observation—are threatened. Insensitivity in its current, politicised usage may also be defined as a version of racism (or sexism etc.) when such attitudes or behavior are difficult to substantiate or observe hence the recourse to highly subjective feelings as the only proof of injury or injustice.

The new level of receptivity to charges of racism was memorably exemplified in the reaction of some white intellectuals and public fig-

ures to the Tawana Brawley case in 1988. Brawley was a black teen-
ager who, with the apparent assistance of the "Reverend" Al
Sharpton and lawyers Alton Maddox Jr. and C. Vernon Mason concocted a lurid story of having been raped and abused by a group of
white men. It was a fable that preoccupied the law enforcement agencies of New York State for almost a year. The lengthy grand jury investigation (as well as that of a team of investigative journalists) established that the charges were an elaborate hoax.

For those who had welcomed the case as the latest evidence of the
persistence of brutal racism and the general depravity of American
society, the matter was not to be disposed of so lightly. Stanley
Diamond, distinguished professor of anthropology at the New School
of Social Research in New York City wrote:

> The grand jury has responded to the technical questions of the case, weighing
> evidence but necessarily blind to its deeper meanings. In cultural perspective, if
> not in fact, it does not matter whether the crime occurred or not. . . . What is
> most remarkable about this faked crime is that traditional victims have re-created
> themselves as victims in a dreadfully plausible situation."[46]

In the same spirit William Kunstler, the radical lawyer said "It makes
no difference whether the attack on Tawana really happened. . . . It
doesn't disguise the fact that a lot of young black women are treated
the way she said she was treated."[47]

In another hoax at Emory University in Atlanta, a black student
claimed to be victim of racial harassment (that included racial slurs
written on the walls of her room) which she herself concocted apparently to divert attention from academic problems (allegations of
plagiarism in a chemistry class). The president of the Atlanta chapter
of NAACP observed: "It doesn't matter whether she did it or not . . .
because of all the pressure these black students are under at these predominantly white schools."[48]

These responses to contrived incidents of racism highlight another
important component of the conditions which shape discussions of racism and the ready acceptance of every allegation of its presence: the
commitment of blacks and their supporters to the victim role. As the
comments quoted above indicate, *what matters is not actual victimization*, but past or potential future victimization. The eagerness with
which the victim role is sought is not hard to explain: it provides both

a position of indisputable moral superiority *and* grounds for both restitution or compensation of a more tangible kind. Virtually every single racist incident on the campuses is followed by demands for various benefits to the alleged victims: a black culture center, more faculty positions, more financial aid for protected minority students, mandatory "consciousness level raising" courses for the entire student population dispensing the approved views on these matters.

Shelby Steele quoted earlier is among the small number of visible black intellectuals willing to challenge the conventional wisdom on racism. He observed that

> a reenactment of past victimization . . . confirms our exaggerated sense of the enemy. . . . Victimization is a form of innocence and innocence always entitles us to pursue power. . . . By exaggerating our enemy in order to define ourselves, we put ourselves in the ironic position of having to deny clearly visible opportunities in order to "be black" and claim a strong black identity . . . the more opportunity one admitted to . . . the less "black" one was.

He also pointed out what has become increasingly obvious but risky to state in public—that racism doesn't explain many problems of the black population such as "The epidemic of black teen pregnancies, the weakened black family, the decline in the number of black college students" or that black students "have the lowest grade point average and the highest dropout rate of any student group in America."[49]

IV

It is the great paradox of our times—and perhaps another phenomenon associated with decline—that the sway of the new orthodoxies is most secure on college campuses which used to be thought of as sanctuaries of tolerance, open-mindedness, iconoclasm, and genuine diversity. Richard Bernstein was one of those who drew attention to this development:

> there is a large body of belief in academia and elsewhere that a cluster of opinions about race, ecology, feminism, culture and foreign policy defines a kind of "correct" attitude toward the problems of the world, a sort of unofficial ideology of the university. . . . The view that Western civilization is inherently unfair to minorities, women and homosexuals has been at the center of politically correct thinking on campuses.[50]

According to an English observer, "PCism has become part of a broader malaise, a factor in the breakdown of social consensus. The most worrying aspect of this is the fashionable contempt for the notion that America shares a common culture, built mainly on the achievements of European ancestors."[51]

One of the best examples of politically correct thinking on campuses is the fervent embrace of "diversity" (or "multiculturalism") already commented upon in connection with "multicultural" studies. Here I wish to stress the extent to which this term has become a codeword for its very opposite: narrow doctrinaire thinking and a euphemism for left-of-center political conformity. What "diversity" has most clearly ceased to mean is diversity of ideas. When it concerns physical or ethnic characteristics diversity denotes, in the words of a Harvard law school student, "being black, or belonging to some other racial minority; being female; being either openly gay or lesbian, and most recently, being disabled."[52] He wondered what these attributes have to do with the "marketplace of ideas" universities are supposed to foster?

"Multiculturalism" was also characterized as "one of the most destructive and demeaning orthodoxies of our time. This orthodoxy . . . is that race is the determinant of a human being's mind, that the mind cannot, and should not, try to wrest itself from its biological or sociological origins . . . 'Multiculturalism' turns out then, to be neither multi nor cultural. In practice, its objective is unanimity of thought on campus . . . "[53]

Moreover the favored categories of "diversity" not only fail to encompass the existing wide variations in ethnic or demographic background or sexual orientation, they also exclude diversity linked to class membership, religious preference, or political affiliation and outlook.

Even within the favored groups that constitute "diversity," political-ideological conformity is expected and demanded. It is not enough to be black to satisfy the criteria of "diversity" if that black person happens to be a Republican or a neoconservative. Indeed Professor Derrick Bell of Harvard Law School categorized blacks dissenting from his leftist (and preferential policy-oriented) world view as blacks who think like whites and don't count as "real" blacks; Bell made clear that they were not those he had in mind to broaden diversity.[54] Nor is it sufficient to be a woman to be included in this rainbow coalition if she happens to be a follower of Phyllis Schlafly or an admirer of Jeane Kirkpatrick. The same may be said about Hispanics of Cuban origin who happen to be anti-Castro and anti-communist. They too would rapidly learn that "diversity" does not apply to thinking or political belief.

"Politically correct thinking" on campuses also nurtures many forms of moral-intellectual vigilantism and novel forms of puritanism. Thus:

> The University of Minnesota has banned its dance line of 16 women from men's athletic events because the performances "sexually stereotyped" them. The women said they should decide that for themselves. The university told the dancers . . . that they were perceived as objects. . . . The dancers greeted the announcement with "shock, anger and sadness" the coach . . . said. "We feel we are intelligent enough women to know when we are considered objects."[55]

It was characteristic of the climate of opinion on major campuses that when one of the regents of the University of Michigan "requested an investigation of whether the bathrooms of a university building were 'being used as a meeting place for members of the homosexual community to perform sexual acts' " this provoked protest demonstrations and demands for his resignation. It appeared that the protest had more to do with his disapproval of the alleged activities in the particular setting than with questioning the validity of his assertions (i.e., that the university bathrooms were used for the sexual encounters).[56]

The increasingly bizarre aspects of current campus life and their connection with politically correct beliefs were highlighted by events on the campus of Mount Holyoke College in Massachusetts, an elite school for women that has been in the forefront of the crusade against "racism." Where such crusades and the spirit underlying them may lead was shown in a recent incident:

> Led by the Association of Pan African Unity . . . several Mount Holyoke student organizations joined with college administrators in a rally . . . calling for the college to acknowledge that discrimination exists on campus and to combat it. . . . The rally was in response to an incident . . . in which a male Hispanic visitor in Mead dormitory urinated on the door of two black women. It is unclear whether the incident was a result of racism, sexism or was simply a drunken act. . . . Mead dormitory has announced that it will conduct workshops . . . to deal with the issues raised by the incident.[57]

It was not made clear how the misbehavior of this visitor was further evidence of discrimination on the campus, nor was any evidence provided to suggest, let alone prove, that the drunken visitor *chose* the door in question to urinate on in the knowledge that black students lived in the room to which it led. But, as has become the rule in similar cases, it was instantly assumed that drunken loutishness was insufficient explanation of his behavior, racist motives had to be summoned up.

In a letter to the college community and addressing the student senate the president of the college Elizabeth Kennan called "the act in question . . . barbaric" and appeared to share the publicly prevailing conviction that it was a form of racism. She was also unhappy that students in the dormitory initially failed to report the incident and recognize its unmistakably racist character.

It remains to be seen how the Mount Holyoke College authorities will determine (in more rallies, workshops, and committee meetings) whether the act was only racist or also sexist and if so which element was predominant? But other troubling questions remain and need to be addressed especially if the college wishes to develop guidelines for future incidents: What if a Hispanic male urinates at the door of white women? Would that incident be classified as racist or merely sexist? What if he urinates at the door of *males*, white or black? Hispanic? What is the proper category to apply if a black male urinates at the door of white women *or* white males? What ideological label would be affixed to this act if it occurs in the stacks of the library or other public places not belonging to particular individuals of any color? When, generally speaking, does urination in places other than a lavatory become a political statement or perhaps a form of speech protected by the Constitution? How do we know that a political statement was intended? Can such a political statement be made in a state of intoxication? Is it appropriate to call a Hispanic person racist who himself belongs to a minority officially defined as disadvantaged and victimized by racism?

Attempts to legislate virtue are not limited to campuses though the most grotesque examples are found there or in adjacent communities. This author has for over two decades been privileged to observe these trends in the neighboring town of Amherst, Massachusetts where public discourse has been dominated by the large, left-leaning academic population. At the time of this writing the Amherst school system was seeking to ban and penalize, "staring or leering with sexual overtones" and was earnestly seeking to define what constitutes an "offensive stare." Furthermore, "Other behavior that would be considered sexual harassment under the proposed policy include: spreading sexual gossip, making unwanted sexual comments, exerting pressure for sexual activity and making unwanted contact of sexual nature. . . . Under the proposed policy, possible consequences for students who sexually harass a peer include detention, suspension, expulsion . . . or referral to the police." In turn, the town of Amherst sought to introduce new bylaws that would ban "racial slurs," "epithets directed at homosexuals," and more generally "harmful words." The proposed bylaw did not specify if calling someone a sexist pig, racist oppressor, patriarchal capitalist, or homophobic creep were to be included in the list of punishable terms.[58]

The attempted overregulation of behavior did not always spring from moralistic sources, often it rested on assumptions diminishing rather than highlighting individual accountability. I am here referring to the growth of litigation in cases where some personal injury—physical, mental, or moral—was attributed to the actionable negligence of other actors or institutions. Underlying such litigation and its supportive legislation has been a trend to expand the responsibility of professionals and businessmen (doctors and landlords in particular) and public bodies (municipal governments, employers, etc.) and to narrow that of individuals. For example, "In one of the largest personal injury awards ever granted in New York State for loss of a limb, a Bronx jury . . . awarded $9.3 million to a dishwasher who lost his left arm after he fell on the subway tracks while drunk and was struck by the train." His lawyers argued that he "would not have fallen on the tracks if transit workers had . . . removed him from the platform when they noticed that he was intoxicated."[59] While the award was unusually high (and might have been reduced on appeal) the spirit in which it was made is not unusual. Its premise was that the individual is to be protected from accidental mishaps of a wide variety even in situations where he is capable of protecting himself and is capable of assuming some responsibility for his own welfare or safety as in avoidable accidents. (Perhaps the award made by the jurors in this case was colored by a notion that getting drunk is also socially determined.)

During the 1980s the idea continued to gain ground that it is the obligation of society or particular social institutions to protect the individual against a wide variety of accident and risk. A British commentator wrote: "America's legalism breeds the shifting of burdens onto someone else. It saps initiative from the economy quite as effectively as the state-sponsored variety." Unconstrained by the taken for granted assumptions of contemporary American culture he also noted that "another facet of this phenomenon is the warped idea that the problem with America's underclass is a lack of self-esteem, and that the answer to poor educational performance is to teach more self-esteem." He succeeded as well in putting his finger on another characteristic of American culture in our times: "the new abundance of euphemisms. Prisons have become 'rehabilitative correctional facilities,' housewives are 'homemakers,' deaf people are 'hearing impaired,' a cerebral palsy society tells journalists never to use the word 'suffer' about those with that 'disease' (forbidden), 'affliction,' (forbidden) condition (allowed)."[60] He could have added "senior citizens" replacing old people and "golden years" to divert attention from the pain and discomfort associated in most cases with aging and the plethora of other terms devised to make us forget the difficulties and indignities associated with physical or mental illnesses and disabilities and death itself.

The determination not to confront semantically the unpleasant realities associated with the condition of the underclass, or the mentally ill or the old, is a form of collective denial that reflects unwillingness or inability to come to grips with these matters either institutionally or psychologically. The euphemisms sampled have a soothing quality; they seek to redefine the problems and liabilities in question. The predilection for euphemisms is also connected with the matter of "sensitivity" discussed earlier. At a time when racial and ethnic sensitivities are inflamed, reflexive charges of racism, sexism, ageism, elitism, or classism may be avoided by appropriate terminology and circumlocutions. Finally, there is the legacy or residue (or revival) of sixties egalitarianism that culminates in the dismissal of all hierarchies and distinctions between groups and individuals which, in turn, exerts an influence on terminology. So pervasive have these beliefs become that people now seriously argue that the blind or paraplegic have as much right to sit next to an emergency exit on a plane as those who are neither, or that mental retardation ought not disqualify a person from seeking public office, and illegal immigrants must be given the right to vote and students should be presented with a high school diploma regardless of their academic performance.

V

In late 1990 the conflict with Iraq emerged as a new development with much potential impact on the domestic life and politics of the United States and a possible new outlet for adversarial energies and activism. While at the time of this writing (in February 1991) public opinion has been generally supportive of American policy the adversary culture has already began to gear up for circumstances that could provide new opportunities for the impassioned denigration of the system in connection with protesting American military intervention. Efforts are under way to compare U.S. involvement in the Persian Gulf to that in Vietnam just as it used to be claimed that U.S. involvement in Central America (that is, its support of the anticommunist guerillas in Nicaragua and the government of El Salvador) paralleled that in Vietnam. Because of the oil factor, the crisis in the Persian Gulf has also led to assertions that U.S. involvement is nothing but a service to the oil companies, another capitalist conspiracy. Once more the churches positioned themselves in the forefront of the protest against American military moves, determined to find parallels with past U.S. policies in Vietnam and Central America. Jim Wallis a dedicated supporter of the Sandinistas and editor of the radical evangelical magazine *Sojourners* urged that "the alleged national consensus of support for U.S. policy [regarding Iraq–P.H.] must be disrupted."[61] The new peace or antiwar movement and its old-style social criticism is examined in the last essay of Part II.

The congressional and gubernatorial elections of the fall of 1990 did not disclose any significant or novel trend as far as the electoral expression of public opinion was concerned. The Democrats, including liberal democrats continued to maintain and enlarge their power in Congress, as incumbents usually do, and the congressional power of the GOP continued to erode. There was one noteworthy election. For the first time an authentic representative of the adversary culture, a former sixties radical from Vermont got elected to national office, to the U.S. House of Representatives. He was Bernard Sanders, former mayor of Burlington, Vermont, admirer of what used to be Marxist-Leninist Nicaragua, self-proclaimed socialist but not of the moderate, social democratic mold. This was a breakthrough for the radical-left which up till now only succeeded in electing its authentic representatives to municipal or state offices as for example Tom Hayden to the California legislature.

Despite all the problems noted above and contrary to what many members of this change-oriented and change-worshipping society had believed, the American system of government has proved far more stable than the communist ones. The latter finally collapsed under the weight of conflicts and weaknesses which they had successfully concealed and suppressed for long periods of time behind facades of unanimity and solidity.

Nonetheless the comparison of the strengths and weaknesses— moral, material or political—of Western and communist systems need not lead to the conclusion that the demise of communism will automatically lead to the reinvigoration of the West or the United States in particular. Although the decline of the threat of foreign aggression—such as the Soviet Union represented for decades—is a welcome relief, and the unravelling of communist systems does reflect favorably on the advantages and benefits of Western democracies and economies, none of these developments will restore social cohesion or cultural vitality in the United States, nor will they revitalize our intellectual and political elites or recharge their deeper values. The outlook and self-assurance of the latter may be more difficult to repair than the budget deficit or balance of payments.

Symptomatic of the trends discussed here and relevant to contemplating the future of social cohesion of American society, the new emphasis on ethnicity and national origin may yet emerge as a serious corrosive force. Questioning the basic values and traditions of society takes specific form when even in a preschool kindergarten children are encouraged to renounce, in effect, their common cultural-national heritage (as they also are when the new cultural diversity programs discussed earlier are imposed upon them). A letter to the editor of the *New York Times* noted that

> The teachers of my son's public school kindergarten class here in Brooklyn have just anounced that the children will no longer celebrate the traditional Thanksgiving. The pictures of Pilgrims and Indians sitting down peacefully to share a meal, they say, are too degrading to Indians.
>
> Instead they will celebrate an "international" Thanksgiving in which each child will be required to sit at a meal with a flag identifying national origin. My son was told that he would have to choose one strain of his English, Scottish, Irish, German and Jewish ancestry. A girl was told that she could be either Philippine or English, not both. . . . The United States flag . . . was allowed . . . after some parents refused to choose any flag. On one of the country's truly national holidays, they [the children] are encouraged to think of themselves as anything but American. . . . What is being challenged here is the whole idea that there is an America—that people of different races, creeds and national origins can be united as a nation.[62]

The questioning of American culture and its traditions (exemplified by such innovations) caries great symbolic weight and does not go unnoticed outside the United States. This is not to suggest that foreign critiques of the United States are mainly inspired by the aversion and doubt displayed by domestic detractors of American society but only that domestic and foreign critiques often converge and stimulate one another.

The position and reputation of the United States remain globally ambiguous and the hostility it has inspired in many parts of the world is not likely to vanish because communist systems proved to be both economically and morally bankrupt. While there is considerable overlap between domestic and foreign critiques of the United States (both tend to be associated with anticapitalism and varieties of leftist outlook) the foreign critiques are also fuelled by nationalism and apprehension about the damage American-style modernization and its cultural carriers inflict on traditional cultures. As a strong and rich country, but also one with many problems constantly in the news, anti-Americanism will be with us for a long time.

As the century nears its end, it is clear that communist systems and the ideas of Marxism which inspired them have failed. At the same time much conflict and confusion remains in the West, especially in the United States. American elite groups in particular continue to question the values and institutions of their society as they seek to alleviate the problems they face.

Perhaps the very notion of the ultimate solubility of problems, collective or individual, is a mirage, itself a product of Western culture, Western ways of thinking.

This is not to deny that American society faces difficulties. But they spring from sources (discussed below) which are different from those designated by the hostile critics who cling to the belief that the United States, Western cultural values and capitalism represent evil incarnate in our times.

Notes

1. Paul Hollander. *The Survival of the Adversary Culture*. New Brunswick, N.J.: Transaction, 1988.
2. To detest Western societies without simultaneously sympathizing with either non-Western or communist ones is possible but not easy and quite uncommon. Those alienated from Western societies almost invariably gravitate toward sympathy or admiration for communist or state socialist systems.
3. Dennis Wrong. Letter in *Contemporary Sociology*, July 1990, pp. 496–497; also relevant is his original review of the book published in ibid., September 1989 where the argument was presented at greater length, i.e. that left-radicalism or the adversary culture is an insignificant presence on the campuses and in American cultural life in general.
4. Cold War revisionism, that is, the view that the United State was primarily responsible for the Cold War has been assiduously propagated by authors associated with the Institute for Policy Studies such as Gar Alperowitz, Richard Barnett, Marcus Raskin, Richard Falk and others. See chapter 8. pp. 000–000.
5. Bill Keller. "At Mrs. Gorbachev's School, Hardly a Communist In Sight," *New York Times*, 4 November, 1990; see also Leon Aron, "What Glasnost Has Destroyed." *Commentary*, November 1989.
6. Perhaps the most notorious has been J. Arch Getty: *The Origin of the Great Purges*. New York: Cambridge University Press, 1985. Other authors of this persuasion include Roberta Maning, Gabor Rittersporn and Lynn Viola. For a critical discussion of some of these efforts see Peter Kenez, "Stalinism, as Humdrum Politics." *Russian Review*, October 1986.
7. "Alienation Under Socialism" (A Roundtable Discussion), *Soviet Sociology*, November–December, 1990, p. 60.
8. *Program of the Communist Party of the Soviet Union*, with a special introduction by N.S. Khrushchev. New York: International Publishers 1963, pp. 121–22.
9. "Excerpts from Solzhenitsyn Article." *New York Times*, 19 September 1990.
10. Robert Heilbroner. "Reflections—After Communism." *New Yorker*, 10 September 1990, p. 98.

11. Murray Hunt. Letter to the editor, *New York Times*, 14 January 1990.

12. Martin Weiss. "Managua Diarist." *New Republic* 26 March 1990, p. 43.

13. James Perkins, Executive Director, Traprock Peace Center. Letter to the editor, *Daily Hampshire Gazette*, 3 July 1990.

14. Dennis Wrong. "On Political Identities." *Dissent*, Fall 1990, 482–83.

15. Jacob Weisberg. "Public Television's Cuba problem: Nobody Watched." *New Republic*, 13 August 1990.

16. Robert Lindsey. "1960s Activists Jailed in New Causes," *New York Times*, 19 May 1987; Tim Golden. "The Defiant Freed Fist Collects a Few Dollars." *New York Times*, 23 June 1990.

17. "U.S. in Moral, Social Decline." Letter by Doug Maren in *Harvard Crimson*, 24 July 1990.

18. Richard N. Goodwin. "A country diminished in possibility." *Daily Hampshire Gazette*, 3 November 1990.

19. Alvin Kernan. *The Death of Literature*, New Haven: Yale University Press, 1990, p. 70.

20. Edward Rothstein: "Roll Over Beethoven," *New Republic*, 4 February 1991, pp. 30, 32, 34.

21. Eugene Genovese. "The Arrogance of History." *New Republic*, 13 August 1990, pp. 35, 38.

22. Diane Ravitch "Multiculturalism," *American Scholar*, Summer 1990: for another critical discussion of multiculturalism see Glenn M. Rickets. "Multiculturalism Mobilizes." *Academic Questions*, Summer 1990.

23. Ravitch, op. cit., pp. 341–42.

24. Shelby Steele: "The Recoloring of Campus Life." *Harper's Magazine*, February 1989, p. 53.

25. Suzanne Daily. "Inspirational Black History Draws Academic Fire." *New York Times*, 10 October 1990; a further display of the new trends toward such inspirational history and Afrocentric studies was provided by the Second National Conference on the Infusion of African and African-American Content in the High School Curriculum in Atlanta, November 1990. The Conference (sponsored by major corporations, including publishers) espoused without hesitation beliefs in the racial superiority of black Africans and characterized much of Western culture as "vomit." "Little protest emerged about the idea of teaching Egyptian hieroglyphs, cleansing rituals, numerology. As to the prospect of such children getting jobs, Nobles [Wade Nobles, one of the speakers] replied, 'When we educate black man, we're not educating him for a job, we're educating him for eternity.' " The Conference also featured a sympathetic representative of the white educational establishment, Thomas Sobol, education commissioner of New York State who exemplified the eagerness of guilt-ridden white educators to accommodate the inflammatory rhetoric and demands of the promoters of Afrocentric and "multicultural" studies. See Andrew Sullivan, "Racism 101," *New Republic*, 26 November 1990, p. 20.

26. Ravitch, op.cit., p. 347–48.

27. ibid., p. 348.

28. Thomas Sowell. *Preferential Policies: An International Perspective*. New York: Morrow, 1990, p. 153.

29. David Lloyd. "Throwing stones in glass houses." *California Monthly*, September 1990, p. 19.

30. Ravitch, op. cit., p. 354.
31. Sowell, op. cit., pp. 15–16.
32. William R. Beer. "Resolute Ignorance: Social Science and Affirmative Action." *Society*, May–June 1987; also by the same author, "Sociology and the Effects of Affirmative Action: A Case of Neglect," *American Sociologist*, Fall 1988.
33. Sowell, op. cit., pp. 128, 129.
34. Ibid., p. 180.
35. The legislation proposed by Hayden requires the California state university system and all community colleges to " . . . strive to approximate, by the year 2000, the general ethnic, gender, economic and regional compositions of recent high school graduates, both in first-years classes *and subsequent college and university graduating classes.*" [my emphasis] Quoted in John H. Bunzel: "Should UC Admissions Set Ethnic and Racial Goals?" *Los Angeles Times*, 1 July 1990.
36. Sowell, op. cit., pp. 123, 124, 127, 184.
37. Glynn Custred. "Onward to Adequacy." *Academic Questions*, Summer 1990, p. 64.
38. *Measure*, October 1990, pp. 3, 4.
39. Stanley Crouch. *Notes of a Hanging Judge*. New York: Oxford University Press, 1990 p. xi.
40. Willard Gaylin. *The Rage Within: Anger in Modern Life*. New York: Simon and Schuster, 1984, p. 182.
41. Edward Alexander. "Race Fever." *Commentary*, November 1990, p. 45.
42. Ibid., p. 45.
43. Marianne Preger-Simon, Ed.D. identified herself as "a consultant on oppression/liberation issues" in a letter printed in the *Daily Hampshire Gazette* on 30 October 1990.
44. Burns W. Roper. "Radical Tensions Are Down." *New York Times*, 26, July 1990.
45. Edward Alexander, op. cit., p. 48.
46. Stanley Diamond. "Reversing Brawley." *Nation*, 31 October 1988, pp. 409, 410; for a book length expose of the case see Robert D. McFadden et al., *Outrage: The Story Behind the Tawana Brawley Hoax*, New York: Bantam, 1990.
47. Jim Sleeper. "New York Stories." *New Republic*, 10 September 1990, p. 21.
48. Quoted in Alexander, op. cit., p. 45.
49. Shelby Steele. "The Memory of Enemies." *Dissent*, Summer 1990, pp. 327, 329, 331, 332.
50. Richard Bernstein. "Academia's Fashionable Orthodoxy: The Rising Hegemony of the Politically Correct." *New York Times* 28 October 1990.
51. Charles Bremner, "The thought police closing off the American mind." *London Times*, 19 December 1990.
52. Brian Timmons. "Fraudulent 'Diversity.'" *Newsweek*, 12 November 1990 p. 8.
53. "The Derisory Tower" [editorial], *New Republic*, 18 February 1991. See also in the same issue Fred Siegel, "The Cult of Multiculturalism" and Irving Howe, "The Value of the Canon." See also John Taylor, "Are You Politically Correct?" in *New York Times*, 21 January 1991; also "Taking Offense: Is this the new enlightenment on campus or the new McCarthyism?" *Newsweek*, 24 December 1990.
54. Ibid.

55. "Female Dancers Banned at Games of Men's Teams." *New York Times*, 1 July 1990.
56. "Gay Rights Group Protests Remarks By an Official." *New York Times*, 14 August 1990.
57. "Mount Holyoke: Students Rally To Overcome Discrimination." *New York Times*, 11 November 1990.
58. Judith Kelliher: "Amherst Schools tackle staring as 'sexual harassment.'" *Daily Hampshire Gazette*, 18 July 1990; Judith Kelliher. "Amherst targets fighting words." *Daily Hampshire Gazette*, 29 August 1990; see also Jim Hillas. "Rights lawyer questions 'fighting words' bylaw.", *Daily Hampshire Gazette*, 5 September 1990.
59. Calvin Sims. "$9 Million Won for Loss of Arm in Drunken Fall." *New York Times*, 21 September 1990.
60. "Hey, America, Lighten Up a Little." [unsigned editorial in *The Economist*], *New York Times*, op-ed, 5 September 1990. See also Walter Goodman, "Decreasing Our Word Power: The New Newspeak," *New York Times Book Review Section*, 27 January 1991. Goodman noted: "The ailment of hypersensitivity, a symptom of political correctness, is breaking out in journalism." He was commenting on a new publication advising journalists how to avoid words or expressions minority members may find offensive.
61. Peter Steinfels. "Church Leaders Voice Doubts on U.S. Gulf Policy." *New York Times*, 12 October 1990; by mid-November the Church leaders went beyond doubts: see Ari L. Goldman. "Council of Churches Condemns U.S. Policy in Gulf." *New York Times*, 16 November 1990.
62. William Ticker. Letter to the editor. *New York Times*, 22 November 1990.

PART I

The Failure of Communism

1

Hungarian Paradoxes

Hungary under the long reign of János Kádár has often been seen in the West as a wave of the future, a model of evolutionary transformation within the Soviet bloc and its only success story. My recent visit provided me with a new understanding of both changing conditions and the limits of change in this small but resourceful nation.

I left my native Hungary without authorization in 1956 and did not go back for eighteen years—on the somewhat irrational grounds that, once there, I might not be permitted to leave, and the U.S. government was not likely to send in the Marines to get me out. In 1974 I finally overcame this reluctance, and have gone back regularly every few years since then.

These visits are not journeys of emotional homecoming since both my parents are no longer living, and I have never cherished illusions about Hungary as my lost homeland. Nor are they motivated, so far as I can tell, by any sort of sociological fact-finding zeal, since I am not a professional student of Hungarian society, politics, or culture and have never before written on the subject. If anything, they are rather like random archeological excavations without a grand plan or expectation of great discovery, which may yet turn up something.

I do not nourish a love-hate relationship toward Hungary and its people. For their part the "natives" are very friendly (I come after all in the dual capacity of former countryman and representative of "the West"). Thus I find myself surprisingly detached, feeling neither hostility nor any great warmth. When in Hungary, I am not quite a native but not simply a tourist, either. I still have a few friends and relatives living there, I still speak the language fluently and without an accent (though with a somewhat diminished vocabulary), I still know my way around Budapest. Yet for all that, I am an outsider with inside knowledge, and I rather enjoy this role. Among other things, it means I can leave whenever I want to, which has not always been the case.

My earlier life in Hungary is fairly well summed up by a few episodes recorded indelibly in my memory. In 1944, when I was twelve, my family and I came close to be killed by an anti-Semitic mob led by Hungarian storm troopers of the pro-Nazi Arrow Cross party; seven years later, during the postwar Communist regime of Mátyás Rákosi, we were exiled as "politically unreliable elements" and transported under armed guard in the middle of the night to a village in Eastern Hungary. This, as it occurred after my graduation from high school, took care of any prospect of attending university.

I spent two years in this village, after which I was drafted into one of the quasi-military units known as "construction battalions." These were special units set up in lieu of military service for young men of draft age whose political classification barred them from regular military service. Our days were devoted to heavy manual labor combined with military drills and compulsory political seminars. The food and living conditions would have caused riots in any American prison. I spent two years in this type of military service.

Since my grandfather's socioeconomic background was the cause of the exile and our attendant classification as politically unreliable, a few episodes from his life too are in order here, if only because they also convey so succinctly what it meant to be a prosperous Jewish businessman in that part of Europe in the first half of the twentieth century.

In 1919, during the Communist revolution led by Béla Kun, my grandfather was jailed and beaten up for being a capitalist by representatives of the short-lived Hungarian Soviet Republic. A year later, having fled to Vienna and then returned, he was once again arrested and beaten—this time for being a Jew, by soldiers of the "white" counterrevolutionary army. Two decades of relative peace ensued, and then in March 1944, following the entry of German troops into Hungary, he was arrested by the Gestapo but miraculously released a few months later, only to suffer a skull fracture during the Arrow Cross pogrom I have already mentioned. In January 1945, following the Soviet entry into Hungary, he was chased through the streets of Budapest at gunpoint by a group of Soviet soldiers as he was running away with my mother and sister (in whom they took a decidedly prurient interest). I recall his hurried efforts in the air-raid shelter to shave off his mustache without water, in order to make it more difficult for the pursuing soldiers to recognize him (my mother and sister we concealed with pillows and comforters). In 1948 my grandfather was tried and imprisoned (for a year or so) by the Hungarian Communist authorities for "sabotaging the five-year plan" (he then still nominally owned a business); in 1951 he was exiled, with the rest of us, for his past socioeconomic sins. He died in exile.

That I can still go back to Hungary despite such memories (and even enjoy it) is somewhat puzzling to me, and I have given some thought to the question. I have no strong feelings about the prevailing political system, or about the people or the social conditions. I am evidently more tolerant than Sylvester Stallone, who after a visit to Hungary observed that "if everybody had to spend two weeks in a Communist country, 'patriotism in America would reach epidemic proportions.'" Also, for reason not entirely clear to me, I am less irritated by Communist party officials in Hungary (with some of whom I am personally acquainted) than I am by those of my American academic colleagues who believe that the Marxist-Leninist authorities in Nicaragua deserve the sympathy of every decent human being.

Perhaps the key to my equanimity lies in the opposite of survivor guilt—what might be called survivor smugness. Having escaped the Nazis and gotten away from the Communists, and having managed in addition to make a new life for myself in the West, I feel lucky and privileged enough to be able to revisit even those scenes of my childhood that carry less than happy associations. On one of my first trips back, I searched out the "Yellow Star House"—where my family and I were given shelter for a time before we went into hiding in 1944—and also paid a brief visit to the village in Eastern Hungary where we spent our exile. I even tried to visit the grounds of the Hungarian Nuclear Research Institute, which I had helped build during my years in the construction battalion (it remains closed to the general public).

Such biographical reflections and links aside, there is no question but that present-day Hungary is an interesting country, a place where, as the cliché has it, East and West meet. (Or, according to a taxi driver, a country which adopts the worst features of both the East and the West; he had in mind state socialism, a gift from the East, and the new taxes, a Western import.) It is a country that readily inspires reflections about the connections between personal lives and social-political arrangements, about the present and future of bureaucratic state socialism, about socialism and modernity.

It is surprising to discover, for example, that Hungary boasts a full quota of the social pathologies we tend to associate with the advanced industrial societies of the West: extremely high suicide and very low birth rates, alcoholism, juvenile delinquency, soaring divorce rates, and serious environmental problems, including especially air and water pollution. Socialism, then, for all its varied attempts at benevolent social engineering, has not provided a shield against the ravages of modernization—that much at least is clear from the case of Hungary.

Other conclusions are not so easy to come by, since Hungary seems to lend itself to both sides of every question, including the question of whether genuine social change can ever take place within the confines of the Soviet empire.

Those who believe in the possibility of such change can cite examples of liberalization. In Hungary, dissidents are not jailed or kept in psychiatric hospitals, only deprived of regular employment and sometimes of decent housing; they may travel abroad; they may also publish their *samizdat* magazines and pamphlets, with occasional interruption by the authorities who sometimes take away their equipment and close their shops.

A friend said to me last summer, "These days you can, even in public, talk or write about almost anything—but it will not make any difference." A striking example of this was provided by a teenage tour guide who was taking a group of some twenty (Hungarian) visitors through an old monastery. Describing the history of the building he noted that during World War II several hundred Jews were hidden in it, and for that reason the Germans had arrested the Abbot. The same Abbot, he added with a straight face, "was again arrested after the war, this time by the Communists, and tortured to death." On another guided tour, of caves outside Budapest, our guide used the opportunity to thunder about the incompetence of the planning authorities who had ruined parts of the natural setting in their zeal to create a tourist attraction.

These and other examples of outspokenness do not mean that people have a greater sense of control over their lives; the complaints as a rule reflect despair and helplessness. The economic hardships, mismanagement, and corruption are here to stay, in one way or another. A friend (just given permission to attend some conference in Western Europe) said wistfully: "Yes, they let us go, but we have to beg for it. I would give a lot for a passport like yours." Although travel restrictions have substantially diminished, travel to the West has yet to become a self-evident right as opposed to something grudgingly doled out. Moreover, some old restraints survive. A cabdriver told me that he could not get a passport allowing him to go to a capitalist country for ten years, because he had served in the missile forces of the army: "They figure that it takes ten years for the technology to become obsolete, so by then I cannot reveal any secrets."

In any event, the concessions are subject to the whims of authority and can be withdrawn at will. So long as Hungary's basic political structure remains unchanged, and so long as the party still holds a monopoly of power, nothing will take place in Hungary or any other Soviet-dominated society comparable to the recent transformation of formerly authoritarian countries like Spain, Portugal, or Argentina.

The case of Hungary can also be used to argue that even in the Soviet bloc, the past has a way of reasserting itself, however gradually, so that a country with close historical and cultural ties to the West will eventually shed the Soviet political straitjacket. The voracity with which educated Hungarians consume Western culture (not only in its blue-jeans/rock-music aspect) would seem to bear out some part, if not all, of this optimistic thesis. So too would the curious revival of social customs, attitudes, and modes of address, along with a more relaxed officiousness and nepotism, associated with the Austro-Hungarian monarchy. Also reminiscent of the monarchy and of the so-called historic compromise which Hungarian nationalism made with it in the latter part of the nineteenth century is the idea of achieving a similar or corresponding compromise with the Soviet Union.

Nationalism in Hungary is not quite so strong as it is in Poland, where it gains support from a uniformly Catholic population (only two-thirds of Hungarians are Catholics). Nonetheless it is still a vital cultural force which has helped to cushion the political regimentation imported from the East. Hungarians believe their culture to be far superior to that of most of their neighbors—and especially to that of the Soviet Union—and this belief contributes to the sense of national solidarity and community. These are further enhanced by the country's small size (the population is just over ten million) and by its unique language, totally unrelated to that of its neighbors or for that matter to any other country in Europe.

How the Jewish minority still living in Hungary (estimated at fewer than 100,000) fits into this community is a controversial question. The regime is officially quite tolerant of Jewish cultural and religious existence—more so than any other in the Soviet bloc. On an earlier visit I saw an exhibit in a major museum devoted to Jewish life and culture in Hungary. But I also recall one of the guards making a disparaging remark about the exhibit.

Opinions differ widely on the extent and tenacity of anti-Semitism within the general population. Individual Jews to whom I talked seemed rather wary of the whole subject and less than eager to assert their Jewish identity in public or even to make it known to fellow workers. Given the history of Jewish life in Hungary, their attitude should hardly be surprising.

If Hungary's Jews seem reticent these days (at least on questions of their identity), the same cannot be said of other sectors of the population. It is the apparent lack of intimidation among Hungarians in most walks of life that is, in my eyes, the most notable development of the last two decades. Politically relevant grumbling and criticism are endemic; I must have spoken, for instance, to at least twenty taxi drivers—you can sit next to them, no bulletproof or other dividers here—all of whom complained with relish and abandon of the declining living standards, rising prices, inflation, corruption, shortages, mismanagement. (Once when a black Mercedes drove by one of them remarked: "I would put away the driver of any of these cars; you can't have a car like that without being a crook of one kind or another.") The taxi drivers generally work ten to twelve hours a day, six or seven day a week. One was a degree-holding engineer who spent the hours of eight to five in his office, and after five drove a taxi. Why? To make ends meet and, in his case, to save for a down payment on an apartment. As many told me, the Hungarian authorities are enthusiastic proponents of "privatization"; the government is getting out of the housing business, and if people wish to get better housing they must pay for it.

In the past, complaints were considerably more muted—not just because informers might be listening, but also because Hungarians felt a genuine gratitude to the authorities at being, if not well off, then at least better off than their neighbors in other Eastern-bloc countries. This brand of limited contentment is no longer in evidence. Today people seem far more beset by economic anxieties, though these very anxieties may reflect higher expectations as much as they do more objective realties. The country's present economic difficulties, well reported in the American press, are due to huge indebtedness, low productivity (at any rate in the public sector), overstaffing, and rising prices which are barely followed by rising incomes. In an attempt to make the economy more productive and profitable, the authorities are instituting new measures: superfluous workers will be let go, new taxes are on the horizon, and government subsidies to housing and other services are being cut back. As a result, people seem, if anything, more gloomy and dissatisfied than they were in the old days. They are no longer as grateful as they once were, for instance, at being allowed to own some little Czech, East German, Rumanian, or Soviet-made car. "Why should a car be a privilege?" one cabdriver asked. And, to obtain this privilege, why should a family deprive itself of other goods and services for years?

In addition to economic worries, there is a new sense of class inequality in Hungary deriving from the limited free-enterprise policies implemented a decade ago. Ordinary Hungarians have always resented the privileged life of the Communist party aristocracy, but now their resentment has been enlarged to take in the new breed of high-living private entrepreneurs who have appeared on the scene in the wake of those policies. Natives of Budapest refer to these successful free-enterprisers as "the upper ten-thousand," and describe—with a mixture of reverence and resentment—the luxurious villas they are having built for themselves, complete with indoor swimming pools and the requisite Mercedes.

To be sure, the private sector also includes doctors, lawyers, computer programmers, owners of small hotels and restaurants, as well as small craftsmen like shoemakers, tailors, plumbers, and electricians. But even these entrepreneurs can earn incomes ten, twenty, or even thirty times higher than those of the average citizen, whose pay ranges between $100–$150 per month. Prices in Hungary are very low, of course, when translated into dollars—a good meal may be had for two or three dollars; a taxi ride for under a dollar—but even so the average income does not go very far.

By reviving private enterprise Hungary has become not only a more productive *and* inegalitarian society, but also one that has done away with the cardinal tenet of all existing socialist systems: the monopoly of public (state) ownership over the means of production. Thus, to the extent that Hungary has become a more livable, more open society it has also become less of a socialist one. Whether or not this evolution will continue it is hard to say, for Hungary's destiny does not hinge on its own decisions.

Even in the Gorbachev era, Soviet power cannot be forgotten, nor can the Soviet presence be ignored as the ultimate factor in Hungary's destiny. (I might also note that nobody I talked to mentioned Gorbachev and his reforms. When I brought up the topic the response was one of skepticism about any sweeping changes in the basic character of the system, both its Soviet and Hungarian version.) Thus, on three separate drives to the countryside, each in a different direction, I saw numerous Soviet military installations and troops, fuel depots, tank proving grounds, truck parks; there were even Soviet soldiers touring local museums.

Such sights are a forceful reminder of the limits of Westernization, and of what are sometimes politely called "certain geopolitical realities." While it is hard to predict the limits of institutional change, especially under the current fluid conditions—much depends both on the degree of change within the Soviet Union itself and on the problems of succession following the approaching retirement of János

Kádár—"Westernization" of several kinds has already made deep inroads into the minds of Hungarians. Educated Hungarians understand, deeply appreciate, and long for the blessings of political democracy, free public expression, institutional restraint on power, and other aspects of political pluralism which educated Westerners tend to take for granted or dismiss as unimportant.

En route to the airport on my way back, I was asked by my youthful taxi driver if I would sell him a one-dollar bill. "What for?" I asked. "For good luck," he said. It was an unlikely talisman for a member of the Hungarian working classes to cherish as protection against adversity under socialism.

2

Social Problems in Hungary

*The crisis means that all the working problems of
the system appear historically at the same time
and this crisis has one crucial message: things
cannot continue in the old way.*
—Imre Pozsgay, 1988

*We are afraid . . . afraid of being fired, of not
knowing that tomorrow we will have as much
bread on the table as today. We are afraid of price
increases and wage freezes, of the weather, the
pollution of the environment, of cancer, AIDS,
unemployment and the new income taxes. In short
of each other and the future.*
—Katalin Dobossy, 1988

How and why has socialist Hungary become a spectacular repository of serious social problems and pathologies which used to be
thought of as characteristic only of advanced, pluralistic, capitalist
societies?

Comments in a Hungarian samizdat journal illustrate the nature of
these problems:

> Was there ever a time when corruption, deceit and stealing became such an inte-
> gral part of our national economy as today? Day by day, the quality of life is de-
> clining: our waters are getting murkier, our crop lands are being poisoned, the air
> is becoming increasingly polluted, and our perspectives are shrinking. Has Hun-
> garian society of any other era experienced a general degeneration of life compar-
> able to that of today? (Demokrata 1986, 69)

Unpublished conference paper written in 1988 when Hungary was still a one-party state although on the way to the changes culminating in the elections of 1990 which for the first time
since 1945 provided the country with a democratically elected government and parliament.

Commenting on the anniversary of the liberation of Hungary from Nazi occupation the writer Gusztav Megyesi asked: "Can one speak of liberation in a country where socially useful labor serves no purpose; where the monster of economic crisis looms incessantly; where housing is not provided to all citizens, nor employment worthy of their training; where it does not really pay to bear and raise children, or to learn or to think; and where one hears and reads only of difficulties and problems?" (quoted in Deak 1988, 45)

At a gathering of intellectuals in September 1987 the writer Istvan Csurka said, "death manifests itself not only in suicides but also in the spreading fatigue, apathy, indifference, and resignation." He called the Hungarians "a nation of waiters . . . a mass without dignity and self awareness" and claimed that "four to five million people live in this country without any social or material prospect" (Radio Free Europe Bulletin 1987, 7). Elsewhere he warned about the pervasive decomposition of Hungarian society, about "the waves of defections, the fateful decline of the willingness to bring children into this world, the unrestrained drunkenness, exceptionally high rates of suicide and indifference toward national identity" (Csurka no date, 48, 52).

In early 1988 a petition circulating in Budapest stated: "The economic and political crisis of our country is rapidly deepening. Society no longer believes that the government is capable of retarding the decline. It deems unjust the burdens it must bear and senseless the sacrifices it must undertake" (*Felhivas*, March 1988).

According to Ferenc Koszeg, another dissident intellectual, "68% of retired industrial workers have slipped below the state-calculated subsistence level. . . . Overwork, alcoholism and unhealthy diets have contributed to a death rate for men aged 35 to 49 that is almost twice the European average" (Koszeg 1986, 23). It has also been reported by Hungarian researchers that suicide rates have been climbing since the mid 1960s "accompanied by dramatic increases in chronic alcoholism . . . established familial and communal ties were weakened or broken" (Kamm 1987a, 14). An editorial in a daily newspaper warned, "We must restore not only the material conditions of family life. We also need moral rejuvenation" (Kovacs, 1988).

The problems of family life were also reflected in the battered wife syndrome (which, unlike many other social problems, cannot be blamed on modernization, quite the opposite, through perhaps it can be blamed on heavy drinking). Apparently the peasant proverb "Only the beaten woman is a good woman" still guides the behavior of many men. An article in a women's magazine jestingly suggested that wife-beating could be averted if only couples of the same weight were allowed to get married and if women were taught karate before marrying (Kulcsar, 1988).

Hungary also has its own underprivileged poor (preeminent among them, the gypsies) and the characteristic problems associated with such strata of the population: "low school attainment, low or missing skills and qualifications, irregular and low income, poor housing, above average fertility . . . residential segregation." Gypsies in particular are overrepresented in the criminal population at large and significantly among violent criminals (Andorka et al. 1988, 84).

The mental health of the population has also been declining. According to the conclusions of a study of mental illness and its treatment,

> One sign of the presence, indeed the growth of insoluble personal tensions . . . is the relentless increase in the problems of mental hygiene . . . high levels of alcohol abuse are commonplace . . . neuroses [are] becoming of epidemic proportion, headaches becoming a mass affliction, [as well as] the taking of tranquilizers and sleeping pills, and the reduction . . . in the resilience of people. . . . Year after year there is an unbroken upward spiral of those retired for mental health problems . . . the traffic at mental institutions and clinics is constantly increasing as is the number of suicides. (Szalai and Vajda 1988, 5)

Preoccupation with the social problems of present-day Hungary is not limited to intellectuals and academic sociologists. The mass media delves all too eagerly into such matters, reminiscent of the corresponding zeal of the Western press. For example a new collection of articles from popular magazines (*Magyar Mozaik* 1988) ranges over topics such as the housing shortage, daily life and bureaucracy, rural poverty, underpaid academics, alcoholism, the difficulties of old age pensioners, the bankruptcy of a collective farm (and its disastrous effect on a village), the firing of "whistleblowers," unemployment, murder and family disputes, suicide and corruption, juvenile delinquents, unlawful institutionalization, corruption in a home for retarded children, the story of a gypsy homosexual prostitute, the mistreatment of orphans, and other problems. Each report or case history exemplifies some type of institutional failure or malfunctioning.

A documentary film shown in the summer of 1988 portrayed young drug addicts and the numerous deprivations and hardships associated with their condition (i.e., family disorganization, lack of housing, lack of education, and plain poverty). Again, the message of the film was that none of the institutions which were supposed to prevent or help to alleviate such disorders work and that nobody is ever rehabilitated.

It is ironic that Hungary, which during the 1970s and much of the 1980s had been perceived and portrayed in the West as the great success story of the Soviet bloc, is depicted quite differently by some of its most perceptive intellectuals, journalists, and sociologists. Western misperceptions are exemplified by the observations of an American sociologists: "Except among the Gypsy population, one is hard pressed to find poverty and insecurity that afflict a quarter of the population of the United States. And the Hungarian welfare system offers basic guarantees in old age, child-rearing and illness" (Burawoy 1985, 45) Evidently Dr. Burawoy, despite his two-month stint in a Hungarian factory, managed to remain isolated from unpleasant Hungarian realities which of late have been acknowledged even by high ranking officials. Not quite incidentally, and reflecting on his predisposition, he succeeded in discovering pleasing contrasts to what he considered the injustices of American society.

Some of the social problems and difficulties of Hungary are reflections of modernity, or modernization; even, if you will, of "Westernization." Thus a Hungarian psychiatrist discussing the problems of teenagers noted with a touch of pride that "We have the same problems here that they have in Munich or Vienna" (Kamm 1987b, 18). Indeed the existence of many social problems requires at least a modicum of material prosperity, personal choice, and levels of expectations which have outgrown and come into conflict with what is available materially and culturally.

In assessing Hungarian social problems we must also make some allowance for the relatively sudden and heady expansion of free expression that may lead to hyperbole, to the temptation to overdo muckraking when taboo topics can at last be freely discussed and ventilated in public. There is also the matter of relative deprivation. Conditions in Hungary used to be reasonably good (by East bloc standards) until a few years ago when the economy began to flounder and the standard of living declined. The new income taxes (introduced in January 1988) have been a particularly hard blow, eliciting widespread resentment but also jokes ("did you know that Hungary is now both a first and third world country; we pay Swedish taxes and receive Ethiopian wages.") But even if there is an occasional rhetorical tinge to the laments over the condition of Hungary there can be no doubt that they have been inspired by genuine difficulties and deprivations, including declining public health standards, rising male mortality rates, and nervous disorders multiplying at the same rate in both urban and rural areas.

It is clear by now that socialism as practiced in Eastern Europe has not succeeded in providing a shield against the ravages of modernization as it had once been hoped. It will be recalled that the major appeal of socialism used to be its promise to bring about technological and material progress without the social disruptions and cultural havoc created by corresponding processes under capitalism. As Peter Berger put it "Socialism . . . promises all the blessings of modernity and the liquidation of its costs, including, most importantly, the cost of alienation" (Berger 1977, 61). Under socialism, community and sense of purpose would flourish; competition would be held in check; the dog-eat-dog world of capitalism would vanish; modern technology would serve human needs; human dignity would be the preeminent value. Most importantly work was going to acquire a new meaning. In the words of Trotsky, "productive labor, having ceased to be a burden, will not require any goad." Moreover, "the distribution of life's goods, existing in continual abundance, will not demand . . . any control except that of education, habit and social opinion" (Trotsky 1937, 45–46).

Amazingly enough it also used to be believed—and some Western intellectuals may still believe—that under socialism the existential terrors of life would also be banished; that greater work satisfaction, improved living standards, and vibrant communal ties would make life meaningful and impart a solid sense of identity to the individual.

(Such beliefs also explain why most socialist states have relentlessly campaigned against religion, perceiving it as both useless and pernicious; socialism was to make life not merely materially secure but also meaningful, hence it could dispense with the crutch of religion.)

Socialism as we have known it did not usher in any of this—neither greater work satisfaction, nor material abundance, nor sustaining social bonds, nor (consequently) a new meaning to life. Admittedly though, the daily frustrations and anxieties introduced by state socialist systems were at least capable of diverting the citizen from the contemplation of the meaning and higher purpose of life.

The state ownership of the means of production in particular failed spectacularly to yield the benefits it was supposed to provide in regard to efficiency, productivity, and distributive justice. Increasingly this came to be admitted even by some of the officials. Thus Imre Pozsgay (a member of the politbureau of the Hungarian ruling party) said recently that "the creation of communal property in the context of state ownership leads to a crisis and it extinguishes incentives; it brings about a wasteful rather than cooperative society, one that is not based on social solidarity" (Pozsgay 1988, 2).

There is reason to dwell on the unfulfilled promises of socialism because they help to understand the rise of social problems in Hungary as they do in other bureaucratic state socialist systems of the Soviet mold. At the same time, the seriousness and complexity of the problems of Hungary and the despair they engender in both the socially conscious intellectuals and the masses call for additional explanation beyond the well-known and widely experienced failures of state socialism.

Although the uneven availability of information makes such assertions somewhat problematic, it is a premise of this discussion that the social problems of Hungary (or some of them at any rate) are in some ways different from those of other East European countries. They are products of both the social-political structure of Hungary (which is similar to that of other Soviet bloc countries) but also of the distinctive Hungarian historical experience (for a lengthier examination of the distinctiveness of Hungarian historical development and underdevelopment see Hankiss 1986, 360–371 and Volgyes 1987).

How does Hungary differ from other socialist states of the Soviet bloc? Unlike them, Hungary had a major, popular and traumatic revolution in 1956 such as no other Marxist one-party system had ever faced in Eastern Europe or elsewhere. Although this Revolution was brutally crushed it led to changes in official policy and in the mentality of the governed. While on the one hand it was a major "learning experience" for the population, making clear that substantial institutional change was not a viable option and that political expectations were thus to be reduced drastically, at the same time from the 1960s onwards, material and cultural expectations began to rise. The Kadar regime abandoned the classically totalitarian policies of regimentation or political mobilization; passive compliance or nonresistance become sufficient and compatible with good citizenship. The population—having been simultaneously granted such a concession and taught the lesson that significant political change was not possible—turned Hungary into what may have been the most apolitical of all East European nations. Although there were many notable exceptions, small groups of dissenters and critics, for the majority a newly intensified pursuit of a decent standard of living and private pleasures took precedence over public concerns.

Vaclav Havel's analysis of such conditions in Czechoslovakia captured the essentials of the Hungarian situation during most of the Kadar decades:

> It is as if the shocks of recent history . . . had lead people to lose faith in the future, in the possibility of setting public affairs right, in the sense of any struggle for truth and justice. They shrug off anything that goes beyond their everyday routine concern for their livelihood; they seek all manner of escape routes; they succumb to apathy, indifference towards impersonal values and their fellow men, to spiritual passivity and depression. (Havel 1987, 10)

Over the past three decades cynicism, well-grounded in historical experience, became entrenched; the gulf between the private and public realm deepened; indeed, the very idea of the "public good" remained questionable or wholly discredited. Material aspirations grew apace while opportunities, though improved, remained modest. Urbanization continued as did the transformation of an agricultural into the industrial sector of the economy. Geographic mobility has continued to undermine communities and stable relationships. In 1981, 44 percent of Hungarians above the age of fifteen did not live at their birthplace and there were approximately one million people (of a total population somewhat over ten million) commuting over long distances to work, returning home only on weekends (Andorka et al. 1988, 76).

Thus in the post-revolutionary period ideal conditions were created for the rise and spread of anomie and the proliferation of social problems associated with it.

There is another circumstance that adds to the uniqueness that the defeated revolution of 1956 has imparted to the Hungarian case. It is the reinvigoration of a certain culture-historical marginality that has for centuries been part of the national consciousness, a collectivized version of personal loneliness. This marginality is in part a consequence of geography, linguistic singularity, a precarious perch between East and West, the collective memories of being the victim of many conquests. The comments of George Konrad conjure up this condition and its connection with expectations:

> It's here in East Central Europe that Eastern and Western culture collide. . . . We have been argued over, agreed upon, traded, sold, dismembered; we have been the subject of peace conferences and settlements. . . . We are bad boys, skeptics, rogues, con artists, wheelerdealers, survivors . . . our historical legacy, our stock in trade, is cynicism. . . . Daily training for grimmer times keeps us in shape; we are consoled by our pessimism (Konrad 1981, 49).

To be sure the connection between such attitudes and statistically measurable social problems is elusive; a sense of historical-cultural marginality and the incompletely suppressed memories of a defeated revolution do not directly translate into high suicide and divorce rates, falling birth rates, institutionalized corruption, or a steady increase in alcoholism. Nonetheless the cumulative historical experience and awareness of defeat may in some elusive way contribute to self-destructive behavior such as suicide and heavy drinking (Andorka et al. 1988, 58).

I am using the concept of social problems here as it is generally used in the Western social sciences. It refers to forms of behavior (or situations and conditions) which—while seen as corrigible to some degree—violate or disrupt widely shared social norms and interfere with the functioning of major social institutions; they are situations that entail societal inefficiencies and institutional malfunctioning. The most widely discussed social problems are crime and delinquency, escapist behavior (alcohol and drug abuse in particular), suicide, mental illness, family disintegration, low birth rates, (sometimes the opposite: overpopulation), the situation of old people, and problems of work (which may include unemployment, excessive mobility of labor and the lack of work satisfaction). Poverty and unacceptable inequalities may be added to the list. Of late, problems of public health and the physical environment must also be included.

It should be stressed that the concept of social problems as applied in the West is largely apolitical: crime, heavy drinking, divorce, etc. are not as a rule, deemed to have political roots—unless the notion of "political" is stretched beyond its customary scope. It is true, on the other hand that many American texts on social problems tend to treat such phenomena as if they were singular products and liabilities of capitalists systems; American textbooks on such topics rarely if ever hint or allow that crime, corruption, poverty, or drunkenness may also be found in countries which insist on being called socialist and treat political pluralism as a harmful luxury and obstacle to economic and social progress.

It is by now conventional wisdom that most social problems originate in the disruptions of modernization, especially those connected with urbanization, industrialization, and secularization—the triad of processes modernization entails. Together they erode or altogether destroy traditional communities which used to perform the dual function of providing informal controls over behavior and inculcate moral values and restraints as well as a sense of identity.

Undergirding several social problems under socialism we find two additional phenomena which may be viewed both as problems in their own right and sources of the other more specific problems noted above. They are estrangement (or alienation) and bureaucracy. The major difference between alienation under capitalism and socialism appears to be that whereas under capitalism it is mostly intellectuals who are so afflicted under socialism alienation has come to be more widely and equitable distributed, it has become a mass phenomenon.

It is not hard to link alienation to social problems such as (certain types of) crime, escapism, and lack of work satisfaction. Bureaucracy, in turn, is a source of and symptomatic of inequality since the bureaucratic position often entails rewards and privileges and the whole bureaucratic design institutionalizes unequal income distribution and the unequal power relations. Bureaucracy also encourages low productivity and all-around inefficiency (by the proliferation of rules, overstaffing and aversion to risk taking and initiative); it interferes with the solution of environmental problems; finally, it stimulates alienation by creating a sense of powerlessness in those it is supposed to serve by reducing the sense of participation and belonging of individuals. As a Hungarian sociological text put it:

> Helplessness, lack of autonomy and dependence are common experiences among relatively broad strata of the population. It is not so much dependence on "the powers that be" but rather on lesser powers, the various bureaucracies, commerce, service agencies, the superintendent of the building where you live, in short such experiences and feelings are stimulated by the intractability of daily problems. (Andorka et al. 1988, 97)

It must be acknowledged that in its earlier, more coercive, indeed totalitarian phases, socialism (in Hungary and elsewhere) did create some impediments to the ravages of modernization, if not by providing a new sense of belonging, then by a coercive regimentation and organization of life that precluded certain forms of deviant or socially problematic behavior. Formal social controls were strong and pervasive, the population was "mobilized," opportunities for escapism were modest, the struggle for survival claimed people's full attention and energy. Material shortages prevented the rise of any sort of "consumerism" or aspirations beyond subsistence.

Under such conditions social problems, or many of them, were kept under control by the successful regulation of expectations, that is, by keeping them low. A Hungarian psychiatrist observed, "When a society is a little liberalized more personal problems come to the surface. . . . Only in societies that remain closed, like Romania, [under Ceauscescu] we hear of no problems" (Kamm 1987b, 18). It was a situation that could be characterized in the words of Durkheim as one in which "each in his sphere vaguely realizes the extreme limits set to his ambitions and aspires to nothing beyond. At least if he respects regulations and is docile to collective authority . . . he feels that it is not well to ask more." More specifically, he also observed, "Lack of power, compelling moderation, accustoms men to it" (Durkheim 1951, 250, 254).

In the same spirit Vaclav Havel noted that "most people are loath to spend their days in ceaseless conflict with authority, especially when it can only end in the defeat of the isolated individual" (Havel 1987, 10–11).

Let us now consider precisely which mechanisms were used to control and keep expectations low.

Generally speaking, it was one of the characteristic attributes of the state socialist systems that the tight control of popular expectations went hand in hand with ceaseless agit-prop efforts to dilute the distinction between the way things actually were and the way they were supposed to be; prospects of personal fulfillment under socialism were portrayed in an unrealistically favorably light which, however, conflicted with the reality as experienced by the population. Thus the official propaganda without intending to do so, increased awareness of the difference between theory and practice even among the least educated. At the same time, since it was backd up by other (coercive) institutions and policies, this propaganda provided a yardstick for adjusting overt behavior to the official norms and expectations.

Several specific measures were used to control expectation of various kind. Comprehensive censorship and travel restrictions eliminated or reduced bases for comparison and thereby helped to keep expectations low (even foreign radio broadcasts were jammed to keep out dissonant views and information from the daily life of the citizen). Free public discussion of any aspect of life different from the official world view was suppressed to avoid the sharing and circulation of discontents and deviant opinions. Prompt coercive responses to deviant behavior of both political and nonpolitical kinds helped to reinforce conformity and the acceptance of the status quo. State control over employment and access to higher education were proof of the power of the authorities to regulate social mobility and determine status. Severe controls over associational life and intellectual discourse further narrowed the opportunities for individual self-assertion and control over one's life and for the shared contemplation of alternatives. All these measures converged on reducing bases of comparison and alternatives to the status quo, in reducing and circumscribing personal choice.

Interestingly enough, the expectations of the individual under state socialism came to resemble the characteristic life of traditional societies. The observations of a Soviet dissident Valentin Turchin capture the result of the conditions here sketched: "The basis of the social order is considered by the citizens as absolutely immutable, given once and forever, absolutely unchangeable . . ." They consider it as a given, as Newton's Law. When you fall down you don't blame gravity (Shipler 1983, 194). Similar sentiments were echoed by the late Georgi Markov, the Bulgarian dissident: "the life of each of us was determined by a very simple and sound principle—to endure somehow. No doubt this is the principle of a man who realizes that he is the victim of unalterable circumstances. It is the principle of minimal hope and minimal resistance" (Markov 1984, 40).

To be sure conditions in Hungary even under Rakosi, the Stalinist leader between 1948–53, were somewhat different from those in the Soviet Union. The system had existed for a shorter time, Hungarians knew more of the world outside and Hungary had always been a more Westernized nation than Russia, Bulgaria, or Romania. Yet the mentality described above was exported to Hungary and has taken root albeit with some modifications. Above all, the presence of Soviet troops and the crushing of the 1956 Revolution were powerful and traumatic reminders that even in the post-Stalin era there still were narrow limits to change and expectations had to be kept low—especially in matters political. Moreover during and after 1956 many of the most discontented elements of the population were killed, imprisoned, or chose to emigrate, hence the pool of those prone to higher expectations shrank. If shortly before and during the Revolution there was an upsurge of political expectations, in its defeat and aftermath they dropped precipitously. One may plausibly argue (though difficult to prove) that this sudden change from high to low expectations contributed to a cultural, social-psychological malaise that was to manifest itself in low birth rates, high suicide rates, and escapism of various kinds.

While it used to be a major accomplishment of state socialist systems to maintain their stability by controlling expectations and regulating aspirations (by the means sketched above), during the 1970s and 1980s this capability has gradually eroded. Nowhere has this been more clear than in Hungary, hence the rise to the surface of massive frustrations and the corresponding proliferation of social problems.

Beginning in the mid-1960s the Hungarian authorities became less repressive; the line separating the public from the private realm was more generously redrawn; the regime declared itself tolerant of apolitical attitudes. The pursuit of material gain became legitimate even to the extent of allowing a private sector to emerge and many semiprivate ways of making money came to be tolerated. Travel restrictions were also greatly relaxed; Western works of art and forms of mass entertainment became more accessible. Western radio broadcasts ceased to be jammed, or less consistently. It was during the late 1960s and the 1970s that Hungary earned the appellation of "the most cheerful barrack in the socialist camp." By Soviet bloc standards dissidents were not harshly punished. Loss of jobs was the most favored retribution and the critics ceased to be imprisoned. As I had observed elsewhere, following my second visit to Hungary in 1979,

> Hungary comes very close, perhaps the closest, to Marcuse's model of the affluent, repressively tolerant society of which change has been virtually banished. . . . Hungarians [are allowed] within the limits to . . . indulge in privatized consumption precisely in order to divert them from politics . . . harsh political repression is absent but the limits of permissible nonconformity are well known and clear to the population. (Hollander 1983, 181).

More recently Miklos Haraszti observed, "The state need not enforce obedience when everyone learned to police himself" (Haraszti 1987, 94). As Marcuse would further argue, the relatively free circulation of ideas, including a wider range of criticism of the authorities, has served the purpose of diverting the more articulate groups from contemplating their powerlessness, while the modest material improvements have generally legitimated the system and provided apolitical preoccupations for the masses. Again Havel offers a penetrating analysis of this state of affairs:

> In the interest of the smooth management of society . . . society's attention is deliberately diverted from itself, from social concerns. By nailing a man's whole attention to the floor of his mere consumer interests, it is hoped to render him incapable of appreciating the ever-increasing degree of his spiritual, political and moral degradation. Reducing him to a simple vessel for the ideals of a primitive consumer society is supposed to turn him into pliable material for complex manipulation. (Havel 1987, 12)

The growth of such short term orientations was also noted, more cautiously, by Hungarian sociologists:

> We are living at a time of the narrowing of societal perspectives and conceptions of the future. This applies especially to collective conceptions of the future. Still even the more personalized aspirations, confined to the family, have these characteristics. This accounts . . . for the desire for urgent and rapid acquisition; the widespread hedonistic life styles; the "go with the flow" mentality, a certain fatalism and a general short term orientation. The frequent suicides among the old—besides the pressure of acute illness—are due to such "using up" of the future. (Andorka et al. 1988, 96)

While the developments outlined above were unfolding social problems increased, resulting from the combination of the new spurt of modernization, the rise (and frustration) of expectations, and the flaws peculiar to Marxist-Leninist one-party systems. The rise, frustration, and less effective regulation of expectations has been the most apparent in regard to the following social problems:

1. Escapism, especially heavy drinking
2. Suicide (the ultimate escape)
3. Family disintegration
4. Low birth rates
5. Crimes against property (state property in particular) as well as corruption (white collar crime)
6. Emigration, legal, illegal or semi-legal

Thus on the one hand the well-known discontents of modernity, much in evidence in pluralistic Western societies, have established themselves in Hungary. At the same time they have been intensified, aggravated, and combined with conditions peculiar to Hungary of the post-1956 era. As noted above these include preeminently, the successive rise and frustration of expectations, especially material ones. (It is important to note that though the expectations associated with social problems were predominantly material, they have been accompanied by an intensification of the claims on privacy and private, apolitical gratifications.)

In Hungary during the last quarter century the individual could choose between blaming himself or the surrounding social setting for failure, especially material failure. According to Ottilia Solt, a Hungarian sociologist, at least until recently the official point of view holding the poor responsible for their condition commanded widespread public assent. Solt also believes that poverty is the single major social problem in Hungary, especially as the ranks of the unemployed are gradually increasing. Pensioners, retired on account of old age or ill health, represent the other major group among the poor (Solt 1988).

To be sure the growth of aspirations in Hungary since the 1960s has not been quite as limitless (as Durkheim described) nor has the decline of the regulatory power of the authorities been quite so pronounced. Nonetheless, the tendencies described are there.

Of late the rise of material expectations and consumerism have been dealt several blows by difficulties of the Hungarian economy. By the mid-1980s it has become clear that the official policies and the economy can no longer sustain the material aspirations of the population; new policies of retrenchment began to undermine the much overrated Hungarian "economic miracle" and the political stability that rested in part on it. In order to maintain the material comforts achieved during the 1960s and 1970s people are compelled to work much harder in the 1980s; many hold more than one job; sixty to seventy hour work weeks are common. The spread of neurotic symptoms and disorders (as well as a widespread refusal to give up smoking) have been associated with such stress (Szalai and Vajda 1988). The word "stress" itself has even entered the Hungarian language. With declining economic conditions, a Hungarian underclass began to emerge comprised of the unskilled, old age pensioners, large families, and those with only one breadwinner.

An article by the sociologist Zsuzsa Ferge appearing in 1983, well before the recent drastic measures (such as the personal income tax introduced in early 1988), addressed the growing economic difficulties and the resulting hardships for particular groups of the population:

> A number of unspectacular, often unpublicized price increases or the disappearance of many less expensive articles of consumption had the most devastating effect on low and middle income families. . . . Further contributing to these trends were the measures of "privatization" over the past years . . . affecting particular groups, including children and the elderly.

Only a small proportion of the population was able to counteract the price increases and reduced welfare benefits by making more money. . . . For the majority an extra income requires substantial extra work, or better paid but worse, more unhealthy jobs. . . . The impact of the factors noted above has been particularly severe on those already facing financial difficulties, those with average or below average incomes, low income families with several children . . . or those which include old age pensioners. Household surveys indicate that in such families, besides a growing frugality, there is a shift toward lower quality foods or physiologically less valuable nutritional substitutes . . .

Of late a new category has been added to these groups: the young . . . there are hundreds of thousands among the young, at the beginning of their careers who are compelled to make compromises with their jobs and accept those below the level of their training, or simply poor jobs . . . they have little hope for rapid improvement of their condition. Here is the root of the frequent complaints about the lack of enthusiasm, of the lack of perspectives and pursuit of pseudo-solutions among the young. (Ferge 1983, 10)

What remains of the hopes and promises of socialism if it no longer delivers even modest material security even as it continues to withhold political freedoms? And how will political stability fare if the regime's control over expectations continues to erode? Will it be possible to preserve, as Western countries have done, political stability while social problems proliferate, or will social problems impinge explosively on the legitimacy of the system?

Conditions in present-day Hungary are extremely fluid to allow for sweeping conclusions, or even persuasive speculations as regards the future of social problems and pathologies. They are likely to remain the price the country has to pay, paradoxically, for both political liberalization and the long-standing, politically inspired mismanagement of the economy.

One thing clear is that while socialism with a somewhat more human face has made it possible for certain expectations to rise it does not have the capacity to satisfy them or to stem the tide of the problems associated with such expectations and with modernity. While in the pluralistic societies of the West the discontents and social problems of modernity coexist with substantial political and personal freedoms and high standards of living, unhappily, under socialism,—as exemplified by Hungary—similar social problems can also flourish but without the compensations and consolations that the availability of options provide to those living in pluralistic societies.

Postscript: Late 1990.

Socialism no longer exists in Hungary. The Marxist-Leninist one-party system was swept away without violence (as was the case all over Eastern Europe in 1989 except in Romania); a coalition of freely elected non-Marxist parties governs Hungary since the spring of 1990; free expression has been completely restored and a free enterprise system is being expanded. Political pluralism abruptly achieved exacts its costs. Unemployment and inflation are increasing and a sense of crippling economic problems pervades public opinion and undermines trust in the new system. Political participation measured by voting behavior is not high. Economic inequalities have increased.

If people initially believed that the newly introduced political freedoms will readily translate into economic improvements, such hopes are being eroded by deteriorating economic conditions. The vanishing fear of authority, a general sense of disorganization, new opportunities for various criminal enterprises, unemployment and greater material deprivations converge to encourage the growth of crime. The new freedoms also encourage the public emergence of social problems which had earlier been invisible, suppressed by the authorities such as homelessness and ethnic friction (i.e., public expressions of anti-semitism and anti-gypsy sentiment). There is less money for social programs and various subsidies. It is difficult to think of any social problem not likely to increase under these conditions.

Some of the questions raised earlier appear now in a new political context: will the material problems and frustrated expectations threaten the stability and legitimacy of the newly established, fragile political democracy? Unhappily it seems that Hungary in the foreseeable future will not be able to bring its social problems under better control since the latter and political pluralism are far from incompatible.

References

Books and Periodicals

Andorka, Rudolf et al. eds. 1988 *Tarsadalmi Beilleszkedesi Zavarok Magyarorszagon* (Disturbances of social adjustment in Hungary). Budapest: Kossuth.

Berger, Peter L. 1977. *Facing Up to Modernity*, New York: Basic Books.

Burawoy, Michael. 1985 "Piece Rates, Hungarian Style." *Socialist Review*, January.

Csurka, Istvan. n.d. *A Magyar Tarsadalom Erkolcsi Allapota* (The moral condition of Hungarian society). Budapest.

Deak, Istvan. 1988. "Hungary: The New Twist." *New York Review of Books*, August 18.

Dobossy, Katalin. 1988. "A Report of the Public Opinion." In *Magyar Mozaik* (Hungarian Mosaic). Budapest: Minerva.

Durkheim, Emile. 1951. *Suicide*, New York: Free Press.

Ferge, Zsuzsa. 1983. "Ki Fizesse a Szamlat?" (Who should pay the bill?) *Heti Vilaggazdasag*, June 4.

Hankiss, Elemer. 1986. "A Megkessett ipari forradalom kenyszerpalyaja" (The restricted trajectory of the late industrial revolution). In his *Diagnozisok 2* (Diagnoses 2). Budapest: Magveto.

Haraszti, Miklos. 1987. *The Velvet Prison: Artists Under State Socialism* New York: Basic Books.

Havel, Vaclav. 1987. "Letter to Dr. Gustav Husak, General Secretary of the Czechoslovak Communist Party." In J. Vladislav (ed.): *Vaclav Havel, or Living in Truth*. London: Faber and Faber.

Hollander, Paul. 1983. "Public and Private in Hungary: A Travel Report." In *Many Faces of Socialism*. New Brunswick: Transaction.

Kamm, Henry. 1987a. "Hungary Seeks Way to Cut High Troubled Youth." *New York Times*, July 30.

_____.v 1987b. "Hungary Takes Note of Its Troubled Youth." *New York Times*, December 2.

Konrad, George. 1981. "Letter from Budapest." *New York Review of Books*, November 5.

Koszeg, Ferenc. 1986. "Hungary Doesn't Deserve Model Communist Image." *Wall Street Journal*, June 18.

Kovacs, Judit. 1988. "Csaladfeltes" (Protecting the family). *Magyar Nemzet*. (The Hungarian Nation), May 26.

Kulcsar, Ildiko. 1988. "Az Asszony Verve Jo?" (A beaten woman is a good woman?). *Nok Lapja* (Women's magazine), May 21.

Markov, Gregori. 1984. *The Truth that Killed*. New York: Ticknor and Fields.

Pozsgay, Imre. 1988. "A valsagkezeles antikatasztrofa politikat tartalmazzon" (The handing of the crisis must entail a policy of dealing with disaster). *Kozgazdasz* (The Economist). Budapest. May 5.

Shipler, David. 1983. *Russia*. New York: Penguin.

Solt, Ottilia. 1988. Taped conversation with the author.

Szalai, Julia; Vajda Agnes. 1988. "A szocialis és egészségügyi ellátás határán" (On the boundary of welfare and public health provision) *Szocial-Politikai Èrtesitó* 1988, No. 1.

Trotsky, Leon. 1977. *The Revolution Betrayed*. New York: Pathfinder.

Volgyes, Ivan. 1987. "Parliamentarianism and Pluralism in Eastern Europe: Assessing the Social Bases." *East European Quarterly*, September

Other Sources

Demokrata, no. 3., March 1986. Cited in Foreign Broadcast Information Service, 13 August 1986.

Felhivas (A petition). Mimeographed, Budapest, 17 March 1988.

RFE Hungarian Language Broadcast Dept. Bulletin, October 10, 1987.

3

Politics and Social Problems
in the Soviet Union

*The Party is engaged in a titanic effort to
eliminate phenomena alien to socialism.*
—T.I. Zaslavskaia

Western Views of Soviet Social Problems

Western discussions of Soviet social problems and their relationship to Soviet political institutions and trends have been influenced by two conditions. One has been the absence, or limitation, of accurate and comprehensive information. As a Western commentator put it, Soviet authorities "can variously publish no information . . . incomplete information, contradictory information, wrong information . . . or, mischievously correct information."[1] This difficulty has, over the years, considerably diminished: There is now more information and more reliable information available as the authorities have increased their willingness to allow public ventilation of domestic ills. Still, detailed and fully comprehensive statistics on major social pathologies such as homicide, drug addiction, prostitution, or mental illness remain to be made public. At the same time, in the spirit of glasnost, the official monopoly on the definition and discussion of social problems has weakened; in fact, their coverage has become a form of social criticism. (Even begging has become mentionable in the news media.[2])

The second influence on Western views of Soviet social problems has been wishful thinking about the connections between Soviet domestic problems and the nature of the entire political system, including its foreign policies. The long-standing Western disposition has been (even more so since the rise of Gorbachev) to believe that domestic weaknesses and problems are bound to exert a basically benign influence on the Soviet political system: they cry out for alleviation and put pressure on Soviet leaders to reform their institutions and policies. Socioeconomic problems have been seen as significantly limiting the freedom of political action of Soviet leaders; at some point they would be compelled to turn inward, away from "adventures" abroad and regimentation at home in order to make the system more rational, productive, efficient, and satisfactory to its citizens. The leaders have also been seen as bound to respond, sooner or later, to public demands to improve living standards—indeed, the need for the modernization of the economy has emerged (or perhaps reemerged) as the most compelling explanation of why far-reaching reforms can no longer be delayed. Such assessments tend to attribute pragmatism to the Soviet leaders and are permeated with skepticism about the importance of ideology.

For many Western commentators, the discrepancy between a highly authoritarian political system—maintaining a huge bureaucracy, fielding vast armed forces, being active abroad, lavishly subsidizing its internal security and espionage services and propaganda apparatus—and a population suffering a great variety of privations, shortages, mismanagement, and assorted social pathologies has been viewed as irrational. The magnitude of social problems cried out for alleviation, even for thoroughgoing structural changes. Gorbachev has greatly encouraged such beliefs and expectations by dwelling on a variety of social problems with unusual candor.

The idea of "social problems" is distinctly modern because by defining anything as a "problem" we mean not only that it is undesirable but also that it is not an immutable condition, that it can be alleviated. As a past president of the American Social Science Research Council put it, "A renewed determination to ameliorate certain longstanding, as well as recently developed, ills of the society has arisen along with a sense of power and confidence in its ability to do so."[3]

Some recent Soviet discussions echo similar confidence. Whether such optimism is warranted either in the United States or in the Soviet Union is open to question. The fact remains that now, in the second half of the twentieth century, we have more "problems"—both as individuals and societies, in the East and the West—because of our growing intolerance of many deficiencies of social and personal life. For example, poverty used to be a normal condition, whereas today it is a social problem (at any rate in Wester societies). Similarly, routinized work, various illnesses, marriages lacking in excitement and intense personal fulfillment, and the underrepresentation of women in various occupational hierarchies used to provide no ground for public complaint, protest, or scholarly inquiry, but they do so today.

Social problems refer to aspects of social life and group behavior that are perceived as undesirable but remediable. In the Soviet Union they are often called "phenomena alien to socialism." Needless to say, what is defined as undesirable (alien) reflects prevailing social-political norms and standards, which in the Soviet case have been authoritatively determined by the political decision makers and guardians of the official values; the link between social problems, political institutions, and values is unusually clear-cut and explicit under such conditions.

To be sure, social problems often are unintended consequences of various social arrangements and attempts at social-economic reorganization, rather than merely matters of political or moral definitions. The chronic food shortages, demographic imbalances, and overall backwardness of the countryside in the Soviet Union have clearly been the unforeseen and unintended results of purposeful institutional change, such as the collectivization of agriculture.

Social problems in the Soviet Union can be separated into at least three distinct groups. In the first group, we find what is often referred to as antisocial behavior. This includes all varieties of crime, delinquency, prostitution, and divorce (antisocial in that it interferes with the upbringing of children, thus with social cohesion). Ethnic and racial discrimination, and its consequences, may also be put into this group.

The second group consists of various types of escapist behavior, including alcoholism, drug addiction, and suicide (the ultimate escape). Escapist behavior, too, has antisocial implications, since it disrupts predictable social interaction, the routines of work and family life.

Third, there are various structural-situational conditions that constitute social problems—particularly relevant to the Soviet case and to the relationship between politics and social problems. Such problems have the most direct connection with the political ordering (or disordering) of society. They include the various scarcities, especially of housing and consumer goods (and the corruption they elicit, which merges into criminal conduct); deficiencies in public health; low birthrates (perhaps, from the authorities' point of view, also a form of antisocial behavior); rural underdevelopment or uneven modernization; bureaucratic mismanagement; environmental problems; lack of work satisfaction; and the excessive mobility of labor. Old age is yet another social problem that falls into this group—it is not antisocial to be old, nor does it represent a form of escapism or violate any social norms. It is a problem created by the combination of improvements in public health and the resulting longevity, the changing family structure and social values (which reduced the respect accorded the old), and lack of resources (required to replace services that used to be provided by the extended family).

Social problems in Soviet society have three major sources, two of which can be defined as political. The first has been the general process of modernization, which always disrupts traditional ways of life, worldviews, modes of production, and stable communities. The second has been the self-conscious application of political-ideological criteria to this process and the associated reorganization of society, creating problems peculiar to Marxist-Leninist one-party systems, such as rural backwardness. Third, some social problems have been created by the application of official conceptions of rectitude and the corresponding (broader) definitions of deviance. The official view of the survival of religious attitudes and behavior provides one example of such a "problem." Insofar as emigration and unregulated internal population movements represent a social problem, it too is a direct result of the imposition of political standards on personal lives and choices. What is socially problematic about emigration in Soviet society is to a considerable degree a result of its prohibition or restriction, which creates pent-up frustrations and discontent and possibly magnifies the attraction of all things foreign, or at any rate, Western. However, allowing people to travel unhindered and to emigrate could create some genuine problems independent of any political label attached to such movements, i.e., the loss of highly skilled citizens, including important scientists, specialists, and artists.

Modernization, in both Soviet and other varieties, is the crucial breeding ground of social problems. It creates high expectations (regarding the various frustrations earlier seen as inevitable or immutable) and the belief that most problems can be solved. Modernization also creates social disruptions more directly as it interferes with stable social relationships and undermines world views that used to impart some measure of security to human existence; it makes behavior more uncontrolled and uncontrollable.

Whereas the reluctance to acknowledge publicly the presence of serious social problems—and their connection with modernization—has been predominant for most of Soviet history, since the mid-1980s this attitude has been undergoing substantial change. Until recently, the official article of faith was that socialist modernization was qualitatively different and less traumatic from modernization under capitalism: the community was not being undermined, or if old communities were being destroyed, they were being replaced by new ones, equally sustaining or even more meaningful and vibrant.

Socialist modernization, however, turned out to be as disruptive as the capitalist variety; the disruption was exacerbated by the lavish and arbitrary use of state power, as exemplified by the collectivization of agriculture and the abandon with which large chunks of the population were moved around, in both punitive and nonpunitive ways.

Nevertheless, socialist modernization did not unduly raise expectations, whereas in pluralistic societies rapidly rising expectations underlie many forms of socially problematic behavior. Under conditions of great political violence, high levels of insecurity, and institutionalized scarcities, the type of expectations that elsewhere contribute to social problems (e.g., to many types of crime, juvenile delinquency, divorce, escapism) was absent. As Marshall Goldman has observed, the Soviet Union could simultaneously experience great economic hardships *and* conduct vigorous expansionist policies around the world "because ordinary Soviet citizens seem willing to endure poor condition at home and . . . allow their leaders to divert so much to defense and heavy industry with a minimum of protest. The Russian people have a higher tolerance for deprivation and suffering than most other peoples of the developed world."[4]

These attitudes were slowly changing in the past two decades, and they have apparently changed quite rapidly since the rise of Gorbachev. Still, over the long haul, the shortages and limits of economic modernization have retarded or circumscribed the development of some social problems: "consumerism" and associated crimes against personal property, certain types of suicide motivated by endlessly spiraling expectations, neuroses and sexual deviations that are nurtured by an excess of free time and choice—these do not flourish under conditions of serious scarcities, limited expectations and opportunities. (However, petty but widespread pilfering of state property has become virtually institutionalized as a way of gratifying simple, basic needs.) The backwardness of rural life also has meant that certain traditions (and informal group controls) have been easier to preserve in areas subject to little centralized control, whereas in the cities, housing shortages often forced three generations to live together, benefiting the upbringing of children. Thus, Soviet modernization has in some ways been more incomplete, in other ways more sweeping and penetrating than modernization in the West, and this has had an effect on the character of Soviet social problems.

The disruption of community in the Soviet Union was not only an unintended consequence, or byproduct, or modernization, it was also a politically motivated process, as was the whole enterprise of Soviet modernization. The connection between the demise of community and particular social problems has been a staple of sociological analysis. The decline of community leads to the loss of informal social controls exercised by people over each other's behavior by virtue of knowing one another and, in some degree, depending on one another. Soviet sociologists have also commented on this phenomenon, noting for example: "People of different cultural and moral levels and of different backgrounds and ways of life mix. They leave behind them traditional forms of control by the family, by the public opinion of the village street, by relatives."[5] The eruption of antisocial behavior is the most direct consequence of the decline of these informal social controls. Formal controls, no matter how enormously strengthened—as they certainly have been in the Soviet Union—cannot replace the informal ones (although they may help, as, for example, does the internal passport system in controlling serious crime).

The Soviet View of Soviet Social Problems

Of late, the Soviet leadership has increasingly acknowledged that Soviet society has not been immune to the problems associated with modernization. At the same time, inadequate, sluggish modernization has itself been defined as a problem, with its perpetuation of techno-logical underdevelopment and a neglected infrastructure, an obsolete system of communications, and a crippling rural backwardness.

Since the mid-1980s there has been a great deal of public discussion and dissection of social problems of a great variety, including hundreds of articles delving with relish into such social pathologies as prostitu-tion, suicide, drug addiction, the neglect of invalids, the unseemly behavior of juveniles, the decay of sexual morality, the hardships of women, and poverty.[6] In contrast to earlier times, today there is less concern with making sure that the social problems singled out for public attention are portrayed as isolated or anomalous phenomena, as alien and unrelated to the major institutions and characteristics of Soviet society.

Gorbachev himself has remarked: "Socialism possesses everything necessary to place present-day science and technology at the service of people. But it would be wrong to think that the scientific and technological revolution does not pose problems for socialist society as well."[7] As the context suggests, Gorbachev's concerns had more to do with managerial inefficiencies and the difficulties associated with adopting the latest technology than with the more profound dis-locations created by modernization. But S. Shatalin, a corresponding member of the Soviet Academy of Sciences, recently acknowledged that socioeconomic problems (especially that of retarded growth) have been virtually systemic.[8] Tatiana Zaslavskaia, a prominent critic of Soviet socioeconomic arrangements and procedures, likewise has repeatedly linked the problems of the economy to the deficiencies of social justice and to "the human factor."[9]

We may be witnessing the beginning of what might be called the "depoliticization" of social problems, that is to say, a new willing-ness to admit their full range and devastating consequences while also attempting to disassociate them somewhat from the ideological and political foundations of the Soviet system. Undoubtedly, the au-thorities would like to make the candid analysis of social problems

compatible with support for major Soviet institutions and an affirmation of the official values. An effort is being made to convey to
the public that no matter how grave and widespread such problems
are, they need not delegitimize the Soviet political system. For this
kind of endeavor to succeed, officials must also convince citizens
that the major political institutions and elites of the system need not
take credit for either all the failures or all the successes of the system, that the political determination of Soviet life is on the wane
and possibly has never been as complete as had earlier been alleged
and believed. Still, the uninhibited ventilation of social pathologies
is something like opening a Pandora's box, as has been recognized
by many in the power elite (for example, Egor Ligachev) who are
concerned that such discussions have gone too far and could erode
the legitimacy of the system no less effectively than the successive
revelations of the misdeeds, errors, incompetence, or corruption of
virtually all Soviet leaders who followed Lenin. This is not an unfounded apprehension.

It may well be asked what remains of the distinctiveness, let alone
the superiority, of the Soviet social-economic system if it is admitted
that its industries pollute the air and earth no less than their capitalist
counterparts; if crime has shown no signs of withering away; if it
turns out that socialist institutions have no edge in sparing people
from personal misery and unhappiness, culminating in heavy drinking, divorce, or suicide; if shortages of essential goods and services
continue to cripple daily life; and if caring for the old and sick is not
more generous and humane than under capitalism.

There have been over time two conflicting pressures in the Soviet
Union exerting influence on the definition, recognition, or denial of
social problems. From the standpoint of the ideological legitimation
of the Soviet system, serious social problems similar to those in de-
caying capitalist societies were not supposed to exist and the less said
about them the better. The well-known, notorious problems afflicting
capitalist, or class, societies—crime, juvenile delinquency, prostitution, alcohol abuse, discrimination against women and ethnic
minorities—were supposed to wither away under the more egalitarian, just, and rational social arrangements introduced by the Soviet
system; if they did not, they were referred to as if they were some
mysterious virus, "survivals" doomed to extinction by the march of

history and the relentless improvements in the outlook and conscious-ness of Soviet people. How indeed could there be such problems in a society that even candid, muckraking Gorbachev described as "a world without oppression and exploitation . . . a society of social sol-idarity and confidence"?[10]

There has thus been, from its earliest days to the present, a tension between the glorification and ideological legitimation of the Soviet system and the acknowledgment of the existence and gravity of so-cial problems in Soviet society. A Hungarian journal publishing in 1988 under conditions of far greater glasnost than obtained in the USSR recently had this to say about the Soviet social problems and their official acknowledgment:

> Institutional assistance for the poor has still not been put on the public agenda in the Soviet Union. After all, the fact that a substantial portion of the citizens live under seriously deprived conditions remains to this day a taboo topic. In a coun-try where until very recently it had not been acknowledged that there were drug addicts and homosexuals, and where it was forbidden to entertain the possibility that anybody could be unhappy, it is hardly surprising that official policy makers were reluctant to take note of poverty.[11]

Modernization under the auspices of, or in the framework of, socialism and inspired by Marxist-Leninist ideology was supposed to be radically and qualitatively different from modernization unleashed by the inhumane forces of capitalism, as both Peter Berger and Adam Ulam have observed. Socialist modernization was expected to spare the participants the deprivations the earlier capitalist variety entailed: both the material deprivations associated with poverty, industrial reg-imentation, and urban crowding *and* the spiritual losses stemming from the undermining of traditional ways of looking at the social and natural world. The major blow dealt to mental hygiene and emotional well-being was the disruption, or complete loss, of community. The still lingering appeal of socialism has been, in the words of Peter Berger, the "promise [of] all the blessings of modernity and the liqui-dation of its costs, most importantly, the cost of alienation . . . [by] projecting the redemptive community into the future."[12]

Although insistence on the distinctiveness of socialist moderniza-tion and the superiority of the new social institutions predisposed the Soviet authorities to deny the existence of social problems, ideology created its own pressures and requirements for discerning and identifying social problems, for defining situations or forms of behavior as politically unacceptable and hence socially problematic. A political system dedicated to the radical transformation of the human condition and committed to the ceaseless perfection of social institutions and human nature was bound to find more forms of human behavior intolerable and problematic than a social system resigned to human and institutional imperfections. Such intolerance was also enhanced by the Leninist stress on voluntarism, on the political will that increasingly gained influence among the Soviet political elite as it became clear that institutional-environmental changes were failing to eradicate a great variety of human imperfections and as social defects continued to lag behind the sweeping transformations of society. An outlook that was highly politicized and shaped by ideology has further contributed to the perception of social problems by the refusal to regard deficiencies of social existence and institutions as sometimes accidental, if not preordained. When nothing can be attributed to accident or to "the nature of things," problems multiply. Hence, novel (by Western standards) social problems have emerged in Soviet society such as "private property mentality," attachment to religious values, crimes against public property, the "misuse" of free time, and more recently, low birthrates. Such social problems tend to shade into political problems; given the "overintegrated" character of Soviet society, the distinction between social and political problems (and spheres) has often been difficult to maintain.

Thus, in the Soviet Union ideology has created social problems by providing new, demanding criteria against which to measure social phenomena and human behavior. At the same time, it has generated unease and denial when social problems have persisted, although they should have been relegated to the dustbin of history by the forces of politically ordained social progress.

The conflict between the ideologically imposed restraint on revealing and analyzing social problems and the ideologically inspired soul searching stimulated by increasingly obtrusive deficiencies of the social order has recently tilted decisively toward revelation and public ventilation, as in the famous speech of Gorbachev at the 27th Party Congress:

While duly assessing what has been achieved, the CPSU leadership considers its duty to honestly and candidly tell the party and the people about our deficiencies in political and practical activity, about unfavorable trends in the economy and in the social and spiritual sphere . . . For a number of years—not just because of objective factors, but also for reasons that are primarily subjective in nature—the practical actions of party and state agencies lagged behind the demands of the times and life itself. Problems in the country's development grew faster than they were solved. Sluggishness, ossification of the forms and methods of management, decreased dynamism in work, growth of bureaucracy—all these things did considerable damage to the cause. Stagnant phenomena began to show up in the life of society.[13]

The Impact of the Political System on Social Problems

The connection between politics and social problems goes beyond the political definition and determination of what constitutes a "problem" and which of them may publicly be discussed. The political realm can in very tangible ways both stimulate and restrain the growth of social problems. I shall first take note of the restraining effect of the political system.

Generally speaking, numerous social problems are linked to the gap between aspirations and achievements. When people accept material deprivations as normal, there will be relatively few crimes against property; when a degree of monotony or emotional-sexual frustration that often is part of monogamous marriage is accepted and taken for granted, the desire for divorce (or adultery) will be more limited; when people cannot conceive of better ways of life than what is provided by their social environment they will not seek improvement by trying to leave their country; when bleak, deprived living conditions are taken for granted, the pressure for escapist behavior will be more modest. There are many such examples of the connection between expectations and social problems.

During much of its existence, the Soviet political system has been highly successful in containing and stabilizing expectations of much of the population, in the way that traditional societies used to be able to do. Durkheim's words capture the essence of the attitudes that prevail under these conditions: "Each in his sphere vaguely realizes the extreme limits to set to his ambitions and aspires to nothing beyond. At least if he respects regulations and is docile to collective authority . . . he feels that it is not well to ask more."[14] In the same spirit Valentin Turchin, the Soviet dissident, has observed: "The basis of the social order is considered by the citizens as absolutely immutable, given once and forever, absolutely unchangeable. . . . They consider it as a given, as Newton's Law. When you fall you don't blame gravity."[15] More recently Natan Sharansky, another leading dissident, made a similar point: "Not only the authorities consider citizens cogs in the wheel of the state, the people so consider themselves too. The Western notion that the government *is* subject to constraints of law is alien to the Soviet citizen. The government is the law. It can grant rights . . . and it can take them away . . . Gorbachev has not changed this principle."[16]

These observations also help to explain why many Soviet citizens are not looking forward to change with joyful anticipation but regard it with forboding or apprehension. They are inclined to associate the known and stable with at least a minimum of security, whereas change, which has almost invariably been imposed from above, may mean new risks and dangers; hence it reminds them of the limited control they exercise over their lives. Such attitudes explain the mixed reception given to Gorbachev's reform proposals by many groups and strata in Soviet society and also the questioning of the desirability of dwelling on the shortcomings of the Soviet system, including its social problems.

Low expectations have been found to prevail not only in political matters but even in regard to the daily diet. In the early 1980s, a study of Soviet emigrants reflected the modest expectations of Soviet citizens about a wholesome diet. Although the researcher established that by Western standards their diet was extremely poor, "28% of those interviewed termed their diet 'satisfactory'; another 10% had no particular opinion which amounted to the same reaction . . . their answers reflected perennially low expectations or an ignorance of what might be bought under more plentiful conditions."[17] To the extent that expectations have risen recently, at least among certain groups, the proliferation of certain social problems may be expected. More of this below.

Whereas on the one hand, the politically inspired controls over expectations imparted a degree of stability to the life of the citizen and prevented or slowed down the rise of aspirations (which could not have found socially *unproblematic* gratification), many social problems in the Soviet Union can be directly traced, on the other hand, to the political priorities, values, controls, and the resulting politically induced deprivations. These social problems include the whole range of white-collar crimes, crimes against public property, and corruption of many kinds. Thus the politically inspired and determined process of modernization has not been the only link between politics and social problems. The political sphere has created or interacted with social problems in other ways as well. Expectations were not only kept under control by scarcities and major political calamities but were also restrained by regimentation and the control of leisure, social mobility, and, more generally, opportunity.

Resource allocation is the most direct link between politics and a wide range of social problems. Scarcities symbolized by the ever-present necessity to stand in line remain a pervasive part of life and a visible reminder of the consistently low priorities given to consumer needs.[18] Insufficient resources have created or intensified social problems, including (1) poor standards of public health, (2) rural backwardness and migrations, (3) insufficient and antiquated housing, (4) the hapless condition of old people, (5) low birthrate (a response to scarcities), (6) threats to the environment, and (7) inadequate treatment and rehabilitation of heavy drinkers and drug addicts (reducing alcohol consumption also conflicts with the need for revenue).

Ultimately it is the politically determined priorities and organizational styles (bureaucratic rigidity, planning, centralization) that underlie the social problems connected with scarcities—problems such as corruption; inequalities, or distributive injustices; as well as waste and mismanagement. Almost all material shortages and deficiencies in services and the provision of consumer goods may be traced to political values and priorities, except for those due to the weather. Even shortages and deficiencies that arise from the Soviet-Russian work ethic can be linked to incentives and thus again to the realm of politics. Above all, these deficiencies are determined by the long-standing, overwhelming bias in resource allocation toward the military-political sector (including state-security and agit-prop outreach activities) as opposed to the civilian-social needs.

Sergei Grigoryants, a prominent social critic, has made a connection between social problems associated with technological backwardness and the political realm:

A society deprived of democratic institutions, that is, of the opportunity for growth, improvement and adaptation to changing conditions, proved to be instinctively hostile to the achievement of human genius. . . . Modern technologies are created by people with a different feeling of responsibility toward society, people who utilize the full range of democratic freedoms for that society's improvement. These technologies . . . cannot be employed to their full capacity and without danger in other (in this case, archaic) social structures.[19]

Another area where the connection between social problems and politics is close and clear is that of the nationality question and the ethnic tensions associated with it. These issues are political in origin, since most of the various ethnic groups did not voluntarily join the Soviet nation-state, and once joined by force, they would have preferred greater political and cultural autonomy than was granted. The ethnic problems have two further dimensions: first, the competition between particular ethnic (or nationality) groups and the dominant Russians, and second, the relationship among particular ethnic groups, as for example the Armenians and Azerbaidzhanis. The display of violent hostility between the latter groups in 1990 provided a striking illustration of the connection between rising expectations due to political relaxation and the eruption of certain social problems. In turn the turmoil in the Baltic states has been an obvious example of national-cultural and political self-assertion and of the determination to achieve greater independence of the Soviet Union. Another aspect of the ethnic problem is the gradual numerical decline of the Russian majority, due to differential birthrates among the various ethnic groups.

While, as noted above, some characteristics of the political system directly impinge on the creation of social problems, others continue to exercise a restraining influence. These include administrative measures, such as a system of residence permits used to keep former convicts concentrated in particular areas and to deprive them of mobility; strict controls over the possession of firearms; and the relatively great freedom of the police and the judiciary to prosecute crimes.

The Impact of Social Problems on the Political System

Thus far we have looked at the ways in which the Soviet-system, in its capacity as a modern and still modernizing society and as a distinctive political culture, contributes to the rise and persistence of social problems. Next we will examine the obverse: how social problems impinge on the Soviet political system.

Although earlier I questioned some overly sanguine Western assumptions about the inevitable connection between social problems and the liberal-rational reform supposedly necessitated by them, I agree that many if not most of these problems represent at least a drag on the political system: They divert energy, resources, and personnel from other areas and interfere with the political-public agenda. A number of Western observers have, over the years, come to believe that a system so hobbled with socioeconomic problems and deficiencies cannot sustain an aggressive foreign policy, that such a policy requires more ample resources, undivided organizational energies, and unified, supportive public sentiment.

Many social problems undermine economic efficiency and challenge the social order, and the Soviet authorities are well aware of this. Such problems include alcohol abuse and disrespect for public property, undisciplined attitudes toward work, excess mobility of labor, and dissatisfaction with available educational and employment opportunities. Nor does society benefit from the quest for personal happiness that results in divorce and a large number of children who grow up in incomplete families. In turn, low birthrates cut deeply into the supply of manpower for labor and the army and are also deemed to weaken a properly collectivist socialization process: one-child families are often deplored as the cradles of individualism, consumerism, and other evils. Still, the commitment of the authorities to the eradication or significant curtailment of some of these problems conflicts with other priorities; for example, the need for revenue conflicts with cutting back of the production of alcohol (or closing the illegal distilleries, though of late steps were taken to ration sugar required for such operations[20]). Nor are the authorities willing to increase birthrates by prohibiting abortion or other forms of birth control because such measures would greatly increase popular discontent.

It remains an intriguing question whether social problems, or some of them, could, in the not-too-distant future, have a benign effect on matters political, exerting a liberalizing, pluralizing pressure, as had been expected by Western observers for decades. To the extent that several of the social problems mentioned here entail certain individualistic values, as indeed many do—be they oriented toward higher living standards through crimes against public property, or greater personal happiness by discarding unsatisfactory spouses, or reducing family size, or moving into already overcrowded cities in pursuit of better goods and services—such acts and orientations may slowly erode collectivism, respect for authority, and public discipline, thereby weakening the political order. All such aspirations and forms of behavior represent a placing of the "private" above the "public" interest, as such things are defined in the Soviet Union. The growth of these aspirations may portend trends that could reduce the gap between the Soviet Union and Western societies and could bring about a limited pluralization of society and some degree of emancipation from the political determination of the direction pluralization will take.

Unquestionably, many social problems drain the public and political domain. To be sure, this could also lead to a strong reaction, a crackdown, or a renewed program of regimentation, or the reintroduction of social discipline. Nonetheless, as Bialer observed, there is "an incongruity between the harsh and honest judgments about the sorry state of the Soviet society and economy and the relatively feeble remedial actions . . . being taken or proposed."[21]

It is also likely that the relationship between politics and social problems is limited, that, with respect to some problems, the political domain may have only a marginal relevance. This may be a surprising proposition from one who has always regarded matters political as the major driving force in the development (or deformation) of Soviet society. However, I also observed as long ago as the early 70s, "If, indeed there is any kind of convergence between the U.S. and the Soviet Union, it can be found in the realm of social problems,"[22] suggesting that I saw many problems as largely or partially apolitical phenomena.

Certain social problems have more to do with the human condition and with modernization in general than with any particular political system. Even in the more repressive, more totalitarian, or more highly politicized period of Soviet history, some forms of human misbehavior and social problems had a measure of autonomy—certain types of suicide, crimes of passion, mental illness, and so forth. At the same time one may also argue that in the more totalitarian phases of Soviet history, it was easier to make the connection between social problems and politics because politics permeated and shaped most aspects of life: even divorce often had political roots (as during the purges or because of housing shortages and the attendant familial friction, which were in turn determined by political priorities in resource allocation).

In all likelihood social problems will continue to multiply under Gorbachev, rather than merely be given more publicity, for reasons that include the rise of expectations stimulated by his rhetoric and his policies as well as by signs of a somewhat greater political tolerance at the top. Although it is very difficult to tell how widespread the rise of expectations has been since Gorbachev's emergence, it is likely that it has not been confined to the urban intelligentsia. Yet, some reports suggest that although expectations have risen, they are far from explosive, at least not in the industrial hinterlands. Thus for example in Semipalatinsk:

> The residents are not about to revolt, or do much more than complain. They have learned to live with bare store shelves, rationed meat, crowded communal apartments, endless waiting lists for telephones and cars, an absence of cultural institutions and serious air pollution. But Mr. Gorbachev has stirred their expectations without delivering a tangible improvement in their lives, a gap that has the potential to undermine his leadership and throw the wisdom of his programs into doubt.[23]

If the appetites of the Soviet masses continue to grow, literally and figuratively speaking, then social pathologies and a decline of political will and regimentation may turn out to be mutually reinforcing.

In the longer historical perspective, the persistence and proliferation of social problems in the Soviet Union also mean that it is possible for a society to have a limited supply of both "negative" and "positive" freedoms,[24] contrary to earlier hypotheses. The abundance of Soviet social problems demonstrates anew and quite conclusively that a politically motivated campaign of modernization, although bringing about a drastic decline of "negative" (Western) freedoms, is compatible with economic stagnation and a minimal growth of positive freedoms (social and economic rights or entitlements); that is, the modernization can be accompanied by prolonged and oppressive shortages and material deprivations, which were supposed to be eliminated at the expense of personal and group freedoms.

Notes

1. Cullen Murphy. "Watching the Russians." *Atlantic Monthly*, February 1983, p. 37.
2. I. Rost. "Miloserdie-ne milostinia" (Altruism, not charity). *Literaturnaia gazeta*, 17 February 1988.
3. Henry W. Riecken. "Social Science and Contemporary Social Problems." *Items*, March 1969, p. 1.
4. Marshall I. Goldman. *USSR in Crisis*. New York: Norton, 1983. p. 174.
5. I. Kasyukov and M. Mendeleiev. "Sociologist's Opinion: Must a Family Man Have Talent?" *Nedelia*, transl. in *Current Digest of the Soviet Press* [hereafter CDSP], 19 April 1976, p. 25.
6. See, for example, the following articles in *Sotsiologicheskie issledovaniia*: S. I. Kurganov, "Motivy deistvii nesovershennoletnikh pravonarushitelei" (Motives of actions of juvenile lawbreakers), no. 5 (1989), pp. 60–63; "Narkomaniia s tochki zreniia sotsiologa, vracha, pravoveda i zhurnalista" (Addiction from a viewpoint of the sociologist, doctor, lawyer and journalist), no. 2 (1989), pp. 38–51; Ia. I. Gilinskii, "Effektiven li zapret prostitutsii?" (Is the prohibition of prostitution effective?) no. 6 (1988), pp. 68–70; Ia. I. Gilinskii and L. G. Smolinskii, "Sotsiodinamika samoubiistv" (Sociodynamics of suicides), no. 5 (1988), pp. 57–64; T. A. Dobrovolskaia, N. A. Demidov, and N. B. Shabalia, "Sotsial'nye problemy invalidov" (Social problems of invalids), no. 4 (1988), pp. 79–83; and O. A. Voronina, "Zhenshchina v j'muzhskim obshchestve'" (Woman in a male society), no. 2 (1988), pp. 104–110. See also the articles on deviance and social problems in *Soviet Sociology* 27, no. 4 (1988).
7. Mikhail S. Gorbachev, "27th Congress Speech," *Pravda* and *Izvestiia*, transl. in *CDSP*, 26 March 1986, p. 6.
8. S. Shatalin, "Sotsial'noe razvitie i ekonomicheskii rost" (Social development and economic growth), *Kommunist*, no. 14 (1986).
9. T. I. Zaslavskaia, "Chelovecheskii faktor razvitiia ekonomiki i sotial'naia spravedlivost" (Social justice and the human factor in the development of the economy), *Kommunist*, no. 13 (1986).
10. Gorbachev, op. cit., p. 36.
11. Ferenc Szaniszlo, "Szegeny emerek" (Poor people), *Heti Vilag Gazdasag* (Budapest), 28 May 1988.
12. Peter L. Berger, "The Socialist Myth," Public Interest, Summer 1976, pp. 89; see also Adam Ulam, *The Unfinished Revolution*. Boulder, Co.: Westview Press, 1979.
13. Gorbachev, op. cit., p. 4.
14. Emile Durkheim, *Suicide*. New York: Free Press, 1951. p. 250.
15. David Shipler, *Russia*. New York: Penguin, 1983. P. 194.
16. Natan Sharansky, "As I See Gorbachev," *Commentary*, March 1988, p. 31.
17. Marvyn Matthews, "Poverty in the Soviet Union," *Wilson Quarterly*, Fall 1985, p. 81.
18. A *Literaturnaia gazeta* article suggested that citizens may spend years of wait-

ing in line. L. Vellikanova, "Na razny temy" (On various topic), *Literaturnaia gazeta*, 20 April 1988.

19. Sergei Grigoryants, "Three Paradoxes of the Modern World," *Glasnost Information Bulletin*, October 1988, p. 20.

20. Bill Keller, "Soviet Moonshiners Drain Sugar Stocks; Rationing Imposed," *New York Times*, 26 April 1988.

21. Seweryn Bialer, *The Soviet Paradox: External Expansion Internal Decline*. New York: Knopf, 1987. P. 123.

22. Paul Hollander, *Soviet and American Society: A Comparison*. New York: Oxford 1973, p. 301.

23. Philip Taubman, "Semipalatinsk JournalIf Perestroika Was Steak, Life Would Be Better," *New York Times* 22 September 1988.

24. Isaiah Berlin, "Two Conceptions of Liberty," in *Four Essays on Freedom*. New York: Oxford, 1969.

4

The Nature of Discontent
with Communist Systems

The Puzzle

There was a time when many Western intellectuals and even portions of public opinion were inclined to judge communist systems more by their intentions and ideals than by their accomplishments and institutional practices. It might have seemed a daring suggestion that "Communist regimes are to be judged . . . not by what they promise, not by what the founders of the socialist doctrine envisioned but by how their people live and are ruled."[1] By the beginning of the 1990s time is ripe to judge these systems in exactly such terms, by what they delivered not by what they had intended to deliver, by their long-standing practices rather than their legitimating theories. This is exactly the kind of judgement being rendered by the people living under these systems who were their intended beneficiaries.

At a time when communist systems in Eastern Europe and elsewhere are in a state of dramatic disintegration or slow unravelling—as the case may be—and when the last arrival among putatively socialist systems has been voted out of power in Nicaragua, it is of special interest to undertake an exploration of the nature of the discontents such systems generate with inexorable regularity and which have led to their current decomposition. It is of more than academic interest to examine more closely the nature and components of these discontents and especially the pervasive sense of frustration and deprivation communist systems create in a highly patterned way.

How is one to explain that communist states established at different times, in different places, and under different historical circumstances nonetheless created remarkably similar discontents among their people in areas as diverse as Eastern Europe, China, Cuba, Ethiopia, Nicaragua, the Baltic states, Soviet Armenia, Angola, Mozambique, Indochina, and Tibet? The question is all the more intriguing since in the decades following the death of Stalin Western scholarship increasingly emphasized the differences among communist states and cautioned against taking a monolithic view of them.

It was for the first time during the 1980s that several communist systems came simultaneously to experience difficulties in maintaining the status quo. Also for the first time the smaller communist states could no longer expect brotherly (coercive) assistance from the Soviet Union in the event their people threatened the local *nomenklatura*'s power and privilege. Several of them—Hungary, Poland, East Germany, Czechoslovakia, Romania, Bulgaria—are undergoing sweeping changes and have in fact ceased to be "communist."[2] More than ever before the discontents of the people living in Eastern Europe and the Soviet Union are being articulated in an impressive and increasingly public manner. In China the process of change was brutally arrested in June 1989 but the signs of massive popular discontent were just as perceptible. Cuba, Ethiopia, North Korea, and Vietnam remain, for the time being, defiantly opposed to change; their rulers apparently retaining the will and capacity to prevent expressions of discontent and continue to govern regardless of the disposition of their people.[3] But even in the communist systems that are still resisting change, attitudes of the governed and especially their discontent are, for the first time in their history, beginning to have an impact on the calculations of the higher authorities as they seek controlled change without compromising their monopoly of power.

While we are too close chronologically to fully explain this process of unravelling, or to assess with any precision its historic significance or institutional consequences—this is a good time to take stock of the enduring and endemic discontents communist societies produce, especially since these discontents have led to substantial political changes that were almost totally unexpected both inside and outside these countries.

It is all the more worthwhile to undertake this inquiry since many in the West remain incapable or unwilling to grasp the depth and uniqueness of the discontent these systems generate. Those writing in *The Nation* are a good example. A recent issue explained:

> The exodus of youthful East Germans across the Austro-Hungarian border cannot be interpreted . . . as an abandonment of the teachings of Karl Marx. To be sure the emigrants are hoping for a better life than they found under the East German regime. But the country to which they are traveling . . . is not Thatcher's Britain or apres-Reagan America. . . . By leaving East Germany the new emigrants have chosen capitalism with a human face. Its humanization was and is the work of the party that Marx founded. And so the newcomers have gone from Stalin back to Marx."[4]

Evidence of the unhappiness of those who were to benefit from communist social systems are hardly new. From the Kronstadt uprising to the recurring waves of East Europeans and Soviet citizens "voting with their feet," to the revolts and rebellions in Eastern Europe to the boat people of Indochina, there have been abundant indications that social harmony and material contentment have eluded these countries, that "the indissoluble link between the Party and the people" was a bit of black humor not unlike Stalin's suggestion during the purges that life was becoming day by day happier for Soviet citizens and human beings were the greatest asset of the system.

Why have communist systems proved so unsatisfactory for so many people in almost every place where they were installed? It may be asked, "unsatisfactory" compared to what? The answer is that these systems have been unsatisfactory both in comparison to the levels of satisfaction found in past and surviving traditional societies and those prevailing in contemporary capitalist-pluralist ones. Not even the harshest critics of Western societies have been seeking to escape their deficiencies and injustices by physically removing themselves (unlike refugees from communist systems) while millions of people around the world seek to gain entry to these capitalist democracies, especially the United States, but also to Canada, Western Europe, or Australia.

Let us first ask what have been the indications of the massive discontents in communist societies and why they have intensified over time?

The Symptoms of Disaffection

The major and most striking indication of the dissatisfaction communist societies generate has been the recurrent, periodic outpouring of people (as well as individual defections) and the extraordinarily stringent and comprehensive measures these systems had introduced to prevent such unauthorized population movements. Despite the historical uniqueness of the phenomena—both the volume of the outflow and the preventative measure—little social scientific attention has been paid to them.[5]

To ask whether or not these refugees and immigrants were primarily motivated by political or economic dissatisfactions is pointless; their political and economic motives were inseparable. Since the economies of the countries concerned have been shaped by their ruling political elites and the prevailing official ideological-political criteria their economic performance cannot be separated from the political system. Even if the refugees were primarily motivated by matters material such dissatisfactions are of great political significance in social systems which have focused their energies on the restructuring of the economy and have sought to legitimate themselves by providing material improvements and security for all. In fact for many decades it has been the standard assessment among Western intellectuals and even many specialists, that these systems while deficient in the realm of political liberties or free expression have delivered economic security and impressively met the basic needs of their peoples.

It should be pointed out that these population movements were not trivial in size, nor were they confined to the upper strata of the populations or to those these governments labelled and treated as politically unreliable: millions of people of diverse socioeconomic background, age, occupation, and ethnicity sought to escape these systems.

First came hundreds of thousands of the so-called White Russians in the aftermath of the October Revolution of 1917; they were followed by at least 2 million Soviet citizens who had been slave laborers or prisoners of war in Germany and refused to return after World War II. (Hundreds of thousands were forcibly repatriated after World War II with the assistance of the British and U.S. occupation forces in Germany and Austria.) Over 200,000 Hungarians escaped after the defeat of the 1956 Revolution and approximately 100,000 Czechs in 1968 following the Soviet invasion. Several million East Germans departed between 1945 and 1961 (when the Berlin Wall was built to end the exodus) and a quarter million Soviet Jews were allowed to emigrate in the 1970s. More recently during the summer and fall of 1989 close to 300,000 East Germans departed (some via Hungary, others through Czechoslovakia) many of them in their own cars—beneficiaries of the highest living standard of any communist country. Confounding some Western theorists of human behavior and advocates of state socialism, they kept saying that they left because they wanted to live in a free society. Millions fled China under Mao to Hong Kong and elsewhere; millions from communist North to noncommunist South Vietnam and from the communist North to South Korea when these countries were divided. In our hemisphere communist Cuba lost 10 percent of its population. Even more remarkable, between 1820 and 1960 (a period of 140 years!) only 92,000 Cubans immigrated to the United States[6] when such activity was easy and unhindered by government imposed interference. By contrast since the establishment of the communist system—in less than three decades—one million left Cuba under very different and far more difficult circumstances.

Nicaragua lost during a decade of communist rule a similar or larger share of its population as an estimated 500,000 left the country with a population of 3.5 million.[7]

Topping all these figures over 3 million Afghans, or 20 percent of the population fled the communist regime since 1979. The communist victory in Indochina was followed by the boat people as well as overland refugees, their numbers exceeding 2 million.

Moreover, as the saying goes, numbers alone do not tell the story. In most instances these defections involved loss of family ties and personal property and considerable danger since illegal departures were punishable by long prison sentences and border guards in several countries were authorized to shoot at the escapees.

At a time when many communist or formerly communist systems no longer prohibit and prevent travel or emigration, the risks and hardships endured by earlier generation of escapees deserve to be recalled because they so tellingly illuminate both the determination to leave and the difficulties encountered.

The dangers faced by those trying to scale the Berlin Wall are well known. Less well known has been the fact that "some East Germans take a 10-to-1 chance in going by the direct route: a dash through barbed wire, electric trip wires and minefields along the country's 860 miles frontier with West Germany." Some looked for a less direct route: "From Romania to Yugoslavia they swam the Danube at the Iron Gate gorge, their few belongings . . . wrapped in watertight canvas. They were in constant fear of being . . . sent back to East Germany. . . . The majority jump East German ships, seek foreign assignments . . . use frogmen's suits to swim in the Baltic or slip gradually westward across less guarded frontiers within the Communist bloc."[8] In 1981, two East German families kayaked 100 miles across the Baltic Sea, paddling much of the time with their hands, to reach the shores of Denmark; in 1989 a Vietnamese man "escaped his homeland by riding for two days on the rudder housing of a Cypriot tanker ."[9]

Similar determination has been shown by many who sought to escape from China under Mao. According to one report "The escaping refugees spend four to eight hours in the water, dodging Chinese gunboats and battling the tides . . . [they] land with their arms and legs cut and bleeding from crawling across the oyster beds. . . . Not all the swimmers reach their destination. Some are picked up by Chinese gunboats . . . other are attacked by sharks, and a large number become exhausted and drown.[10] Earlier the Chinese authorities issued a directive which said that "anyone caught while trying to flee should be given prison terms of 'more than 10 years.'" It adds that border defense units should "'pursue and execute on the spot' individuals who defy arrest."[11]

Cuban refugees also took great risks: "A 22 year old man fled from Cuba . . . in the wheel pod of a jet airliner surviving an acute shortage of oxygen and temperatures of 40 degrees below zero during the nine-hour flight. A companion fell to death."[12] In another incident "the desperation of those who want to leave is evidenced by the long series of almost suicidal attempts to flee . . . in stolen boats and even inflated inner tubes. . . . A group of 150 . . . used a trailer truck to ram through the Cuban Army defenses around the U.S. Guantanamo Naval Base . . . 88 men, women and children defied the gunfire of Cuban troops and made it through the barbed wire obstacles to sanctuary. . . .

The rest were captured or shot by Cuban guards."[13] Seventeen years later such incidents are still common as in the case of two Cubans who made a 250 mile voyage in a "makeshift raft of inner tubes." An American immigration official commented "I am repeatedly amazed that these Cubans are so willing to risk their lives to come here . . . you have to be awful desperate to try something like this."[14]

The Indochinese boat people faced life-threatening risks in unsafe boats, lacking navigational skills, victimized by pirates, and without any assurance that any country would take them.

The attempt to depart legally had its penalties too: applications for exit visas in most of these countries usually led to loss of employment (sometimes housing as well) and other forms of stigmatization and disadvantage. The willingness to face such risks bears witness to the unusual intensity of the discontents of those attempting to depart either legally or illegally.

The second major indicator of the discontent has been the uprisings and revolts. They include the rebellion of Soviet sailors in Kronstadt (1921), the civil war in the Soviet Union in the early 1920s, the taking up of arms by disaffected Soviet citizens under General Vlasov in World War II; the East German uprising in 1953, the Posnan one (in Poland) in 1956, the Hungarian Revolution in 1956, the Czech attempt at political transformation in 1968, the Solidarity movement in the early 1980s in Poland; the guerilla war in Afghanistan since 1979. Anticommunist guerilla wars also broke out and endured in Angola, Mozambique, and Nicaragua; few remember the largely peasant, anti-Castro guerillas in Cuba who fought for years in the Escambray mountains in the early 1960s.

The third important reflection of discontent (actual or potential) among these populations has been the institutional structures and official policies imposed upon them to reduce and possibly eliminate political choice and to forestall or crush expressions of discontent. The most notable of them has been, needless to say, the one-party system itself and the lack of associational rights and freedoms it entails. The combination and stringency of these measures, and their insistent ideological legitimation led at earlier times to the designation of these systems as totalitarian.

The state-party monopoly over the means of mass communication and the thorough and comprehensive censorship likewise originated in the desire both to eliminate expressions of and the possible incitements to discontent and to remove any material from the educational or recreational diet of the population that could provide bases of comparison for evaluating their lives.

Finally, among these institutional structures mention must be made of the highly differentiated political police forces of virtually unlimited power, the most obtrusive institutional expression of the official determination to suppress discontent and to intimidate those willing to express it publicly. They, like other institutions of control, were generally modelled on the Soviet KGB; member states of what used to be the "socialist commonwealth" would also provide fraternal assistance to one another in setting up such police forces (the Soviet Union, Cuba, and East Germany were particularly active in providing such assistance).

The fourth indication of discontent can be found in the public statements and testimonies of individuals who live or had lived under these systems, in the huge literature of disenchantment and disaffection that sprang up almost as soon as the first communist system, the Soviet Union, was established. It was replicated by natives of each country where subsequently similar systems were imposed. They include classics of the genre by authors like Tamas Aczel, Humberto Belli, Liu Binyan, Vladimir Bukovsky, Milovan Djilas, Yue Daiyun, Carlos Franqui, Evgeniya Ginzburg, Piotor Grigorienko, Miklos Haraszti, Vaclav Havel, Liang Heng, Marek Hlasko, George Konrad, Victor Kravchenko, Milan Kundera, Anatoly Marchenko, Georgi Markov, Tibor Meray, Mihajlo Mihajlov, Czeslaw Milosz, Carlos Montaner, Andrei Sakharov, Victor Serge, Andrei Sinyavski, Alexander Solzhenitsyn, Boris Souvarine, Truong Nhu Tang, Doan Van Toai, and many other representing every major communist system in existence.

The Nature and Types of Deprivations

The intensity and endemic character of the discontent communist systems produce differ from those experienced in other societies, both the traditional ones and those of a capitalist-pluralist type. The key difference lies in the fact that many of the deprivations and frustrations citizens of communist systems experience do not appear to them in any way necessary, inevitable, "in the nature of things," but rather arbitrary, unnecessary, and capriciously man-made. This is so because the deprivations and restrictions experienced in communist systems are associated with rapid, large scale social change abruptly and ruthlessly imposed from above, with social engineering, and the prodding and coercing of people into new institutional arrangements and ways of living, with regimentation and "social mobilizations," with the political determination of priorities, *involuntarily* deferred gratifications, and above all with the newly imposed definitions of what is in the best interest of people, whatever they may think about their own best interests.

At the same time it is undeniable that communist systems emerge at certain historical moments partly in response to widespread social and economic problems, dislocations and injustices; they propose and promise sweeping transformations and improvements, nothing short of changing the human condition. These systems are or claim to be revolutionary—at least in the beginning—and therefore the dissatisfactions they create resemble in some measure those produced by every revolutionary movement and government. In its essentials, this is an old story: revolutions raise expectations (more often than not without gratifying them) and by doing so also create an intensified awareness of the discrepancy between the way things are and could or should be, between "is" and "ought", theory and practice.[15]

The aftermath of communist revolutions is especially disillusioning because expectations are dashed with great force and ruthlessness as revolutionary idealism vanishes and the tasks of retaining power and organizing the new society (and its economy) become paramount—the process Trotsky called "the Soviet Thermidor."[16]

The triumph of revolutions and their struggles to survive is followed by a profound change in the composition of the revolutionary vanguard—the supply of selfless idealists quickly runs out. Joseph Conrad grasped this phenomenon well before the proliferation of communist revolutions and their transformation:

In a real revolution the best characters do not come to the front. A violent revolution falls into the hands of narrow-minded fanatics. . . . The scrupulous and the just, the noble, humane and devoted natured, the unselfish and the intelligent may begin a movement—but it passes away from them. . . . Hopes grotesquely betrayed, ideals caricatured—that is the definition of revolutionary success.[17]

Trotsky noted the same process in his *The Revolution Betrayed*: "the outstanding representatives of the working classes either died in the civil war, or rose a few steps higher and broke away from the masses. And thus after . . . hopes and illusions, there came a long period of weariness, decline and sheer disappointment in the results of the revolution."[18] Thus a process of counterselection may operate in these societies: those who survive the struggles for power are likely to be the most ruthless and power-hungry, though not necessarily also the most unprincipled. On the contrary, their value commitments are likely to bolster the ruthlessness required for survival and their retention of power and for the implementation of blueprints the masses object to and fail to recognize as beneficial. They are the kind of people with the mentality of a surgeon who may declare an operation a success whether or not the patient survives.

As communist systems mature they seek to reduce expectations and often succeed in doing so for long periods of time; arguably their stability used to rest as much on the control of expectations as on that of behavior.

We are now in a period when the capacity of these systems to control expectations is slipping, indeed collapsing, hence the new expressions and explosions of discontent. It now seems increasingly true that in the long run, despite all the efforts at manipulating expectations, most people in communist systems end up feeling cheated, their expectations frustrated. These frustrations and dissatisfactions are of dual character. On the one hand, there is an abundance of tangible, objective reasons for them, such as shortages of food and housing; on the other hand, the widespread dissatisfaction is also due to what social scientists call "relative deprivation," relative, that is, to expectations, to notions of what might be possible, fair, or reasonable. The huge volume of propaganda citizens are exposed to, even when not taken seriously, enhances the awareness between "is" and "ought" and deepens contempt for the chronic failure of the authorities to deliver on their promises. (Affluent pluralistic societies also create vast amounts of relative deprivation but these have different sources, manifestations, and consequences.)

By the beginning of the 1990s little mystery remains regarding the specific grounds for dissatisfaction with life in communist systems. The highly articulated discontents of former and current citizens of these lands range from complaints about not having enough to eat to the restraints upon artistic creativity and self expression—deeply felt deprivations and frustrations encompassing the body and should in almost equal measure.

It is important to emphasize that although scarcities of food, housing, and consumer goods provide a major and perhaps the most tangible source of discontent in communist societies, such deprivations by themselves would not account for the pervasiveness and intensity of dissatisfaction. As noted above these deprivations become especially irksome against a background of promises and claims these regimes have habitually made, and that conflicted head on with the realities experienced daily by their citizens. Even groups enjoying preferential treatment may experience discontent. For example Armenians who returned from the United States to Soviet Armenia after World War II and subsequently tried desperately to leave the Soviet Union "have sometimes received preferential treatment." Most of them have been given apartments in new housing developments."[19] One of them who succeeded in returning to the United States when asked what "bothered him most about life in Soviet Armenia . . . [said] 'it was a place for the old people, a place in which to die. There was nothing for the young. If you weren't the relative of an official there was little chance to make progress in work, education or social life'."[20] While personal connections may also be useful in noncommunist countries, the latter do not bombard their citizens with an egalitarian ideology or insist that merit is the only determinant of social advancement and material advantage.

If only material deprivations motivated people to escape from communist countries it would be hard to explain why members of elite groups—ranging from Stalin's daughter and Castro's sister, to distinguished writers, dancers, musicians, scientists, and other successful professionals—have also been well-represented among the refugee populations. For example, as early as between 1954 and 1963, East German refugees included 3981 doctors, 1513 dentists, 708 lawyers and notaries public, 779 university lecturers, 18,062 other teachers, 19,289 engineers and technicians, 135 judges and prosecutors, 1162 pharmaceutical chemists.[21] Professionals and highly skilled workers (and the young) also dominated the most recent exodus of East German refugees who left in 1989. Likewise the first wave of Cuban immigrants were mostly professionals and, less surprisingly, business people.

According to a study of Soviet defectors (who escaped individually not as part of a wave) between 1969 and the mid-1980s there were hundreds of scholars and intellectuals, musicians, singers, dancers, athletes, military and security officers, diplomats, and various officials—in short, highly skilled people of privileged positions.[22]

None of the above is intended to belittle the importance of material shortages and deprivations as sources of discontent in these societies. The endemic scarcities of food are particularly important both as a symbolic expression of the inability of these systems to nurture their people and because of the all too obvious deprivations such scarcities inflict.

The problem of adequate food supplies has been emblematic of almost every communist system ranging from huge famines (in the Soviet Union, China, Ethiopia) to nagging, periodic shortages of one staple or another. Not only has food been scarce and badly distributed, much of it has also been expensive; according to a recent report 59 percent of the average family budget in the Soviet Union goes to food.[23] At this point in time when the Soviet Union is wrestling with serious economic reform, food production remains a special vulnerability of the system. As reported from Moscow, "there is consensus that the key to the impasse is food, that until there is enough food in the shops, energies needed to move the economy won't be released. But not only have reforms announced so far failed to spur deliveries, there is little confidence that this can be expected any time soon."[24] As the winter of 1990–91 approaches there is talk of emergency food supplies from the West to stave off hunger.

The discontents discussed here have two important characteristics. They are experienced by a wide variety of social groups (as is also reflected in the composition of refugee populations) and they are intense as is shown by the often desperate attempts refugees made to escape noted earlier.

But most societies that we call communist have always been poor hence economic hardships by themselves do not adequately account for the massive discontent that has made so many people inclined to vote with their feet.

Discontent over economic hardships is combined with resentment of regimentation, of political interference in daily lives, the lack of political, personal, and group freedoms. Large numbers of people rarely flee their country—when such actions are difficult and dangerous—merely to escape poverty.[25]

Jeane Kirkpartick put her finger on the peculiarly alienating character of communist autocracies, which until recently were also totalitarian (several of them remain totalitarian to this day):

Traditional autocrats leave in place existing allocations of wealth, power, status and other resources, which in most traditional societies favor an affluent few and maintain masses in poverty. But they worship traditional gods and observe taboos. They do not disturb the habitual rhythms of work and leisure, habitual places of residence, habitual patterns of family and personal relations. Because the miseries of traditional life are familiar they are bearable to ordinary people. . . . Such societies create no refugees.

Precisely the opposite is true of revolutionary Communist regimes. They create refugees by the millions because they claim jurisdiction over the whole life of the society and make demands for change that so violate internalized values and habits that inhabitants flee.[26]

There is another important reason people come to detest living in communist systems: it is the pressure to lie, to pretend, to dissimulate, to wear "the party mask," to drastically sever the connection between the public and the private self. A most extreme result of such pressures was observed in Mao's China where even language came to reflect this split. As Simon Leys wrote,

In China people have now at their disposal two levels of languages: one, human and natural which allows them to speak in their own voice, and which they use to talk about their health, the weather, food . . . and so forth, and another one, mechanical and shrill, to talk about politics . . . during one conversation, the person . . . may well switch to a kind of ideologic ventriloquism, according to the topics. In private life . . . ordinary people *never discuss politics*."[27]

Such a profound distaste for matters political was achieved by ceaselessly pressuring the population not merely to desist from opposing the government and its policies but to show enthusiastic support for them. In their zeal to create the "new man" these systems aimed at more than passive compliance; they wished to squeeze out of their citizens positive approval, active, vocal conformity, a show of enthusiasm. Hence the "mobilization" of the population, the endless demonstrations, rallies, marches, meetings, political indoctrination classes for all.

Ideological indoctrination has been a special source of resentment. Thus it was symbolic that one of the first demands Czech students made in late November 1989 was to expunge Marxism-Leninism from the curriculum: "the students at Prague's universities had placed a high priority on doing away with the obligatory Marxist-Leninist approach to virtually all academic disciplines. For them, this achievement was a moral victory without comparison."[28] Hungarian universities got rid of similar courses of study even before the great political changes of 1989–90.

To sum up: the profound discontents widespread and strongly felt in communist societies consist of a triad of mutually reinforcing deprivations and hardships:

1. material scarcities, often including those of basic necessities such as adequate food and shelter
2. a repressive regimentation, or political interference with personal and group autonomy and the associated pressure to engage in prolonged displays of political loyalty totally at odds with the inner beliefs and values of the citizen
3. a persistent sense of the gap between the claims and promises of the authorities and the way things are.

This potent mixture accounts for the intensity and varied expressions of the discontents sketched above.

Why Have Communist Systems Proved to be Peculiarly Depriving?

It remains to explain *why* communist systems create the discontents sketched above.

The most general explanation of the failures of communist systems and of the dissatisfaction they generate is to be found in the tension between their aspirations and promises and their inability to make good on these promises.

Communist systems promised spectacular material improvements and benefits, as well as modernization without alienation, without damage to the human fabric of society; they also promised social justice, the attainment of, or substantial progress toward socioeconomic equality; they were to establish what idealistic Americans call "a caring society"; they were also going to construct a social order that was to encourage and maximize political participation; even more importantly, they promised a society permeated by a sense of community and sustaining purpose; they held out the prospect of exceeding all historically known levels and forms of individual fulfillment. In this historically unique social system there was to be no conflict between the individual and society, social and personal interest, between various groups of society, society and the state, the leaders and the led.

These were, needless to say, unrealistic promises born out of the original, utopian impulse that motivated many of the early leaders and founding fathers of communist states. They tried to change the human condition and forms of social organization beyond what seems attainable in the light of historical experience, available social scientific knowledge, and common sense. These systems did indeed operate with an unrealistic conception of human nature: initially far too optimistic, later on exceedingly pessimistic (this pessimism can be measured by the growing restrictions imposed on people and the associated fear that if left alone, they will make unwise choices). Hence the seemingly inexorable growth of huge controlling bureaucracies reflecting the massive mistrust of the rulers toward their subjects.

The misconceptions of human nature and motivation manifested themselves most clearly in the realm of economics, in matters of production and work. Thus the collectivization of agriculture rested in part on a monumental error, the belief that people would work hard without owning the land (or at least without some substantial control over their working conditions and the fruits of their labor) and that such a collectivized mode of production would be far more productive than that based on private ownership.

Speaking more generally, it may be argued that the mismanagement of the economy—a major source of dissatisfaction in these societies—has been rooted in erroneous conceptions of human nature revealed in the endless debates about motivation and incentives (moral vs. material) and notions of self and group interest. As Milovan Djilas summed it up: "Communism is contrary to human nature. The Communist party is monopolistic and totalitarian. . . . If human nature was perfect, communism might be possible. . . . Capitalism functions better because it is closer to human nature. It permits the human being to express more freedom. Communism has failed . . . because human nature cannot live without freedom, without choices, without . . . alternatives."[29]

The poor performance of the economy, as is so often noted these days, has also been related to overcentralization, to the replacement of the market by central planning. These tendencies in turn are linked to the concentration of political power which interferes with feedback processes.

Of course the poor performance of these economies and the neglect of the consumer sector also had to do with the priorities set at the highest levels: guns always came before butter. This is still the case. As an American commentator put it recently: "The Soviet Union has the means to solve its economic crisis independently [of Western help, that is] if the Party is ready to renounce expansion and share power. To have the resources necessary to help awaken the productive capacities of the population, it would be enough to decollectivize agriculture, abandon a few expensive overseas clients, and reduce the size of the Soviet armed forces to a level sufficient for security but not for intimidation."[30]

While residues of utopian thinking, erroneous conceptions of human nature, and misplaced priorities (associated with expansionism and domestic political controls) provide more than adequate explanation of the chronic economic difficulties of communist societies, we must look to somewhat different factors to account for the type of dissatisfaction elicited by the regimentation of daily life, the ubiquitousness of controls[31] and the sense of a confined existence.

Why have most communist systems been highly coercive through most of their history?

The simple answer is that communist systems have been repressive because their policies and ruling elites have been unpopular yet had no desire to share or relinquish power and because they could not get the population to cooperate with or acquiesce in their policies without punitive pressures and threats. Moreover their particular coerciveness, until recently, was rooted in ambitious blueprints for changing the insitutions of society and the life of their citizens, indeed in the very notion of creating a new human being and radically improving human nature. The more such changes were attempted or implemented, the more coercion became necessary.

There was also a predisposing factor underlying and encouraging the concentration and abuse of power to be found in the philosophical legacy. Marxism-Leninism had great aversion to the concentration of economic power in private hands, but indifference regarding the same process in the political realm. Or, perhaps more accurately, it was an outlook that took it for granted that if, in some unspecified way, the economy would be taken out of the hands of the "exploiters," political democracy and participation would almost automatically follow. The possibility that the removal of the ownership of the means of production from private to public realm would in practice mean some kind of state control and with it the rise of a new and more powerful bureaucracy did not seem to concern the founding fathers, nor their descendants seeking to implement their vision. It was more than implicit in Lenin's outlook that the concentration of political power by itself was not something problematic and threatening that would require some institutional response or safeguard, provided that the power was concentrated in the right hands, in the hands of the people of goodwill, integrity, insight, discipline, understanding of history, and so forth. He proposed no mechanism for identifying and selecting such people.

There have been other, more specific elements in the pattern of dissatisfaction here discussed. In a number of communist systems, such as those of Eastern Europe, (and among numerous nationalities of the USSR) the dissatisfactions noted above have been intensified by their combination with nationalistic grievances. In these countries (and regions) the communist system was an alien import, imposed from the outside, offensively "unnatural," inflaming indigenous sensibilities.

Why the Recent Upsurge of Discontent?

Why has the public expression of dissatisfaction with communist systems increased so explosively in the last few years in both Eastern Europe and Soviet Union? Why indeed have these systems undergone profound change? This is an extremely difficult question to answer because it amounts to asking and explaining why social change occurs, and, even more difficult to explain, why it occurs at a particular time?

We heard much about the long stagnation and corruption of the Brezhnev era which led to pent-up desires for change and improvement in the Soviet Union personified by Gorbachev. Such developments, in turn, spilled over into Eastern Europe legitimating existing discontents. On the other hand, it could also be argued that the growing discontents in Eastern Europe, as for example in Hungary and Poland, had no discernible connection with events in the Soviet Union and had predated the Gorbachev era. One can pinpoint, in the case of Hungary and Poland, economic deterioration as a specific component and explanation of intensified discontent in recent years, contributing to the rapid unravelling of the legitimacy of the system—a legitimacy that has never been deep or strong. As George Konrad put it, at present "it is the regime's mismanagement of the country that is increasingly upsetting people . . . the national debt . . . now stands at $17 billion. That money was simply wasted on subsidies for industries . . . which are . . . money-losing."[32]

While the Soviet presence and domination has always been unwelcome in Eastern Europe, of late the apparently weakened will of the Soviet leadership has encouraged nationalistic self-assertion and the massive public expressions of discontent, first in Hungary and Poland followed by East Germany, Czechoslovakia, and even Bulgaria and Romania. Local leaders no longer certain that their power (once a gift of the Soviet Union) would be propped up by Soviet force were further undermined by an unexpected factor: the subversive spectacle of a reform-oriented Soviet leader. In turn, the Soviet system came to face its own severe problems presented by the nationalistic self-assertion on the part of its own minorities in the Baltic States, Armenia, Azerbajdzhan, Moldavia, the Ukraine, and elsewhere. As of this writing in late 1990, virtually every one of the fifteen republics of the Soviet Union made some declaration of sovereignty and took steps to broaden the margin of self-determination.

Why the System Failed?

In the final analysis communist societies failed to deliver on their promises because of the intractable problem of ends and means and the similarly insoluble problems of reconciling the long and the short run. Future-oriented systems lacking transcendental credentials have difficulty legitimating themselves especially when daily experience routinely conflicts with the promised future. The good intentions of the early days are inadequate to provide the wherewithal for the prodiguous transformations anticipated; moreover, as time passes the idealistic components of these intentions increasingly give way to the determination to cling to power at all cost.

Most recently several communist elites displayed an unanticipated loss of nerve, their determination to cling to power eroding as they faced surging popular discontent. It is not easy to know what came first: the loss of nerve—which in turn made it easier for public expression of discontent or surface—or the discontent which the rulers increasingly sensed and which contributed to their demoralization? While these systems in Eastern Europe never enjoyed popular legitimacy it appeared for a long time that the rulers at least convinced themselves of their own right to rule unhindered by the preferences of their subjects. This no longer seem to be the case.

In the light of recent developments several conclusions may be drawn. One is that motivationally speaking, the will to power even when bolstered by a combination of self-legitimating ideology and material privilege is insufficient to hold on to power when it becomes clear that those possessing it have become totally isolated from their own people and can no longer count on external (i.e., Soviet) assistance.

It is also of interest to note that contrary to widespread Western views, these systems embarked on the road to democratization at a time of declining living standards and growing economic difficulties and not when their economies were functioning better and their peoples benefitting from improved standards of living. We have been often told that communist systems cannot democratize until and unless they reach material comforts and security and therefore it is in the Western interest to assist them on the road to economic improvement. (By contrast many East Europeans believe that should the Soviet economy recover, the political system could return to its old authoritarian and expansionist ways as there will be no longer incentive for reform.)

Recent developments have also made clear that the discontents these systems create have as much to do with matters material as they do with personal and group freedoms—another point worth stressing since for decades it was another part of the conventional wisdom in the West that communist systems greatly improved standards of living, public health, housing, but unfortunately they did so at the expense of democratic freedoms, or—it was also often said—at the expense of our ethnocentric, Western notions of freedom. In fact these systems were incapable of delivering either what are sometimes called procedural (negative) or substantive (positive) freedoms.

Many of the ends communist systems pursued were morally questionable to begin with, others, clearly unattainble, were abandoned; in turn, the means regularly undermined, discredited, or contradicted even the more laudable ends. Retaining and maximizing power became a goal in itself and communist political elites proved as corruptible as any other, or more so.

While overwhelming state power can discourage resistance and suppress expressions of discontent for lengthy periods of time it is clear by now that it cannot legitimate—and thus sustain in the long run—systems which can neither satisfy the spirit nor nourish the body.

Notes

1. "The Myths of Revolution." *New Republic*, 29 April 1985, p. 9.
2. I use "communist" to apply to political systems which (a) seek legitimay by adopting some version of Marxism-Leninism as the official belief system; (b) are one-party systems and (c) established political (state) controls over most of the economy.
3. Apparently matters economic had little to do with the policies of the systems resisting change since their economies are no more productive, efficient, or abundant than those of the countries which embarked on the process of liberalization. Geographic, cultural, and historical explanations of such resistance to change may be more plausible. Each of these systems has been characterised by

long periods of extreme concentration of power in the hands of single individuals; in two cases (Cuba and North Korea) the original revolutionary leaders are still in power; in one, (Albania) such a revolutionary leader was in power for several decades. Also noteworthy that in two of the countries mentioned—Cuba and North Korea—the leaders established, as it were, dynasties, as the supreme leader is grooming members of his family for succession. The other commonality is geographic isolation.

4. "Borderline Marxists." *The Nation*, 2 October 1989, p. 333. These writers were unable or unwilling to grasp that there have been some rather obvious reasons for East Germans to go to West Germany rather than to England or the United States,—other than revulsion from capitalism as practised in these countries and other than the search for capitalism with a human face! Indeed the belated recognition that there is such a thing as "a capitalism with a human face" is itself a novelty among *Nation* authors, presumably forced upon them by the narrowing of alternatives produced by the developments of the communist world.

5. For two exceptions see Paul Hollander: "Border Controls: An Integral Part of the Soviet Social-Political System," in *The Many Faces of Socialism*, New Brunswick: Transaction, 1983; and Vladimir Krasnov, *Soviet Defectors*, Stanford: Hoover Institution Press, 1986.

6. *World Almanac and Book of Facts*. New York: Newspaper Enterprise Association, 1985, p. 254.

7. Paul Berman. "Double Reality—People's Revolution vs. Sandinista Revolution." *Village Voice*, 5 December 1989, p. 43.

8. Hans Stueck. "East Germans in West Tell of Desperate Escapes." *New York Times*, 26 October 1968.

9. United Press International. "2 East German Couples Feel With Child Across Baltic Sea." *New York Times*, 21 October 1981; Associated Press "Asylum for Vietnamese Refugee," *New York Times*, 2 November 1989.

10. Ian Stewart. "Chinese Refugees Swim Across a Perilous Bay to Hong Kong." *New York Times*, 22 June 1972.

11. Tillman Durdin. "China Acts to Bar Escapes to Hong Kong." *New York Times*, 12 January 1971.

12. Richard Eder. "Cuban Hidden in Landing Gear Survives Flight to Spain at −40." *New York Times*, 5 June 1969.

13. Juan DeOnis. "Why Some Will Risk All To Leave." *New York Times*, 12 January 1969.

14. Associated Press. "Eight days at sea on raft: Cubans survive 'miracle' voyage." *Daily Hampshire Gazette*, 22 April 1986.

15. Paul Hollander. "Marxist Societies: The Relationship Between Theory and Practice." In Hollander op. cit., 1983, p. 201–237.

16. Leon Trotsky. *The Revolution Betrayed*. New York: Pathfinder, 1972 (first published 1937), p. 86. see also Adam Ulam: *The Unfinished Revolution*. Boulder: Westview, 1979.

17. Quoted in Josef Skvorecky, "A Revolution Is Usually the Worst Solution" in *The Writer and Human Rights*, edited by the Toronto Arts Group. New York: Anchor/Doubleday, 1983 p. 115.

18. Trotsky, op. cit., p. 89.

19. Henry Tanner. "American-Armenians Who Left U.S. for Soviet Yearn to Return." *New York Times*, 18 March 1964.

20. Martin Gansberg. "Armenians Glad To Be Back In U.S." *New York Times*, 22 March 1964.
21. *Escapes from the Soviet Zone* [pamphlet]. Bonn: Federal Ministry for Expellees, Refugees and War Victims, 1964, p. 7.
22. Krasnov, op. cit., pp. 200–207.
23. Bill Keller. "For Russians, Food Buying Is No Bargain." *New York Times*, 16 September 1988.
24. Flora Lewis. "Young Marx and Old Lenin." *New York Times*, 11 September 1988.
25. The poor who came to America were not in any way hindered or discouraged from doing so by their governments; they were not treated as traitors or potential traitors for wishing to migrate and did not have to confront "iron curtains" and border police forces. They could take what property they had. Today the worst thing that happens to illegal entrants such as those from Mexico is that they are sent back by bus.
26. Jeane Kirkpatrick. *Dictatorships and Double Standards*. New York: Simon and Schuster, 1982, p. 49–50; see also Peter Berger. "Are Human Rights Universal?" *Commentary*, September, 1977.
27. Simon Leys. *Chinese Shadows*. New York: Viking 1977, p. 168.
28. Esther B. Fein. "Czech Students Rejoice At News of Concessions." *New York Times*, 29 November 1989.
29. "Communism, Religion, Freedom." *Freedom at Issue*, May–June 1989, p. 6.
30. David Satter. "Why Glasnost Can't Work." *New Republic*, 13 June 1988, p. 21.
31. For example Ceaucescu favored the conversion of all telephones in Romania into listening devices. One of his officials described the advantages of the new device: "This is not just normal telephone. It also serves as a very sensitive microphone, capable of recording all conversations in the room where it is installed. If this telephone is approved as the only kind legally allowed . . . it will open a new era of broad-scale electronic surveillance, without the need for surreptitious entries into private homes to install microphones." Ion Mihai Pacepa. *Red Horizons*. Washington D.C.: Regnery Gateways, 1987, p. 134. The story is of course reminiscent of the project described in Solzhenitsyn's *First Circle*.
32. George Konrad. "Middle-Class Opposition in a Communist Country." *Uncaptive Minds*, September-October, 1988, p. 43.

5

Postmortem on Soviet Propaganda?

From my earliest days as a student of Soviet society in the West (after observing it from Hungary between 1945–56), I have been baffled by the lack of interest Western specialists on Soviet affairs have shown in Soviet propaganda. Not only are there few monographs devoted to it, major texts on the Soviet political system make hardly a reference to this prominent institution. Although the Soviet propaganda effort has by now passed its peak, it is of interest to look back on its golden years and decades.

As has been the case with Western assessments of other Soviet phenomena, the neglect of propaganda can be explained not by the part it has played in the Soviet system but by circumstances peculiar to the West, by the outlook and attitudes of Westerners contemplating the Soviet Union. Its neglect is all the more startling since from the earliest days of the existence of the Soviet Union propaganda has been a massive, obtrusive, and ubiquitous presence; its importance reflected both in official statements extolling its social-political contributions and in the willingness of the authorities to invest prodigious material and human resources in it production and dissemination.

The intellectual and academic-disciplinary background of Western students of the Soviet system helps to explain the lack of attention to propaganda. They were mostly political scientists and historians not trained in or predisposed to the study of phenomena such as propaganda. Those more plausibly attracted to and trained for its study, social psychologists and sociologists, have always been in short supply among Americans specializing in Soviet affairs.

There has also been a connection between indifference toward Soviet propaganda and a dismissal of the significance of ideology, or official beliefs in Western studies of the USSR.[1] After all, much of propaganda is applied ideology consisting of the dissemination of either watered-down versions of the official ideology, or of exhortations derived from attempts to implement ideology and its promises. No propaganda can be understood without knowing its ideological underpinnings. One may also think of political propaganda as the systematic dissemination of wishful thinking for the benefit of the masses (a usage that comes close to the meaning of ideology developed by Karl Mannheim) on the part of political elites.

Belittling the importance of ideology in Soviet politics has been a longstanding Western habit, perhaps in part because doing so was congenial with *both* a critical and sympathetic view of the Soviet systems. Those who were critical could argue that ideology has been little more than a smokescreen for official scheming and that it had lost all connection with the real objectives of the system; that ideology was a travesty of the original ideals, a device to rationalize duplicitously the powerhunger of the rulers and their aggressive designs. In turn those sympathic could find relief in asserting the unimportance of ideology, suggesting that the system had ceased to be zealously committed to its messianic and missionary designs, that it was becoming more pragmatic and rational, ready to adopt less threatening and more conventional patterns of great power behavior and accept the global status quo, seeking accommodation with the West, while also becoming more responsive to the wishes of its people at home.

Discounting the importance of ideology was also supported by the argument that most Soviet policies, domestic or foreign, are determined above all, by age-old Russian historical traditions and aspirations, and especially, the drive to modernize. It was also often noted that ideology could not be important and taken seriously as a determinant of policy in view of the frequent and often drastic shifts in the party-line and the corresponding opportunistic reinterpretation of sacred doctrines. While all these propositions had large elements of truth they failed to grasp the role ideology played in the exercise of power, the self-justification of the ruling elites, and the bolstering their political will. Developments since Gorbachev—which coincided with the decline of Soviet propaganda—indirectly confirm this view.

The neglect of propaganda in Western inquiries into the nature of the Soviet system was also connected with the vast amount of political violence and coercion during much of Soviet history. There seemed little point in studying propaganda—which, after all seeks to mold behavior in nonviolent ways—when to all intents and purposes Soviet rule and the overt conformity of the citizens rested on coercion and intimidation. At the same time it was hardly ever asked why the regime bothered to pour huge resources into propaganda if it could attain its goals through the formidable institutions of coercion readily available and lavishly utilized. More often than not Soviet propaganda was regarded as a peculiar ritual or reflex, an odd institutional compulsion which hardly served any discernible purpose besides providing some assurance to the leaders that the population was acquainted with the cardinal articles of faiths and properly instructed about the policies currently pursued and provided with standards against which to measure the permissible limits of behavior.

Since Soviet propaganda was typically deployed in combination with coercion or its imminent threat, it was always difficult to assess what part precisely it played in the maintenance and stability of the system, in molding the behavior of the citizen, and how essential it was for regimenting and mobilizing the population. Whatever its actual functions and accomplishments have been, it is at least appropriate to regard it as part of the doctrinal heritage bequeathed by Lenin who was fully persuaded of the utility of ideas as weapons in the political struggle.

Among the reasons that may further account for the Western indifference toward Soviet propaganda one should also mention its notorious dullness; students of Soviet affairs in the West were not anxious to immerse themselves in the study of something so painfully tedious, repetitive, and predictable. Moreover Western, and especially Anglo-Saxon students of politics have been reluctant to rank propaganda among the truly powerful influences over human behavior due to their more rationalistic view of human nature and their corresponding skepticism about the degree to which human beings can be manipulated. The Western liberal tradition as a whole resists the notion that people can be diverted by mere words from the pursuit of their genuine interests as perceived by themselves. Westerners, more in control of their lives and leading a far less politicized existence, are less inclined to give much weight to what propaganda may accomplish and they are especially unfamiliar with the peculiar mix of coercive persuasion and regimentation that long prevailed in Soviet society. The American public in particular is handicapped in understanding Soviet propaganda by their own experience of American electoral propaganda campaigns. Pandering campaign commercials do not help to grasp the nature of Soviet propaganda, which is at once relentlessly self-congratulatory and demanding of exertions and sacrifices of one kind or another. Soviet propaganda campaigns always had an energetic quality and thoroughness which conflicted with the image of the Soviet Union in more recent times (especially during the Brezhnev era) as a lethargic, problem-ridden country, anxious to attend to its domestic needs and weaknesses. There is reason to believe that after the military and the KGB, the agit-prop apparatus has been the most lavishly funded of all Soviet institutions during much of the Soviet history.

Western political propaganda reflects the institutional pluralism and basic values of the political culture in which it is generated. American electoral propaganda in particular is conveyed by personable candidates for office vying with one another in promising how to make the life of the voters effortlessly easier, not unlike advertisements for consumer goods and services.

Soviet propaganda for much of its existence was monolithic and enjoyed an uncontested monopoly over all means of mass communication; the official values it articulated could not be publicly challenged; it was also firmly backed by the power of the state. Soviet propaganda was in fact a product of the publicly and unhesitatingly proclaimed belief in the infallibility of the Party and its leader in power at any given time. Such conditions had profound consequences for the character and quality of the propaganda produced. Above all the lack of competition or public challenge imparted a freedom to redefine or misrepresent reality, boldly and sometimes imaginatively. The mendacity of Soviet propaganda could take flight in a throughly noncompetitive communications environment. Moreover the possibility of coercive sanctions for disrespect or noncompliance strengthened rather than weakened the impact of propaganda. The alternative to being "persuaded" might have been the loss of job, promotion, housing, or residence permit; or in more serious cases, a stay in a psychiatric hospital or imprisonment. There were powerful incentives for aligning overt behavior with the messages and suggestions of the official propaganda. If in the opinion of Marcuse and his followers "repressive tolerance" assured stability in the West, in the Soviet Union repressive intolerance—embodied in the coordination of propaganda and coercion—yielded results in securing conformity.

Another important source of Western indifference to and incomprehension of Soviet propaganda and its role in the exercise of political power was an unawareness (at any rate among the general public, not the experts) that in Soviet political culture propaganda was never viewed with the distasted found in Western, liberal societies. "Propaganda" has been an honorable and respectable concept in Soviet political discourse (thanks largely to Lenin) and not something the government or the ruling party had to engage in apologetically, surreptitiously, or half-heartedly. Nor has it been widely realized in the West that the rise of Soviet propaganda, or the Soviet "propaganda state"[2] was virtually predetermined by the circumstances under which the Soviet Union came into existence. Given the circumstances, the sluggish forces of history had to be replaced or supplemented by human will and organization. The Soviet system was not, to say the least, irresistibly propelled into power by the elemental and overwhelming support of the masses; nor has it stayed in power by relying on such support. The masses, at every step along the road to power and during the consolidation of power, had to be prodded, exhorted, purged of false consciousness, or "persuaded"—hence the unique role of propaganda and the steady demand for its services throughout Soviet history. While many Westerners are under the impression that like all bad things associated with the Soviet system, propaganda, too, was introduced by Stalin, Peter Kenez documented the crucial role of propaganda in the establishment and consolidation of the Soviet state between 1917 and the mid-1920s. It was after all, even in its early days, a political system with a very modest popular backing, hence efforts to expand popular support, to assure, motivate, and exhort the population were important. Kenez concluded that "The regime could not have existed without its special brand of propaganda . . . propaganda played a large role in the 1917 victory of the Communists and an even greater part in their ability to retain their power . . . during the 1917–1921 Civil War . . . ideological struggle, indoctrination, propaganda . . . matter."[3]

It should also be noted that "persuasion," Leninist-Soviet style, was not to be confused with Western rational-liberal notions of changing minds by reasoned argument, by exposing people to new information. The goal of the Soviet leaders was not so much to alter the world view of their audiences. Rather, as Adam Ulam suggested, Soviet propaganda "might be described as ideological noise, intended to crowd out any voices of protest, or doubt and to stultify minds into conformity." Or, as Peter Kenez put it, "the main achievement of the Soviet regime was something negative: It succeeded in preventing the formation and articulation of alternative points of view. The Soviet people ultimately came not so much to believe the Bolsheviks's world view as to take it for granted. . . . In circumstances where only one point of view can be expressed the distinction between belief and nonbelief, truth and untruth is washed away."[4] Simon Ley's summary of the basic principles of Chinese propaganda under Mao makes a similar point:

> It soon becomes obvious that this gigantic enterprise . . . is animated . . . by frightfully rigorous and coherent intention. The aim is to anesthetize critical intelligence, purge the brain and inject the cement of official ideology into the emptied skull; once hardened, this will leave no room for the introduction of any new idea.[5]

Among the roots of Soviet propaganda, reference must also be made to Lenin's and his followers' pessimistic view of human nature. The workers were prone to "trade union consciousness," that is, putting their (contemptible) short-term economic interests ahead of the grandiose schemes of social-political transformation Lenin favored; the peasants were even worse as far as their political consciousness was concerned; the intellectuals, unless closely disciplined by the Party were not to be trusted either. Lenin and his successors were haunted by fears of "spontaneity"—hardly a concept with romantic connotations for them, but one that signified human fallibility and mindlessness, short-sighted, impulsive political behavior. If the people were untrustworthy to begin with, and if the institutional transformations failed to raise their political consciousness adequately, there was all the more reason for the generous use of propaganda. As Kenez put it, "the major elements in the Bolshevik ideological heritage were a clear understanding of the important role of ideas in history and a belief that some people knew better than others; therefore it was unwise to allow people to look after their own interests."[6]

In contrast to the lack of Western social scientific interest in Soviet propaganda, Nazi propaganda attracted considerable attention and was carefully studied. It is instructive to ponder why there was greater interest in Nazi than Soviet propaganda. The wartime context is one explanation. Understanding and countering Nazi propaganda was part of the war effort to defeat a cunning and ruthless enemy. It was also believed that Nazi propaganda was highly skilled and effective and a key to early Nazi successes, especially on the domestic front. It seemed plausible that a system as evil as Hitler's could only seize and retain power if it managed to deceive and trick people, that it could not have any rational appeals.

Certainly Nazi propaganda, domestic or foreign, was more colorful and vivid than its predictable and plodding Soviet counterpart. Nazism became in Western eyes inextricably linked with propaganda which enthralled the masses and encapsulated the evil essence of the regime and it messages of hate. Soviet propaganda even during the height of the Cold War was less of a threat; moreover Americans in particular did not know, and did not care to know, about the venom spewed forth at them by the Soviet propaganda apparatus and those who did shrugged it off. Most importantly not even during the classical Cold War years—between the late 1940s and the mid-1950s—was the Soviet system perceived as being as vicious and dangerous as Nazi Germany.

Unlike much of the propaganda of Nazi Germany, Soviet propaganda demanded of people forms of behavior which did not come readily to those it was aimed at: to work hard, to be disciplined, to surrender personal to (questionably defined) public interest, to defer gratification. Even as late as 1987, the official May Day slogans exhorted the Soviet people to "Be in the vanguard of restructuring! Display activeness and innovation in work! Struggle with revolutionary persistence . . . persistently deepen restructuring . . . increase labor productivity . . . ensure the fulfillment of the plan . . . increase effectiveness . . . strengthen discipline. . . . Master up-to-date methods . . . increase political activeness . . . increase the role of socialist competition . . . protect . . . the gains of socialism."[7]

This is not to say that Soviet propaganda has been limited to such vacuous exhortations, or that it did not provide opportunities for enjoyable scapegoating and the buttressing of a sense of collective self-righteousness which is far from alien to the Soviet masses. In the words of George Feiffer, "Soviet propaganda's skillful selection, misrepresentation and jingoistic distortion of news effectively manipulates the Russians' propensity to see their long-suffering selves as the injured party in world affairs."[8] The latter observation also helps to understand the enduring commitment to the otherwise peculiar notion of "provocation" as in the case of the violation of Soviet airspace by the Korean airliner subsequently shot down.

Neither the contributions of Kenez nor his few predecessors,[9] nor the recent efforts of the U.S. Department of State[10] (which annually catalogues Soviet propaganda campaigns and organizations abroad) have succeeded in increasing either the scholarly or popular appreciation of Soviet propaganda in the United States. The deeper roots of these attitudes—in addition to those already noted—may be found in the favorable attitudes toward the Soviet Union that prevailed in the West during the 1930s and World War II when Americans in particular were subjected to a propaganda campaign by their own mass media seeking to induce sympathetic attitudes toward the great wartime ally. In those days dwelling on the nature of Soviet propaganda and its contribution to the maintenance of the totalitarian system would have been utterly improper. More recently Soviet "peace" propaganda aimed at Americans has had a soothing effect on American public opinion and contributed to a reluctance to take a critical view of the Soviet system.

The rise of Gorbachev and the associated changes further diminished Western interest in Soviet propaganda and this time with better reason than in the past. Glasnost undermined the official monopoly on truth and on the means of mass communication; it also legitimated challenges to the official views of reality, including those of the past; it became possible to reject altogether official values and policies in public. Most importantly the political changes since the rise of Gorbachev damaged severely and possibly irreparably the idea of the infallibility of the Party, its leader and the authorities—an idea which had heretofore been the key determinant of the character and quality of Soviet propaganda. The decline of Soviet propaganda under Gorbachev confirmed the interdependence of the unchallenged official monopoly on power, the ideologically derived self-righteousness and intolerance *and* the large scale production of political propaganda.

To be sure the process has been gradual. In the earlier Gorbachev years old style misrepresentations of reality persisted. For example it was under Gorbachev that the Soviet propaganda apparatus embarked one of its most remarkable campaigns of disinformation designed to persuade global audiences that the AIDS epidemic was the result of American experiments in biological warfare and that the U.S. was working on biological weapons specifically designed to kill blacks and/or Arabs.[11] It has also been noted of Gorbachev's much acclaimed book, *Perestroika*, published in several Western languages that it "aims at a very low level, one that Soviet experts must have decided represents the common Western denominator of ignorance and wishful thinking. Not the least depressing feature of this work, hailed by the *New York Times* as 'the international publishing event of the year' is what it reveals of the Soviet establishments's contempt for the West."[12]

But the changes which gathered force were bound to undermine the Soviet propaganda state revealing once more its dependence on the official monopoly of power, which, in turn, used to rest on an untroubled sense of legitimacy of the rulers. That sense of self-assurance and legitimacy is gone. Under Gorbachev, Soviet leaders and official spokesmen engaged in an unprecedented series of revelations that culminated in the admission that Soviet realities have been profoundly different from what official propaganda proposed all along. As a Soviet emigré scholar put it, "In Gorbachev's Soviet Union, almost every legitimizing myth is being shattered."[13]

Soviet people thus learned that not only is their country not superior materially or in regard to social justice to those in the West but that it is also burdened with a spectacular collection of social problems and ills of its own; that the whole history of the system has been riddled with repression and falsehood; that none of the alleged accomplishments have been genuine or substantial; that Soviet life is deeply imbued with corruption and inequality; that there is hardly anything in the Soviet past that would justify and legitimate the system and the sacrifices it exacted and that even the greatest figure of Soviet history, Lenin, was not without faults and shares some of the blame for the degeneration of the system.

By the late 1980s the Soviet propaganda apparatus had become seriously threatened by the relaxation of censorship (which used to be its essential complement), the expansion of free expression, and the overall impact of social forces unleashed by Gorbachev. At the time of this writing in late 1990, the line between official and unofficial and dissenting views and voices has become blurred. The new publicity given to the great historic crimes of the past (including the collectivization campaign, the massacre of Polish officers in the Katyn forest, new details of the purges), the malfunctioning of the economy, the plight of the poor and old, the discontent of ethnic minorities, the gradual questioning of Lenin's accomplishment—all these developments altered what remains of Soviet propaganda beyond recognition. Moreover these developments took place at a time when "persuasion" is no longer backed up by coercion and when the self-assurance of the leaders has vanished.

Soviet propaganda as we have known it for almost seventy years is not compatible with the developments of the last few years, with the loss of the official monopoly of the means of communication, access to legitimate information, and indeed truth itself. It is hard to conceive of Soviet propaganda bereft of its habitual mendacity, shrillness, selfrighteousness, dogmatism, and sloganeering.

Whereas in the past Soviet mass media portrayed Soviet society as united, harmonious, purposeful, contented, strong and stable, lacking in any serious problems (other than those connected with some foreign intrigues or the survivals of the past), a society which had not even traffic accidents and reports; today there is an endless stream of revelations and reports about the problems and difficulties of Soviet life. In one of the most astonishing reversals, the Soviet mass media increasingly resembles those in the West as it wallows in bad news. As a recent observer noted, "The cracks in Soviet society are so visible these days that they have become part of the landscape. . . . Bad news pours in all over, and headlines read like chapters in the Apocalypse. . . . The revelations are relentless."[14]

At times when all Soviet official verities are crumbling and being questioned it is tempting to conclude that the Soviet propaganda enterprise also turned out to be a monumental failure, that it could not create (at least in overwhelming numbers) loyal Soviet citizens impervious to skepticism, willing to defer gratifications, ready to give every benefit of doubt to their leaders, convinced of the moral superiority of their system of government. Certainly the eruptions of popular discontent alternating with pervasive cynicism, the eagerness on the part of many citizens to set up or join new, unorthodox organizations, the determination to probe and expose every departure of practice from theory—all these phenomena suggest that propaganda made little durable impact on many vocal segments of the population.

At the same time it is difficult to separate the failure of propaganda from all the other failures of the system, notably from the apparent collapse of the sense of mission and self-assurance of the leadership that used to motivate the agit-prop enterprise. It is difficult to produce propaganda on behalf of a cause that is no longer embraced without reservation. Nor are there many or any sacred values or entities left to promote and defend. Finally, the machinery of coercion no longer imposes overt conformity and a respectful attitude on the citizens that in the past used to make it difficult to know if people were "persuaded" by propaganda or merely intimidated by the agencies of coercion. But even if propaganda has ceased to be an important institution in Soviet life today this should not lead us to conclude that it *never* was important, only that its use was inextricably tied to the proclaimed infallibility and power of the rulers. To understand why and how the sense of self-vindication and legitimacy of the rulers vanished remains a challenge to students of the Soviet system and also a key for a better understanding of the official propaganda of the past.

Postscript, February 1991

As noted earlier the nature and fortunes of Soviet propaganda have always been tied to the manner in which power is exercised. With the apparent reemergence of conservative forces in Soviet political life in late 1990 and early 1991, official propaganda has also revived although it has not yet gone unchallenged by the voices of glasnost. Two developments in particular are ominous. One was the distorted coverage in much of the Soviet mass media, including television, of the disturbances in Lithuania in January 1991 in the course of which Soviet elite troops killed fourteen civilians. As a Soviet television viewer put it "she felt as if she had stepped back in time to the years before . . . Gorbachev became the Soviet leader and began encouraging honest and truthful reporting." Not only was it falsely reported that the civilians fired first on the Soviet troops, even more ominous was the claim that the military action was in response to "a call for help from a National Salvation Committee that nobody had heard of until last Friday." As may be recalled it was such "calls for help" from officially conjured groups which were used to justify Soviet intervention in Hungary in 1956, Czechoslovakia in 1968, and Afghanistan in 1979.[15]

Another discouraging development suggesting the revival and strengthening of official propaganda has been the new legislation proposed by Gorbachev "to insure objectivity [in the press] as determined by the Soviet government." Also symptomatic of these trends has been the threat to close down *Komsomolskaya Pravda* "if it continues the critical tone of its current coverage."[16]

Notes

1. One has to go back to the monumental and greatly neglected study of Nathan Leites, (*A Study of Bolshevism*. 1953, Glencoe: Free Press) to find an example of serious concern with the animating ideas of Soviet leaders and their belief in the use of such ideas which links ideology to propaganda.
2. Peter Kenez. *The Birth of the Propaganda State: Soviet Methods of Mass Mobilization 1917–1929*. University of California Press, 1985.
3. Kenez, op. cit., 13, 1, 252.
4. Adam Ulam. *The Unfinished Revolution*. Boulder: Westview Press, 1979, p. 259; Kenez op. cit., p. 253.
5. Simon Leys. *Chinese Shadows*. New York: Viking 1979, p. 167.
6. Kenez, op. cit., pp. 6–7.
7. "The CPSU Central Committee's Slogans for May Day 1987," *Current Digest of the Soviet Press*, 27 May 1987, p. 11.
8. George Feiffer. "Russian Disorders." *Harper's Magazine*, February 1981, p. 55.
9. They include Alex Inkeles, *Public Opinion in Soviet Russia* (1950) Cambridge: Harvard University Press; Fredrick C. Barghoorn, *The Soviet Image of the United*

States (1950) New York: Harcourt, Brace Jovanovich his *Soviet Foreign Propaganda* (1964) Princeton: Princeton University; Gayle D. Hollander, *Soviet Political Indoctrination: Developments in Mass Media and Propaganda Since Stalin* (1972) New York: Prager; David Powell, *Antireligious Propaganda in the Soviet Union* (1975) Cambridge: MIT Press; Barukh Hazan, *Soviet Impregnational Propaganda* (1982) Ann Arbor: Ardis; Roy Godson and Richard H. Shultz, *Deinformatsia: Active Measures in Soviet Strategy* (1984) Washington, D.C.: Pergamon Brassey.

10. *Soviet Influence Activities: A Report on Active Measures and Propaganda, 1986–87*, Washington, D.C.: Department of State 1987.
11. State Department Report, op. cit., pp. 33, 53.
12. Richard Pipes. "Where is Glasnost?" *Wall Street Journal*, December 1987, p. 34.
13. Leon Aron. "What Glasnost Has Destroyed." *Commentary*, November 1989, p. 30.
14. Celestine Bohlen. "Some Soviet Items Aren't Scarce: Crime, Strikes, Fighting, Pollution." *New York Times*, 18 August 1990.
15. Esther B. Fein. "Credibility, Too is a Victim of the Repression in Vilnius" *New York Times*, 15 January 1991; Craig R. Whitney. "The Kremlin Revives on Old Refrain", ibid.
16. Esther B. Fein. "Gorbachev Urges Curb on Press Freedom," *New York Times*, 17 January 1991; see also Serge Schmemann, "Soviet TV Reflects the Kremlin's Grimmer Picture," *New York Times*, 8 February 1991. This article presents several indications of old-style propaganda regaining influence and prominence on Soviet television.

6

A New Look at the Russian Revolution

It is fitting that a new, comprehensive, and thought-provoking history of the Russian Revolution written by a distinguished historian of modern Russia* should appear at a time when the social system built upon its foundation has entered a state of profound decay and disorganization. If through much of its history the Soviet Union was regarded by many observers as a success story of sorts, few would be certain at the present time—as was, for example, the English historian E.H. Carr—that "the sum of well-being and human opportunity is immeasurably greater in Russia today," nor would many subscribe to his belief that the Soviet system represents the "achievement that has most impressed the rest of the world."

In the light of the developments since the mid-1980s it will be increasingly difficult to chronicle the October (Russian) Revolution, and its continuation, as a step in the right direction, as progress achieved at some cost, something both inevitable and in the final analysis desirable. As the 75th anniversary of the Revolution approaches, one by one almost every single argument and justification that used to be part of such conventional wisdom is being questioned and discredited. This is being accomplished less by Western writers (some of whom were quite recently still seeking to drastically reduce the numbers of Stalin's victims) than by indigenous Soviet voices engaged in a wholly unexpected and unprecedented campaign of delegitimation of almost everything the Revolution and the system stood for and claimed to have accomplished. Those in the West who

*Richard Pipes: The Russian Revolution. Knopf, 1990.

sought to justify or vindicate the Revolution, indeed the Soviet system as a whole, by reference to a future that would lead to its humanization are also in a difficult position since the current crisis of the system does not augur well for any projection of evolutionary continuity or improvement. Professor Pipes never shared the view that the Russian Revolution was ordained by the forces of history and legitimated by the glories of rapid industrialization. Unlike many students of Soviet society and Russian history he will not have to execute various deft movements to bring his scholarship in line with the events of the last few years. It is thus hardly surprising that this book will soon appear in the Soviet Union.

The Russian Revolution comes with excellent illustrations, glossary, chronology, a profusion of notes, and a list of one hundred selected works on the Revolution; it contains eighteen chapters approximately half of which address the character of the Old Regime and the events and processes preceding the October Revolution including, preeminently World War I. The other half of the narrative includes an analysis of the part played by Lenin, the character of the Bolshevik movement, the February Revolution, the October Coup, War Communism, the murder of the Tsar and his family, the policies toward the peasants, and the "Red Terror."

We expect of historians three important services. One is to tell us what happened, in a more or less straightforward, descriptive way; second, to explain why the events in question took place, and third, to put the events into a broader context and enlighten us as to their significance. The author of this uniquely informative study fully satisfies the reader on each count. The book is of absorbing interest, lucidly written, unsurpassed in detail and comprehensiveness yet never loses its thrust and direction. Professor Pipes does not shrink from offering causal explanations which he often locates in the motives of "identifiable men pursuing their own advantages" and ideals. Among the factors shaping the Revolution he emphasizes (besides the personality of Lenin) the character of the Russian intelligentsia—its easily perverted idealism, detachment from ordinary people, hatred of the status quo. Indeed, it included many people "in whom commitment to extreme utopian ideas combined with a boundless lust for power."

Especially appreciated is the stand taken on the relationship between scholarly objectivity and individual values; for Pipes scholarship "does not call for ethical nihilism, that is, accepting that whatever happened had to happen and hence beyond good and evil." He is not one of those who would argue that the Russian Revolution can no more be judged than the coming of the Ice Age or an earthquake, sentiments favored by those who lean toward historical and social determinism.

There is ample confirmation and documentation in this volume for the view that there were no radical discontinuities between the disposition of Lenin and Stalin; the latter could build on Lenin's beliefs, attitudes, and policies, including the "Red Terror" which, Pipes points out, "served the Bolsheviks not as a weapon of last resort, but as a surrogate for the popular support which eluded them." In this as in other respects the regime came to reflect Lenin's personality and especially his "obsessive destructiveness." He was incapable of tolerating dissent and as "a stranger to moral qualms . . . [he] resembled the pope of whom Ranke wrote that he was endowed with such 'complete self-reliance that doubt or fear as to the consequences of his own actions was a pain unknown to his experience.' " It is not widely realized in the West that although not in the same class as Stalin and deriving little pleasure from the contemplation of violence, Lenin had few reservations about its lavish application. Such was his incapacity for compassion that he "habitually described those whom he chose to designate as his regime's 'class enemies' in terms borrowed from the vocabulary of pest control, calling kulaks 'bloodsuckers,' 'spiders' and 'leeches.' " He favored preventive terror sharing with Robespiere (to whom Trotsky compared him) the desire "to build a world inhabited exclusively by 'good citizens.' " He impressed Gorky as a person for whom "individual human beings held 'almost no interest . . . [who] thought only of parties, masses, states.' "

Among the conclusions to which this monumental study is likely to lead is that given its beginnings there was little reason to expect great humane accomplishments from the Soviet system; there was a certain symmetry not merely between the Lenin's revolution and Stalin's consolidation (if it can be called that) but also poetic justice to the unravelling now in progress. This book establishes with exceptional clarity that given its foundations it was a mistake to expect the Soviet system to prosper, either morally or materially.

7

The God That Failed Revisited

Although communist systems have been collapsing at an unexpected rate since the late 1980s the specter of communism will continue to haunt us—if no longer as a threat, then as the sum of painful memories and as one of the great mysteries and tragedies of our century. At a time of the disintegration of communist states and the discrediting of their supportive ideology it is especially worth recalling and contemplating their past attractions and power over the hearts and minds of people in many parts of the world. There are several questions to be pondered if anything is to be learned from history and from the spectacular blunders and bizarre misjudgments of individuals who were drawn to these systems and movements, many of them talented, creative, and full of goodwill.

There is the historical question of why entire countries came under communist domination and the entirely different psychological and sociological question as to why particular individuals became entranced with the ideas and institutions linked to communism. The recent, dramatic unravelling of communist systems presents another set of puzzles; it is not easy to grasp how these countries and their people managed to shake off these beliefs and forms of government it imposed on them. To what extent were these developments prefigured or mirrored in the inner struggles of individuals as they freed themselves of beliefs which used to justify the now abhorred practices?

Questions concerning individual disenchantment with communism have been raised before; ever since the Soviet Union was established there has been a lively traffic of commitment and conversion, infatuation and disenchantment, and corresponding soul searchings. The failure of the Soviet-Communist God has been quite thoroughly explored by a long line of Western authors from Emma Goldman to Leon Trotsky and Bertrand Russell, from Arthur Koestler to Ignazio Silone and their colleagues who gave us the volume *The God That Failed* and by latter day supporters who were released from their thrall by Khrushchev's revelations at the 20th Party Congress.

There has been far more reticence about the collapse of faith in more recent times, about disillusionment with the newer communist systems (such as Cuba, China, Vietnam, and Nicaragua) which, since the 1960s stimulated sentiments virtually identical to those once lavished on the Soviet Union. The paucity of this type of literature is all the more remarkable since these systems attracted a huge following which subsequently dwindled (under the impact of various events and revelations) yet these political involvements and disenchantments produced only a modest output of published reflection (as for instance a collection edited by John Bunzel and the writings of David Horowitz and Peter Collier.)

While a history of the Western veneration of Third World communism is yet to be written, the events of 1989 ought to prompt new efforts to come to grips with the specter of communism and its transient yet recurring hold on significant numbers of Western intellectuals. The novelty of the current occasion for reexamining this phenomenon is that for the first time in history communist systems are being transformed into noncommunist ones while simultaneously they are producing vast amounts of new evidence not merely of their repressiveness—that we have known for a long time—but of their total lack of legitimacy and failure to meet the most modest material and human needs of their people.

To be sure it was no mystery why Eastern Europe became communist: it was an offer made by the Soviet armed forces upon their arrival after World War II that residents of these parts could not refuse. In the Soviet Union, of course it was an indigenous growth, not a transplant; so it was in China and Cuba. But even in the countries where it emerged from homegrown revolutions, popular support soon wilted while the systems persisted. How did political systems so thoroughly lacking in popular support and legitimacy manage to perpetuate themselves for so long? Some of the answers are obvious: through terror, coercion, and the resulting sense of intimidation, atomization, and apathy. But how did these systems produce this pyramid of intimidation? What mixture of idealism, commitment, opportunism, and fear motivated those who propped up the authorities? Did those at the top know how unpopular they were and how little the people benefited from their policies? Were they aware of the cultural, political, and economic wasteland they created? How important were individual leaders—Castro, Mao, Stalin—possessed of a megalomaniac drive for power and sense of mission, in perpetuating these systems? Did the most committed members of the elite waver or persist in their beliefs until the last moment, when they were swept away, as in Eastern Europe during 1989? If they too lost their faith what precisely led to this?

It is in some ways a greater mystery why communist systems, in their various (but essentially similar) incarnations exercised such strong attraction for those who did *not* live under them and had no tangible, interest-bound reason to support them. The simple and quick answer, of course, is that, they were attracted precisely because they lived far away and had far less opportunity find out what these systems were like. Still, what needs better explanation is how *successive generations* of educated and well-meaning Westerners were capable of idealizing and admiring political systems quite similar to one another in their oppressive qualities and regularly discredited by various historical revelations and especially by the massive outflow of their discontented citizens whenever the opportunity presented itself.

There is no need to dispute the idealism of the generations of fellow travellers, political pilgrims, tourists, and sympathizers of every variety. It is my belief that, unlike the situation in countries where these systems were in power and support was a matter of self-interest, a precondition of a better life, support in the West was uncontaminated by such factors. The hopes and the infatuation of the sympathizers, old and more recent, was largely untainted by material or status interests and, for the most part, by power drives. To be sure Western intellectuals enjoyed publication of their books in huge printings in communist states and relished being treated as people of great importance when visiting these countries; they could absorb without difficulty huge amounts of flattery, some of it quite unsubtle. It gave them pleasure to be entertained by heads of state or chaperoned by high party officials. Still it must be granted that initially their reverence and admiration for these systems and their leaders was largely disinterested. They were persuaded that these governments significantly improved the lives of their people, that they expunged the ills and evils they had known in their own society, they believed that their leaders were selfless idealists, and that these governments enjoyed massive and spontaneous popular support.

These attitudes were especially understandable in particular historical periods, as for instance the Depression years when American and Western European intellectuals were impressed by the contrast between a Soviet society that apparently banished unemployment, hardship, waste, and irrationality from its economic life, and their own, afflicted by a faltering economy and great social injustices.

The deeper mystery is not why Western intellectuals were initially impressed by particular communist systems, but why their propensity *to remain impressed* by such societies persisted for so long and was capable of renewing itself after each particular episode of disenchantment. In other words the truly puzzling question is why a susceptibility toward communist systems—which kept turning out to be repressive, inhumane, and mendacious—so tenaciously survived? (At the time of this writing, in August 1990, we have been treated to a television program, on tax-supported public television entitled "Cuba: Two Views," the major premise of which was that reports of human rights violations were not facts but "accusations," that a view of Cuba as progressive and humane, and Castro as benign, was as tenable and respectable, if not more so, than the darker vision which stressed its police state aspects. On the same program a veteran admirer and popularizer of Castro, Saul Landau, reverently followed Castro around on a model politically conducted tour of hospitals, factories, research institutes, and beaming citizens while the great leader held forth on the accomplishments of the revolution with hardly a skeptical peep from his interlocutor.

And even if at this point in time it would seem that with the dissolution of the Soviet bloc and the electoral defeat of the communists in Nicaragua (preceded by the boat people, the Tiananmen Square massacre, the waves of Cuban refugees) there is little left to idealize, we must not rule out the possibility that before long a new contender to the title or status of an authentic socialist system will arise and capture the hearts of suitably predisposed Westerners unhappy with life in their own society. So the question stays with us: why has it been so difficult for many morally sensitive and idealistic people to learn something from historical experience?

Some answers to these questions may be found in the reflections of those who travelled the road from commitment to disillusionment and who, in traversing this difficult terrain, survived intact the loss of faith. Their reflections and accounts of their own resistance to and grappling with the loss of faith offer the best hope for understanding why the systems and ideals in question exercised such powerful attraction, why breaking with them is so difficult and why, consequently, many have been tempted to find, time and again, substitutes for the discarded ideals.

Bertam D. Wolfe, perhaps best known for his classic *Three Who Made Revolution*, has been among the great figures of Western intellectual-political history who after a long period of active commitment to communist ideals and practices (embodied at the time in the Soviet Union) broke both with the communist movement and its ideology. Subsequently he became and remained until his death in 1977 (at age 81) one of the most knowledgeable and authentic American interpreters of communism, Marxism, and the Soviet political system.

A recent posthumous collection of his writings entitled *Breaking With Communism** consists of a selection of his letters written between 1938 and 1976 and Voice of America scripts he produced between 1951 and 1954 analyzing substantive issues having to do with Soviet affairs. The letters are addressed to a variety of public figures, scholars, and politicians including presidents Ford, Kennedy, Nixon, and Reagan and Mexican president Echeverria; Senators Henry Jackson, Humphrey, and Taft; Jay Lovestone; authors such as Pearl Buck, William F. Buckley, James T. Farrell, Stephen Cohen, Leopold Labedz, Eugene Lyons, Kenneth Rexroth, Manes Sperber, Boris Souvarine, Edmund Wilson, and Karl Wittfogel among others. These lucid commentaries and lively polemics lend new historical perspective to some of the questions raised earlier and provide further examples of Wolfe's superb understanding of communist theory and practice alike. In putting together this collection Dr. Hessen sought to provide a documentary for the second half of Wolfe's life since his uncompleted autobiography ends with the late 1930s.

*Robert Hessen, ed., Palo Alto: Hoover Institution, 1990, 311 pp.

Wolfe was one of the founders of the Communist Party of the United States in 1919 and subsequently a dedicated supporter of the Soviet Union. He began, as Robert Hessen points out in his informative introduction, by "comparing Lenin's professed ideals with the worst flaws of the United States"—a procedure still characteristic of American supporters of communist systems. His early critiques of the United States were no different from those put forward by present day social critics: he deplored inequality, an uncaring society, the conflict between high ideals and sordid realities; he despaired of poverty and lack of brotherhood, and abhorred dog-eat-dog capitalism.

Between 1919 and 1929 he was active in the communist movements of both the United States and Mexico and was communist candidate for both the New York State Assembly (in 1919) and the U.S. Congress (in 1920) but the voters of Brooklyn did not elect him. During the 1920s he made several visits to the Soviet Union attending meetings of the Communist International. In 1929 the Comintern (that is Stalin) severely rebuked the U.S. Communist Party for its alleged factionalism and sought to strip it of "any illusion of independence or self-direction." Such denial of autonomy for a national communist party and the heavy-handed Soviet methods to accomplish it was apparently the first blow to Wolfe's pro-Soviet beliefs. Complete disillusionment was a gradual process and took several more years. Subsequently Wolfe was expelled from the Communist party and he aligned himself with Jay Lovestone and his faction.

The next decisive stage in distancing himself from the Soviet-communist cause came in 1938 during the purge trials and in particular, Bukharin's frame-up which he could not swallow. He still refrained from repudiating communism, only "its perversion by Stalin"—another strategy preserved among latter-day leftists. Next came the questioning of Lenin and his authoritarianism in the late 1930s and early 1940s and the recognition of continuity between him and Stalin. Some years later he finally rejected Marxism too, as he traced Lenin's intolerance to Marx's dogmatism. During World War II when wartime alliance predisposed Americans to particularly absurd beliefs about the Soviet system, he was among the few critics of the Soviet Union and suffered for it. He spent the rest of his life producing many books and articles delving into aspects of the Soviet system and Marxism-Leninism and seeking to inform Western audiences of their true character. At a time when communist systems in the Third World became fashionable in the United States he recognized their moral and institutional kinship with the Soviet model. During the 1960s and 1970s when anti-anticommunism became a reigning attitude, if not explicit ideology among many American intellectuals, he was often assailed by a sense of hopelessness, feeling, not without reason, that he was swimming against powerful currents of public and intellectual opinion.

Wolfe's observations bolster the idea that there are few if any significant differences between the mindset or predisposition of those who in the 1930s found the Soviet system heartwarmingly humane and those who half a century later were irresistibly drawn to the charismatic Castro or cosy communist Nicaragua and its authentic peasants. This has been the case not because the Soviet Union in the 1930s and Cuba or Nicaragua in the 1980s were similar countries but because the two sets of supporters, their needs and wishes, were similar. As Wolfe put it in a letter written in 1967 to a Jesuit priest enamored of the "young Marx," "As men of goodwill, you are peculiarly eager to deceive yourself"—an observation further vindicated by the continued flirtation of the clergy with "liberation theology" and the recurring delusions of an affinity between Marxism and Christianity.

Wolfe has also durably identified the characteristic attitudes of fellow travellers in his 1944 correspondence with a Quaker author (Anna Melissa Graves) of a book on the Soviet Union. Like others producing such travelogues, she was prone "to generalize too far from . . . limited experience" as for instance when she presumed that because she did not observe religious persecution in the course of her visit, religious freedoms were fully respected. Wolfe also pinpointed another attitude that recurs with monotonous regularity in each generation of sympathizers with different communist systems: "The real trouble, I have come to feel, is that you are not opposed to evil on principle, but only to evil when it comes from your pet source of grievance, the peculiar inverted nationalism which sees the evil thing only when your own country does it"—another observation that brings to mind Ms. Graves' colleagues in the American Friends Service Committee today as they steadfastly avert their eyes from the massive human rights violations in their favorite Third World dictatorships or else manage to find ways to blame the West for them. In 1952, commenting on a book of a British Quaker, Paul Cadbury, Wolfe wrote to Norman Thomas: "The great Quakers of the 19th century would be shocked . . . that one who spoke in their name could lecture on the Soviet Union without saying one word on the new slavery . . . Mr. Cadbury's address . . . is a determined 'Christian' attempt to 'understand' the rulers and not the ruled, the slave drivers and not the slaves." Such selective attempts at "understanding" have remained central to the attitudes of the sympathizers to this day; they appear in combination with a moral absolutism reserved for Western societies and a moral relativism that allows them to take a more charitable view of the flaws of the communist systems in question. Thus Wolfe's gentle polemics help to discern that, contrary to much recent conventional wisdom, there are important similarities between the mindset of those belonging to the old and the newer left.

Although primarily a student of Soviet affairs Wolfe did not flinch from criticizing New Left extremists such as Bruce Franklin whom he observed at Stanford, and Angela Davis. His comments in 1970 on her qualifications to teach philosophy remain relevant to the present not only because she has been doing ever since exactly what he expected her to do, but also because her approach to teaching (including, in Wolfe's words, the wide use of "lethal and mind-deadening slogans") has gained increased acceptance on campuses over the past two decades.

These writings also remind one that an important part of political sanity consists of the capacity to make distinctions, a capacity fellow travellers lose as they are carried away on the tides of moral indignation against the evils of their own society. They have little knowledge of and interest in the specifics of the comparative magnitude of these evils since they automatically assume that no system can be more unjust or inhumane than their own. Wolfe was well aware of this tendency as he disputed (in 1971) the propriety of calling a person jailed for violating drug laws in the United States a "political prisoner." In doing so he also touched on a perverse and destructive tendency that has also been with us since the 1960s, namely, the predilection to expand the meaning of the concept of "political" to cover a wide range of attitudes and activities which have little to do with matters political as the concept has been generally used and understood:

> It is impossible for me to regard the smoker in prison as a "political prisoner" as your circular letter suggests or to have any connection with the slogan peace and power which your letter also invokes. . . . Smoking pot neither makes one a political prisoner, now does it involve peace and power. Smoking pot is not a political act.

Wolfe was of course well aware that it is in truly repressive political systems that so many aspects of life are given a political dimension and where the authorities deliberately seek to blur the line between the political and nonpolitical, or between the public and private spheres in order to expand their control over the lives of their citizens. In the West those who so eagerly attach the label "political" to aspects of life not regarded earlier in that light are engaged in a different enterprise. They are seeking new ground for enlarging their critiques of society; the more things frustrating, depriving or problematic are labelled "political" the firmer grounds there are for rejecting the system, the institutions, and values of society. Simultaneously individual responsibility for personal pain and suffering is reduced or removed and righteous anger justified.

While Wolfe's reflections help to understand the mentality of estranged social critics of various generations and the connection between such estrangement and reverence for political systems presumed to be a superior to those in the West, his writings have some limitations for understanding some of the more recent manifestations of the phenomena here discussed. We must remember that at the time Wolfe became disenchanted with the Soviet system (and Western communist movements servile to it) it was the only such system in the world, hence, arguably, both his illusions and his disenchantment had different sources and dynamics. On the one hand it was easier to see the Soviet Union as a unique, progressive country when it was the first communist society and historical evidence of its monumental failures and defects was only beginning to accumulate. On the other hand, and for the same reason, it would seem that disenchantment would have been more strenuously resisted by the committed. In fact pro-Soviet attitudes vanished more thoroughly than similar sentiments associated with putatively socialist Third World dictatorships of the more recent vintage; the latter appeared to have had a wider, if shallower, support and linger on as only small numbers of the former adherents seem willing to make a clean break.

Perhaps the pro-Soviet attitudes of the 1930s were more of an elite (and sectarian) phenomenon whereas the newer varieties of leftism, "third worldism," and fellow travelling represent more widespread if more superficial commitments, less important to confront and exorcise. This possibility is further suggested by the ease with which more recent political sympathies are transferred from one country or setting to another: from the Soviet Union to China, from China to Cuba (or vice versa), from Vietnam to Grenada or Nicaragua, or the PLO, or ANC, or from any specific country or movement to the more diffuse entity of the Third World. These sympathies survive, even if in an attenuated form, because they are upheld by large numbers of mutually supportive people in fairly cohesive (usually campus based) subcultures which earlier generations of fellow travellers did not share.

Wolfe's case also confirms patterns present in other instances of political commitment and disenchantment. Thus Western idealists usually begin by projecting certain generalised values upon a particular communist system which promise to realize or pursue these ideals with more determination than their own society (Wolfe began by thinking that the Soviet Union was a force for peace as World War I was coming to an end); for Wolfe (as for many of his peers) the Soviet Union also "seemed to be the first country that would institutionalise the ideals of the 18th century" as Hessen put it. In such instances, political infatuations are reminiscent of romantic ones which also involve the wholesale projection of idealized qualities on a particular individual who may be highly unsuited to carry such burdens. As long as the enamored person does not discern too much of a discrepancy between the ideals and the person who is supposedly embodying them, the involvement persists. Distance and obstacles to consummating the relationship help, as the distance between the Western admirer and the country he chose to admire helped to perpetuate his illusions. As evidence or information begin to emerge and

accumulate suggesting that the person (or the political system) is unlike the ideals and expectations projected upon it—or, as the theory-
practice gap begins to reveal itself—disenchantment begins to set in.
This, however, is usually resisted and the affair prolongs itself as the
emotionally involved person seeks to explain away, or rationalize the
discrepancies between ideals and realities, theory and practice.
(Wolfe wrote: "I longed to retain some shred of my old ideals and beliefs, longed to believe that I did not have to write off the spiritual
investment of *a decade* as a total loss.") It must be conceded that in
personal relationships abrupt, dramatic breaks are more common than
in political involvements which are more drawn out and in the course
of which more strenuous efforts are made to explain away the discrepancies between theory and practice. The most fascinating question is most dependent on the elusive nuances of personality and individual psychology: what particular event or experience is the final
straw that at last demolishes a commitment already weakened by a
series of disappointments? It is by no means a rational or predictable
process and not one necessarily related to the volume of disillusioning information available.

It is regrettable that Bertram Wolfe did not live to see the collapse
of the Soviet empire and its massive public rejection by its people.
While he was among many who did not anticipate these developments, the anticommunist outlook, to which he made a durable and
learned contribution has been fully vindicated by these events.

Part II
Discontents in the West

8

The Institute for Policy Studies:
A Case Study in Radical Social Criticism

Our job is to expose the moral and political bankruptcy of the ideas and assumptions now governing America.
—Robert Botosage, *IPS Report*, 1983

IPS is engaged in a longer and deeper struggle, a struggle over the underlying principles and future direction of the political culture itself.
—*IPS Report*, 1983

There are certain types of people who are political out of a kind of religious reason . . . trying to abolish the present in favor of some better future—always taking it for granted that there is a better future.
—Doris Lessing, 1982

Locating the Institute on the Political Spectrum

Most Americans, including most educated and politically aware Americans, have either never heard of the Institute for Policy Studies (IPS) or have no clear idea of what it is, what it stands for, or what it opposes. Educated and politically involved residents of Washington, D.C. are somewhat more likely to have heard of IPS, but even those who are vaguely aware of its existence will probably disagree about its character, significance, or influence. Yet the Institute exemplifies with particular force and clarity certain broad trends and currents in American society.

145

The Institute, founded in 1963, has persisted because a substantial audience resonates to its messages. For example, those who believe that American intervention almost everywhere in the world is without moral justification, columnists who urge U.S. leaders to let events take their course (in Central America and other places) without American involvement, and Americans who are convinced that the United States bears the lion's share of responsibility for the sufferings of the poor in the world. They also include white voters who are likely to support Jesse Jackson for reasons unrelated to racial pride, people opposed to draft registration, as well as those for whom virtually all American military expenditure is wasteful. IPS speaks to citizens who press for making their towns "nuclear-free zones" (or "sister cities" of towns in Nicaragua or the USSR), to those who instinctively place the blame on the United States in any global confrontation, and to intellectuals and journalists who are persuaded that Orwell's *1984* captures the characteristics of contemporary America.

In short, many supporters of the IPS are people of frustrated idealism who believe that in no other country are social ideals and practices as far apart as in the United States.

Indeed, over the last two decades, a generally critical disposition toward existing social arrangements has established itself among sizeable portions of the educated strata of American society. Intellectuals, journalists, clergymen, social workers, and especially academics have become increasingly disturbed by what they perceive as inequities in the American system. What used to be called alienation (or estrangement) has become the more-or-less accepted attitude among these groups—as the rational and legitimate response to the observable defects of society. Especially noteworthy is the increasingly unself-conscious yet totalistic nature of this perspective, reminiscent of what Karl Mannheim called a "total ideology," that is, "fundamentally divergent thought systems . . . widely differing modes of experience and interpretation . . . underlying the single judgement of the individual." (Mannheim 1936, 57, 59) Even as the most vocal rejections of American society died down, a residue of collective doubt and aversion toward major American institutions and values persists. The concept of "adversary culture" best captures the attitudes and beliefs in question.

Lionel Trilling introduced the concept of the adversary culture in the 1960s as a way of describing and conceptualizing a certain detachment of the individual from the prevailing culture and social order that began in the eighteenth century and that has, over time, taken an increasingly political coloration and standardized forms of expression (Trilling 1965). Social historians tend to date the spread of these attitudes from the 1960s and the social-political changes and events associated with that decade.

The Institute for Policy Studies has been closely connected with, indeed in the forefront, of the attitudinal changes noted above. Its major activity has been the production, elaboration, and dissemination of ideas intended to influence and inform the climate of opinion and politics of the past quarter century. Emerging in the early 1960s and still going strong at the end of the 1980s, the Institute has been deeply involved in the ideological and political currents and conflicts of recent American social history, embodying all varieties of "Leftism." As Garry Wills said, "Whenever things were happening on the left . . . the Institute was bound to be represented" (Wills 1971, 98).

The precise role of the Institute in political developments remains a matter of debate. Does it merely reflect the spirit and trends of the times or does it shape them? Has it exerted a substantial influence over public opinion or over politically important elites? To what degree are its activities appropriate to a research institute (or think tank), and in what ways have they gone beyond the customary scope of such activities to partisan advocacy? Even more controversial used to be the question of whether or not IPS has been a "subversive" organization, assisting and nurturing contacts with hostile forces outside the United States. Far from being an academic question, at one point federal law enforcement agencies examined this question without fully resolving it.

I do not seek to settle questions connected with the past political role and activities of IPS. Rather, my curiosity about IPS is part of a broader and more general interest in the sociology of ideas, in their origin and impact, and the relationship between ideas and their social settings. Specifically, I am interested in the "adversary culture," of which the Institute provides an excellent example. Those sympathetic toward the phenomenon of alienation tend to call it "The Movement"; critics refer to it as the adversary culture. A sympathetic commentator, Peter Clecak defines the Movement to include aspects of the counterculture as well as the more political sectors . . . the Movement was a multifaceted critical response of elements of a new postwar generation (and a number of radicalized, in some cases reradicalized elders) to the emerging shapes and imagined trends of that world: the persistence of social injustice within American society; the growth of a relatively affluent consumer culture . . . the quasi-imperialist stances of both superpowers, but especially the United States; the rigid, sclerotic authoritarian "socialisms" of nations in the Soviet sphere; and the deep unrest and revolutionary ferment in . . . the third world.

Other characteristics included:

a vague but insistent sense of spiritual malaise . . . anxiety and alienation from the technological, affluent culture young white people were expected to inherit. A sense of injustice and a sense of meaninglessness: these . . . were the two principal sources of dissent.

Finally,

The distinctive characteristics of the Movement emerge from a central concern with personal authenticity and the corollary conviction that the structures of social power, the liberal ideological consensus and their cultural apparatus formed multiple obstacles to self-fulfillment and community. (Clecak 1981, 529, 503, 531)

The critics' definitions of the adversary culture are very similar, but unlike the sympathizers, the critics don't like what they see (e.g., Kristol 1983, 27–42).

The concepts of "The Movement" and the adversary culture may be linked by suggesting that The Movement merged into, or has given rise to, the adversary culture—the former more dynamic and action-oriented, an aggregate of social and protest movements, the latter a more static reservoir of values and attitudes that only occasionally gives rise to organizational activities.

One can look at IPS as a part of The Movement, as its institutional embodiment and inheritor of its legacy; but it may also be seen as an integral and durable part of the adversary culture. IPS embodies the values and spirit of this culture, it gives it a concrete form, and seeks to translate its aspirations into specific policies. Moreover, after a quarter century of existence, it represents its most enduring manifestation. Of all the organizations and groups that emerged during the

1960s, none proved as long-lived and resilient as the Institute—a fact that by itself attracts attention.

Two additional concepts from the 1960s are relevant to understanding and locating IPS on the ideological-political and cultural spectrum: the "counterculture" (Roszak 1969), and the "New Left," popularized by C. Wright Mills. The counterculture differs from the adversary culture in that it is less political; it represents ways of life and of "self realization" through new forms of art, communal living, personal relationships, and methods of escapism. The New Left, by contrast, was clearly a political entity, defined against the Old Left, that is, independent of established Communist parties and free of the worship of and servility to the Soviet Union; more democratic in both its ideals and organizational practices than its predecessor. Said a New Leftist of Old Leftist parents, "The old left of my mother and father emphasized organization, ideology, party, history, economics, work, the factory, unions, class struggle, marriage and stressed Europe and the Western world, especially the Soviet Union. The new left of my sisters and brothers emphasized action, anarchy, spontaneity, sex, grass, consciousness, the street, the gun, and stressed the Third World (especially Cuba and Vietnam) and race." (Raskin 1974, 211)

It has also been said that the New Leftists "shared a vague feeling . . . that somehow the form of existing institutions discouraged authentic personal relations" (Matusov 1984, 310). The pursuit of "authentic" personal relations hardly preoccupied Old Leftists.

Close as it has been, the IPS kinship with the New Left and its values must not be overstated. According to David Riesman (who was a founding trustee of IPS but later resigned) the Institute has not been a typical New Left outfit, certainly not in its early days. He regarded the founders as generally quite sober, not radicals or counterculture types. He argues that IPS became more radicalized and "New Leftist" under the influence of younger people and some minorities who joined in the later 1960s (Riesman 1986).

Among the core IPS activists have always been Old Leftists, individuals uncritical of and even sympathetic toward the Soviet Union, such as Cora Weiss (who has played a key part in Institute affairs all along as a major and most reliable source of funding), Saul Landau, and Michael Parenti. IPS never, to say the least, regarded criticism of the Soviet system as among its tasks and has been inclined to look upon such criticism as an irritating diversion from its central task: the formulation of critiques of the United States, and its efforts to influence U.S. policies.* The Institute's warmth toward Castro (especially in his second and third decades in power) also suggests a greater affinity with the Old rather than the supposedly free-spirited New Left since Cuba has, since the late 1960s, been one of the most regimented, repressive, and unspontaneous among the Communist systems.

While Institute members tend to be united in their rejection of existing American institutions, there is diversity about the alternatives, especially about the possible foreign models and sources of inspiration. Co-founder Marcus Raskin, unlike many of his colleagues, appears to be well aware of the flaws of contemporary political systems which claim socialist credentials. He has written: "Like many sound ideas, socialism has been the victim of twentieth-century murderers . . . socialism, a concept which referred to the potential for everyone's liberation, has not taken into account the person or unofficial group's freedom to say *no* without fear of terrible retribution." Or: "As any citizen of an East European country knows, socialism as mediated through state power is seriously flawed, indeed deformed" (Raskin 1986, 16, 15). Such remarks reflect the legacy of an uncompromising idealism associated with the beginnings of the New Left and its suspicion of bigness, bureaucracy, and concentrated power rather than the more opportunistic position of other social critics embracing the axion that "the enemies of my enemy are my friends."

Rather than trying to define IPS as either predominantly of the New or Old Left, it seems more accurate to say that the Institute has synthesized these mindsets; in fact, its strength and durability seems to be based on its capacity to reconcile and bring together attitudes, methods and factions of *both* the Old and New Left. Such a synthesis has been made easier, among other things, by the well-defined distaste, even outright hostility toward liberalism, shared by Old and New Left. While not widely recognized—especially among those

---

* It should be noted here that although I refer to IPS as a fairly coherent entity and feel free to generalize about "IPS positions," certain distinctions (as noted above) must be made among its associates (the term used loosely here to refer to various forms of affiliation with the Institute).

who look back upon the 1960s nostaligically—the rejection of liberalism was a major defining characteristic of those who may be regarded as founders of the New Left, including C. Wright Mills (see also Matusov 1984, 343).

The Institute partook of and intersected with all the adversarial political entities and currents of the 1960s and their remnants and has given an enduring institutional framework and expression to them. Perhaps its major political-cultural contribution has been to develop and give a voice to what may be called a respectable estrangement, at once detached from the excesses of the 1960s (while incorporating their major premises), appealing to traditions of American idealism and, unlike other radical groups, embracing a more hard-nosed prag-matism. As such IPS has also proved to be an exemplar of successful lobbying and networking, of patient coalition building.

The Radical Thrust

In order to understand the Institute for Policy Studies one must, above all, grasp its vision of American society. It is an intensely, and often bitterly critical vision which provides the basis for its existence, animates and recruits its members, and brings unity and direction to its intellectual, political, and organizational activities.

This grim vision steadfastly held for over two decades has enabled IPS to become the institutional core of the adversary culture, and a major force within, what might be called "the Protest Establishment." This outlook has also made it possible to bring together under Institute auspices new and old leftist, populist, anarchist (advocates of "creative disorder"), feminist, third world enthusiasts, and other groups and schools of thought. Thus the political-philosophical orientation of IPS is best described as eclectic—a mixture of individualism, com-munitarianism, existentialism, and strands of Marxism-Leninism held together by the glue of a profound, animating rejection of American society. Most importantly, the Institute had few enemies on the left. Michael Parenti, a long-time associate, raised the question in another context: "what is obscene about associating with Communists?" and concluded to his satisfaction that it was not (Parenti 1983).

The examination of IPS critiques of American society give considerable insight into the institution itself. Unlike many earlier studies of IPS* which tended to focus on its activities, organizational ties, and political involvements, I will focus more on the substantive ideas embraced. IPS's values and priorities shed further light on its political objectives and the wide range of organizational activities, campaigns, and lobbying it undertakes in the service of these objectives.

It is not an exaggeration to suggest that anybody who was active or influential in the protest movements of the 1960s, or who had contributed the sharpest critiques of the United States in the last quarter century had some connection, fleeting or enduring, with IPS. With good reason did Garry Wills call IPS "the Rand Corporation" of the "Left" (Wills 1971, 98). While many movements and forms of social criticism associated with the 1960s have fallen by the wayside, IPS remains a substantial political-intellectual presence. In the words of one of its associates, even "in the encroaching shadows of Reaganism and of the lethargy of the American Left, the Institute remains a beacon of scholarship and moral resistance" (Friedman, ed. 1983, xiii).

The survival of IPS is not merely a result of the insistent elaboration of the adversarial outlook. It is also a due to adequate funding, organizational skills, and the personal dedication and prudence of its members and associates.** It should be emphasized that the perpetuation of a negative vision of America is not a mere intellectual exercise for IPS. Although there is a utopian, romantic strain in the critiques of America and the so-called "social inventions" proposed to remedy its failures the Institute regards ideas as weapons to be wielded in the struggle for radical social-political change. Jorge Sol, director of the Institute's International Economic Order project put it this way: "I consider it the role of IPS . . . to prove the invalidity of the ruling ideology and to provide popular movements with the information and analysis needed to justify their opposition and give content to their struggle" (IPS Report 1983, 5).

*(For example, Dickson 1971, Blumenthal 1986, Heritage 1977, Isaac 1980, Kelley 1976, Kincaid 1983, Muravchik 1981 and 1984–85, Powell 1987, Wills 1971.)

**Again, I am using here and below the terms "associate" or "member" to refer to all types of close affiliation with IPS. In fact the Institutite has senior fellows, fellows, and associates receiving different remuneration.

The same action-orientation was apparent in an Institute publication describing the considerations that led to its establishment:

> Government has become unresponsive and destructive in part because all fresh political ideas and moral truths were smothered in the bureaucratic process . . . the universities were churning out false images and ideas because they insisted that social action be kept totally distinct from social theory except where it served the status quo.

> So they decided that there should be a place for thought which was . . . based on the premise that social theory must be informed by, as well as inform, social action. They believed that it was time for a new kind of scholarship. (*Beginning the Second Decade* 1974, 4)

A commentator on IPS put it this way: "The IPS is attempting to lay the groundwork for the new society that will replace the present collapsing one. It not only has dedicated itself to ushering in the new society by inquiry and experimentation but is also doing what it can to hasten the demise of the present one" (Dickson 1971, 276).

In treating ideas as guides and aids to action IPS is more Leninist than Marxist. It believes that the relentless critical analysis of the defects of American institutions is a vital precondition of their transformation, to be brought about by a variety of means, including the struggle to raise the level of consciousness of the various elite groups.

An examination of IPS' intensely critical view of America provides conclusive evidence of its political coloration and its defining values and beliefs. It makes it abundantly clear that—contrary to widespread misconceptions—the Institute is not a "liberal think tank" or a collection of mildly left-of-center intellectuals. This is a matter of some importance since much of IPS' influence and credibility rests on its supposedly liberal, mainstream credentials.

How, then, has this impression, so much as variance with reality, been created? And how has the Institute succeeded in making so many observers overlook the depth and intensity of its hostility toward American society, even though this hostility has been key to most of its ideas and actions. This hostility has been overlooked not because few bother to read carefully IPS texts, or because of a strenuous effort on the part of IPS to conceal it. The hostility towards

American society nurtured by the Institute has gone unnoticed in large measure because it touches a responsive cord in many groups and strata of American society. It is congenial and is taken for granted, to different degrees, by many of those IPS addresses and seeks to influence. The visceral aversion toward American society and institutions has attracted little attention because there has been, over the past decades, an ongoing redefinition of what constitutes radical as opposed to moderate social criticism, indeed, a redefinition of concepts such as radical, liberal, moderate or conservative (Hollander 1986). These shifts in the climate of opinion have contributed to the survival of IPS and have increasingly allowed it to shade into a broader adversary culture, sometimes also associated with the "New Class" (Bruce Briggs, ed. 1979).

My contention is that if the term "radical" (or radical left) has any meaning, the Institute fully qualifies as a radical organization motivated by an uncompromising hostility toward the Americal political-economic system and a strong determination to change its basic characteristics. Such radicalism is however compatible in its day to day practices with allying itself with more moderate groups and causes, without losing sight of its basic goals and values. This policy used to be called "popular front tactics" in the 1930s and 1940s. As Staughton Lynd and Gar Alperowitz, two IPS associates, wrote, "the question is how to work creatively within a mass organization which is somewhat radical (which is why you are in it) but not as radical as you yourself are. *The art of radicalizing reformist structures*, including the structures we have helped to create, requires relearning" (Lynd and Alperowitz 1973, 35, emphasis added). An Institute memorandum dated 15 November 1971 further illuminates the above:

> In terms of strategy, the movement must distinguish between the short-term and the long. The purpose of the short term action is to (a) create more political room for radicalism in which to organize [and] (b) win reforms. . . . The long-term strategy is to win—literally—the revolution. [IPS Memorandum 1971]

There is little mystery in what defines IPS as radical and sets it apart from the mainstream liberal-moderate currents and critiques of American society. Radicals and liberals differ most characteristically in that radicals find few if any aspects of American society to be a source of pride, or worth preserving, although they may admire, in the manner of C. Wright Mills, a largely imaginary past which is contrasted to the corruption of the present. They may even appeal (somewhat opportunistically) to the example or legacy of past political figures and precedents—uncongenial as they might otherwise be—in the service of particular political objectives, as was the case when Marcus Raskin contrasted favorably the prudence of Warren G. Harding and Herbert Hoover, in matters of defense expenditures, with the recklessness of Ronald Reagan (Raskin 1981). Thus the radical rejections of America are often combined with affirmations of an ideal system rooted either in the past or projected into the future. Irving Kristol commented on such attitudes:

> The fact that one can so easily imagine a better nation is . . . irrelevant. People who permit such imaginations to dominate their thinking are in the grip of political delusion . . . Americans . . . who are hypercritical of their countr[y] while pompously proclaiming their loyalty to an ideal version are in fact "anti." Authentic loyalty is to one's incarnate country—as to one's incarnate husband or wife— not to some ideal version. (Kristol 1981, 51)

Liberals, by contrast, may be critical of specific shortcomings but do not reject the entire social system or call for its demolition or basic transformation. They too may find social conditions lagging behind their social ideals but regard the divergence partial and temporary rather than total and irreversible. The liberal critic often playing the part of loyal opposition—seeks to improve the system through reform, making it more resilient and durable, which is why he often becomes the target of the most violent denunciation by radicals, as was often the case in the 1960s and 1970s.

IPS cofounder Marcus Raskin unhesitatingly dissassociated himself from such liberal reformers:

> The liberal reformer in the United States assumes that the basic hierarchic structure of the society is correct . . . that no fundamental changes are necessary, that adjustments are necessary. . . . His only task is to find a way wherein individuals are able to accept the opportunities of finding their niche in the authority structure . . . no matter what the motivation is, the fact remains that reform itself is a necessary instrument of colonization because it is one specific method which updates the colonized structure. (Raskin 1971, 186–87, 190–91)

More recently Raskin refined his views on liberalism by introducing a distinction between two kinds of liberalism, that of "establishment" (or "conventional") as opposed to "progressive." The latter was upheld by "left and humanist liberals, those who did not support the cold war, or had doubts about the course of capitalism, were blacklisted and thrown out of virtually every institution of American life." The "establishment" liberals, on the other hand, were champions of "the national security state, large defense budgets, covert operations abroad and anti-civil liberties legislation at home." They were responsible for "an arms race that has grown to disastrous proportions . . . the development of sovereign oligopolistic corporations, . . . increased poverty, class stratification and reliance on an authoritarian police state to keep the poor and the wretched in their place while stifling protests about their plight" (Raskin 1980, 588).

Raskin's effort to shape the concept of liberalism to his political agenda is reminiscent of the uses made of the word "democracy" by many radical left wing systems and movements (for example, "people's democracy," "guided democracy," "true democracy," "economic democracy,") which also claimed to restore the genuine substance of the concept.

The critic of the IPS mold, unlike the reformist-liberal, views the ills of American society as intrinsic and systematic, and scorns a piecemeal approach to their alleviation. As Michael Parenti, the prolific associate of IPS, observed grimly:

> Rather than being treated as a cause of groups oppression, the capitalist system is accepted as the neutral framework within which groups try to rectify the inequities they suffer. This approach to oppression is congruent with the prevailing ideological orthodoxy that defines all social injustices as aberrant offshoots rather than systemic outgrowths. Like other systemic symptoms, be they military spending, pollution, urban decay, fiscal insolvency, inflation, crime . . . [they] are treated as "issues" separate from each other and from the politico-economic system that produces them. (Parenti 1978, 74–75)

Housing shortages are among such systemic defects that implicate the entire social order. An IPS approach is to "try to understand and explain the housing crisis not in isolation but as a central and emblematic part of a broader crisis of the U.S. economy and social system. . . . Just as the current system cannot house its people decently, it cannot feed them adequately, or provide them with decent

health care, education, environmental protections, and bodily security" (Hartman, ed. 1983, 8). The deficiencies of health care similarly
"demonstrate that even the most liberal form of national health insurance is incapable of dealing with the structural inadequacies of the
American health system" (Lander, in Raskin, ed. 1978, 312). Arthur
Waskow, one of the founders of IPS concluded that the Establishment
is "unable to reform itself" (Waskow 1970:167).

Not only do these critics differ from liberals regarding the methods
and conclusions of their criticism, sometimes they explicitly reject
the idea of liberalism itself, as for example Alan Wolfe, a sociologist
associated with IPS: "Liberalism is very much an ideology of social
control and repression, and for those who are the victims of repression, it matters little whether the guns that shoot at them are in liberal or fascist hands" (Wolfe 1978, 193). It was also reported that
"Frances Fox Piven and Richard A. Cloward, [also Institute as-
sociates] proposed that poor blacks forget about electoral politics and
instead get their assorted entitlements by creating large-scale 'disturbances'" (Seligman 1982: 63).

So sweeping is the rejection of American society that the radical
critic often needs an entirely new vocabulary and conceptual
framework to convey his indignation and distaste for the American
system. Alan Wolfe favors concepts such as "elitist democracy," "corporate ideological repression," and "repressive liberalism," while
Marcus Raskin has reconceptualized America as a colony, or "col-
onized society." (Raskin 1971, xiii).

Apocalyptic imagery often accompanies these radical portrayals: collapse, crisis, garrison state, colony, revolution, and armageddon are
commonly used. In Arthur Waskow's vision, "The substructure of
America, what keeps people alive, has been allowed to rot for a generation while money was put into the Superwar Machine. Sewers are
ready to fail, the health system is collapsing, houses haven't been
built" (Waskow 1971). Elsewhere he spoke of "environmental diseases
getting worse . . . lung cancer, emphysema, mercury poisoning, DDT
poisoning, ad infinitum" (Waskow 1971, Social Policy: 46).

As for Raskin, "the arms race is growing more severe, and the pollution of our lands, food, air and water has reached the crisis stage and
the decay of our cities continues unabated" (Raskin 1975, Op-ed).
Gore Vidal writes in a preface to a collection of IPS writings, "The

United States is now in serious disrepair. The educational system, never much good, is being cut back. Inner cities resemble Calcutta. Productivity is almost as low as England's—and that is low indeed. . . . Our success story is turning sour indeed . . . fantasy now governs in that Disneyland by the Potomac where the Great Cue-card Reader preaches simple-minded sermons of hate, and the last best war of all draws nearer and nearer." (Vidal in Friedman, ed. 1983, x).

Whether we move back or forward in time, the IPS indictments and dire images vary little. The Institute's ten-year report announced that "By 1972 most of the [Institute] Fellows had concluded from their work that a concentration of vast power in the hands of a few had become typical of the American policy, economy and culture, and that the structures of racism and militarism, the exhausting work-place and the exhausted family, the mandarin university and bureaucratized religion, deforested and depeopled Appalachia and devastated Vietnam, were results of this concentration of power" (*Beginning the Second Decade*, 7).

Worse was yet to come as Raskin discovered that "the majority of Americans . . . are at the edge of economic, social and psychological panic" (Raskin, ed. 1978, xi) and that "the sensibilities of people are deformed through economic privations and societal dislocations" (Raskin 1975, *Progressive*, 19). Parenti has envisioned "the mass of middle Americans" afflicted by "occupational disability, job insecurity, job dissatisfaction, constant financial anxieties, mental stress and depression, alcoholism and conflictual domestic relations." Moreover, "even if not suffering from acute want, few if any exercise much control over the condition of their lives." Children in particular "constitute one of the largest and most vulnerable low-power groups. They do not participate as decision makers in most of the arrangements directly affecting their lives" (Parenti 1978, 66–67).

By 1987, Gar Alperowitz and Jeff Faux saw "the American Dream of owning one's home disappearing rapidly . . . millions of Americans not able to afford three square meals a day . . . pessimism widespread in a country built on optimism and hope . . . a majority of the people feel 'alienated and powerless' " (Alperowitz and Faux 1984, 3–4). Ronald Dellums, U.S. Representative and a very close congressional friend of IPS, offered a similarly sweeping, apocalyptic view of the disadvantaged of America: "America is a nation of

niggers. . . . If you are black, you're a nigger. If you are an am-
putee, you're a nigger. Blind people, women, students, the handicapped, radical environmentalists, poor whites, those too far to the
left are all niggers" (Tolchin 1983).

In 1978 Dellums presented the following analysis of the relationship between the inequities and corruptions perpetrated by the U.S.
on its own people and those abroad:

> In the United States, intelligence agencies bug our phones, commit dirty tricks,
> keep enemy lists. . . . In the Third World, U.S. intelligence agencies bribe offi-
> cials, wage secret wars and spawn and train foul replicas of themselves like
> KCIA, SAVAK and DINA.

> In North America, multinational corporations buy elections, rip off consumers,
> conflict with labor and carry jobs out of the country. In the Third World, multina-
> tionals buy countries, bribe officials, exploit workers and despoil resources. (De-
> llums 1978: n.p.)

Alan Wolfe based a whole book on the premise that "repression
is—continues to be—an everyday aspect of American politics . . .
[and that] the history of the United States is a history of repression"
(Wolfe 1978, xii, 4).

Barnet and Raskin believed that so repressive were the authorities
and such a climate of fear had been created that Americans were
ready to "repress themselves" and that "peace and social justice in
America" could not be achieved unless American were "liberated
from the dead hand of authoritarianism" (Barnet and Raskin 1970,
46, 90). Parenti pointed out that "The FBI does its job . . . but it
cannot quite do its job the way that it would want—which . . . explains why it turns to Nazis and Klansmen to do its dirty work. The
Freedom of Information Act is the only thing we have left to keep
them from rounding us up" (Powell 1988, 83). Bertram Gross projected the same state of affairs into the future: "Looking at the present, I see a more probable future: a new despositism creeping slowly
across America" (Gross 1980, 2). As to Saul Landau (otherwise
specializing in the production of films and writings supportive of
communist Cuba and Castro), he thought that "America is a society
whose values even George Orwell might not have imagined" (Muravchik 1981, 2).

It is abundantly clear by now that the radical critic—unlike the lib-

eral—is disinclined to balance the positive features of American society (e.g., legal protections, free circulation of ideas) against the
negative ones. Instead, he almost invariably considers them inconse-
quential facades, superstructures which conceal social injustice,
greed, and the unequal distribution of power and wealth. Not only
does the radical critic regard the pluralistic political process as a
fraud and sham, he has little appreciation for free expression (from
which he greatly benefits), taking it either for granted or dismissing
it as unimportant. He will not grant American societal processes any
benefit of doubt, as he routinely gives to left wing police states
spouting some variety of Marxist-populist rhetoric and professing to
uplift the poor.

Thus Raskin sees "institutional madness structured as rationality,
and the domination of forces that are destructive and genocidal. . . .
The System has become a luxury the people can no longer afford."
Moreover, "the American System, by its nature and development, is
jerry built. It never quite resolves fundamental problems. It merely en-
gulfs them in new ones . . . masking them through the pleasing language of problem solving, coordination and efficiency" (Raskin 1974,
2, 6, 127). Elsewhere he asserts that "in a rich, technologically advanced mass society, politics is reduced to the ability of small groups
of people to dictate suicide for the rest" (Raskin 1971, 62). Not surprisingly he also believes that "today political parties have little relevance
because they are merely vehicles of personal ambition and unexamined
vested interest" (Raskin 1975, Op ed). In an earlier work he and Barnet declared that "in the United States government is a network of private preserves of privilege" (Barnet and Raskin 1970, 27). Celia Eck-
hardt, a director of the Washington School founded by the Institute in
1979, concurred with such sentiments as she assured her audience (at
a commencement exercise at Hampshire College in Amherst, Massachusetts) that "Congress is run by mediocrities, sycophants and special interest" (Russell 1982).

It is also difficult to attribute liberal convictions and values to a
group of people who consistently give vocal support to highly illiberal political systems. This has been illustrated not only by the enduring cordiality between Cuba and IPS (and more recently IPS and
Nicaragua), but also the sympathy and support extended to com-

munist Vietnam even in the era of the boat people and re-education camps.

Richard Barnet and Cora Weiss were among the last-ditch defenders of the Vietnam government (against the charge of human rights violations made by many prominent former antiwar activists) in an advertisement which claimed, among other things, that "The present government in Vietnam should be hailed for its moderation and for its extraordinary effort to achieve reconciliation among all people. . . . In fact all the Vietnamese who worked for the Saigon regime . . . have by now returned to their families and are pursuing normal lives" (Advertisement 1977). Such assessments have in part been motivated by the conviction that the United States has no moral edge over any other system, especially not over those systems opposed to it. Irresistibly drawn to the enemies of their enemy, the critics reserve special sympathy for political systems which maintain an adversarial relationship to the United States.

Perceiving the United States as a historically unique political-economic malignancy unrivaled in its social and moral deformities, helps one understand why these radicals so consistently object to the assertion of U.S. power in almost any part of the world: they seek to curb this malign influence. Correspondingly, they endorse and applaud virtually all foreign critiques of the United States and any encroachments on its power abroad.

Inculcating False Consciousness

It is also characteristic of the radical worldview of the Institute to dismiss any endorsement or approval of the United States by its own citizens as meaningless and delusionary—a reflection of false consciousness and of being programmed by the system. The concept of false consciousness—its alleged inculcation by the mass media and educational institutions—is of great importance for the radical critic as he contemplates distastefully the electoral (or other) legitimation of the system. He cannot accept as genuine any endorsement of the social order by those who are supposed to be its victims—the masses, the working classes, the majority. Indeed, acknowledging the legitimacy of the endorsement would amount to accepting the legitimacy of the system itself. Hence, the critic utilizes the time-honored device of imputing false consciousness to the masses (who are unaware of their true interests), and who are manipulated into displaying a misguided loyalty towards a status quo they ought to reject.

While the Marxist origins of the concept are well known, notions of false consciousness have gained greater strength and popularity through the efforts of the Frankfurt School and have become central to the recent analyses of the defects of capitalist mass society usually exemplified by the United States. American social critics, including those of IPS, have gone to great length in discoursing on false consciousness and the part it plays in "system maintenance." In this respect Herbert Marcuse has been a major influence and inspiration (along with C. Wright Mills) to the associates of IPS engaged in the exposure of the mechanisms and institutions the ruling classes deploy to deprive the population of the proper understanding of its true condition. Alan Wolfe called these activities "ideological repression, the attempt to manipulate people's consciousness so that they accept the ruling ideology" (Wolfe 1978, 8). He would have agreed with Marcuse who once said that it was not worthwhile to grant people the freedom to vote "if they are going to make the wrong use of their freedom" (Hook 1987, 595).

False consciousness takes many forms, some of them probably unanticipated by Marx. According to Parenti, for instance, "Self-hate becomes a valuable asset for the powers that be, directing antagonisms of racial minorities, women, children and other oppressed groups on themselves." Consumerism is a similar device since "the socialization of people into consumerism serves to retard class consciousness." By consumerism Parenti means the desire "to accumulate more than they need" (Parenti 1978, 99, 101). Like other similarly disposed critics, he is apparently ready to inform people of what their true needs are.

Another form of false consciousness is "atheoreticalism," or the inability "to relate isolated events one to the other in a way that makes sense. . . . The democratic state has a vested interest in preventing the emergence of patterns of thought in which two things can be related to a common third thing that caused them" (Wolfe 1978, 118).

A more specific form of false consciousness arises when the citizen is induced to believe the political system is democratic and representative, and to accept one of its central myths, namely, that it institutionalizes the separation of the political and economic realm. Institute writers argue vigorously that such separation does not exist. According to Frances Fox Piven and Richard Cloward, "the experience of politics available to most Americans was organized by particular and elaborate institutional arrangements that concealed the alliance of state and property . . . the economic activities of the government on behalf of property were rendered almost invisible" (Piven and Cloward 1982, 81).

Education is a major villain in the inculcation of false values and consciousness. According to Gore Vidal, "For more than a century, our educational system has seen to it that 95.6% of the population grow up to be docile workers, consumers, paranoid taxpayers and eager warriors in the Bank's never-ending struggle with atheistic communism." (Vidal 1982, 227)

For Parenti "the real goal of education is not to produce the critical independent minded individual . . . but the person conditioned to working at compulsive and mindless tasks, able to suspend autonomous judgments, to suit it to the regulations of superordinates, and to assume his or her place in the elite-controlled institutions (Parenti 1978, 118).

He also quotes approvingly Jonathan Kozol, who was persuaded that American public schools were "in business to produce a man like Richard Nixon, and even more, a population like the one which could elect him" (Parenti 1978, 118).

Raskin, too, saw the citizen as helpless, manipulated object of the elites determined to nurture his false consciousness:

> The state assumes great power and with the corporations organizes the attitudes and operational beliefs that reinforce the individual's sense of loneliness and sense of helplessness. Massive propaganda and advertising are devoted to deflecting any personal or political consciousness which might lead to independent and purposeful action. (Raskin 1974, 4–5)

In an early, major work Raskin devoted a lengthy chapter to the thorough examination of the debilitating characteristics of the American system of education which he called "The Channeling Colony." While much of the book displays the spirit and utopian aspirations of the 1960s, there is little evidence elsewhere in his later writings that the premises which underlie Raskin's thinking in these matters have changed substantially or at all in the intervening years. For Raskin (as for Parenti and other IPS authors and social critics outside IPS such as Bowles and Gintis [1976]) formal education is the tool par excellence for inculcating false consciousness and servility to the state, the American state, the only one specifically referred to in his book, *Being and Doing*:

> On all levels in the school . . . the young person is expected to learn the *basic* economic and political lessons which the modern nation-state teaches and requires so that it may remain authoritarian and pyramidal. The school thus serves as the training instrument for the state. [Moreover]. . . . Children in a colonized world [i.e., the United States] . . . are expected to be tools of forces that they cannot see, understand or control. . . . Nothing is revealed to the individual and the possibility of his wholeness is explicitly denied through the Channeling Colony where the individual learns that he is to see himself functionally in the performance of a specialized series of tasks. . . . In the Channeling Colony, students are essentially in the same position as the peasants of the Middle Ages. (Raskin 1971, 111, 113, 118, 119)

Raskin's conception of the American school—a monstrously impersonal, repressive institution, tainted by the original sin of the division of labor (specialization)—is so outlandish that it can only be understood as a reflection of a heightened intolerance for any externally imposed discipline, an intolerance produced by correspondingly excessive expectations about the creativity of children and the freedom from restraint they must be granted—attitudes also reflected in a remark of Parenti quoted earlier regarding the repression of children.

Repression of another kind has concerned Gore Vidal who has written that

> Although our notions about what constitutes correct sexual behavior are usually based on religious texts, those texts are invariably interpreted by the rulers in order to keep control over the ruled. Any sexual or intellectual or recreational or political activity that might decrease the amount of coal mined, the number of pyramids built, the quantity of junk food confected will be proscribed. (Vidal 1982, 151)

From such reflections Vidal turns to a novel explanation of discrimination against homosexuals, persecuted, as he sees it, "because men who don't have wives or children to worry about are not as easily dominated as those men who do" (ibid.)

In many of the critiques of American institutions surveyed so far, a diffuse (and largely misdirected) antiauthoritarian impulse looms large which also helps to explain Raskin's comparison of school "identification papers, records, tardy slips" to those required to get out of concentration camps, prisons, or hospitals (Raskin 1971, 112). On these pages Raskin seems to embrace in full the romantic anti-authoritarian impulses of the 1960s which undermined the capacity of many social critics to distinguish, among other things, between the hardships of college students and blacks (as exemplified in the memorable volume entitled *The Student as Nigger* (Farber 1969) or between the regimentation prevailing on campuses and military barracks.

Much of this undifferentiated antiauthoritarianism found expression in a deeply emotional aversion to bureaucracy and hierarchy of almost any kind. These objections were in turn rooted in a passionate individualism which erupted in the 1960s, taking the form of protest against regimentation, restraint, and regulation. It also entailed abhorrence of impersonality inherent in the bureaucratic mentality and handling of the individual. The Institute, large a product of the 1960s, fully shared this preoccupation with the evils of bureaucracy which, however, failed to dampen its sympathy for left wing regimes in the Third World which became rapidly bureaucratized themselves. Some of this had to do with simple ignorance of conditions in Third World countries. Many of the radicals were as ignorant, for example of the mistreatment of homosexuals in socialist countries as they were of the reach and power of state bureaucracy in countries like Cuba or North Vietnam. But they also displayed a general inability (or unwillingness) to differentiate, a trait that increasingly became a hallmark of the New Left and the social criticism it had inspired. Waskow explained some of this phenomenon as follows:

> students [i.e., student protestors of the 60s—P.H.] have in mind something quite special when they think or speak of "totalitarianism." They mean the generally machine-like, dehumanizing quality of great bureaucracies, not the specially dehumanizing system of secret police and thought control. This is . . . why some of them can in one breath damn the University of California as "totalitarian" and

deny that Cuba is. For Cuba seems to be "turned on," live, unbureaucratic, full of sex and unexpectedness even if its government controls the press; but the multiversity is gray and chilly. (Waskow 1970, 86)

The quote also helps explain the IPS attitude toward Marxist-Leninist regimes in general and the compatibility of its intolerance of the slightest taint of authoritarianism in the United States (such as requirements for regular school attendance) with the good natured tolerance of the far more consequential authoritarianism of Marxist-Leninist systems. Apparently different standards apply at home and abroad. It is a curious aspect of this radical outlook that while it is imbued with a heightened notion of individual rights and potentials, it also admires Marxist-Leninist systems which treat the very notion of individual rights with utter contempt both in theory and practice.

The individualistic values of these social critics, and their belief in the virtually unlimited potential of the individual, leads them to exaggerate the limits American society places upon the unfolding of such gifts. These beliefs also inflame their capacity for moral indignation and a readiness to discern "repression."

A psychologist observed of such attitudes that

The underlying feeling is one of outrage that society should have mechanisms . . . which inevitably restrict . . . the individual within it. This outrage seems to derive from a truly radical belief in the sacredness of the individual, a belief which is . . . typically American. (Kreilkamp 1976: 43; see also Shils 1969)

A logical corollary to this concern with the individual and his unique needs and rights is the preoccupation with impersonality. As will be seen below, the charge of impersonality is also a key element in the critiques of capitalism, (of its standardized treatment of the individual) weighing perhaps even more heavily in its indictment than the more traditional charge of exploitation. Raskin uses the term "channeling" to denote impersonality. It refers to a "pervasive" process which eliminates possibilities of personal growth and fulfillment in "Western industrialized society" (Raskin 1971, 118). Given this formulation, the reader must presume that this singularly dehumanizing process only makes its appearance in the West, while in socialist industrial societies no such channeling takes place. The implication seems to be that in other societies, the individual seeks the form of higher education and type of career most congenial to his unique personal interests and needs, unhampered by economic need, political pressure or unwanted attention from the authorities.

Impersonality, according to the radical critics, is associated with dehumanizing and mistrust. As Alan Wolfe sees it, "Americans distrust everybody. . . . Strangers are not to be talked to, because if friends are not trusted, who could strangers be?" (Wolfe 1978, 117). This is the kind of assertion which suggests that there may be a connection between impassioned social criticism and a severely impaired capacity to observe how people actually live and behave. For anyone who has lived for any length of time in the United States, the idea that people in this country won't talk to strangers is surrealistic.

The most telling summary of the concern with false consciousness was offered by Arthur Waskow when he proposed that "the system tries to expropriate our heads and hearts as well as our bodies," (Waskow 1970, 163). In other words, this system seeks total domination of the individual by shaping and corrupting both his values and emotions, as well as the more conventional exploitation of "bodies" through military service and other forms of servitude. What most disturbed Waskow was no mere social injustice or political oppression detectable by the naked eye, but a deeper deformation of human beings and their psyche, that social critics often attribute to capitalist societies, unconcerned with the higher ends of life.

The IPS worldview is based at least in part, on the high expectations American culture tends to generate ("much radical thought in America partakes of the deeply conventional American belief in perfectibility, fundamentally a form of chronic optimism" [Kreilkamp 1976, 34–35].) For example, Alan Wolfe, after enumerating the attributes of a just social order (e.g., "work would result in feelings of wholeness and mutuality," no more prisons, "collective living arrangements" replacing the nuclear family, etc.) concludes: "Such a vision is within our grasp. It requires only one [sic] change: the replacement of a system based on private power and exploitation with a system based on participation and control, the replacement of an undemocratic, illiberal and repressive capitalism with a democratic and liberating socialism" (Wolfe 1978, 206). Such utopian optimism is also apparent in Waskow's Draft Constitution for the United States which proposes, among other things that "All citizens over 13 shall have equal personal incomes, and all citizens under 13 shall receive two-thirds of that income. . . . All labor shall be voluntary. . . . All property shall be owned by a Collective, Comradery or Commonwealth. . . . No person shall own any property. . . . The level of the personal income of each citizen, to be set in January each year. . . . There shall be no Continental or Commonwealth armed forces" (Waskow 1971 March, 74, 76).

The impassioned denunciation of American society is thus anchored in the deeply held belief that society is, or ought to be, a good deal more than an arrangement that takes limited care of certain basic needs. Instead, the critics see the social system as a vital instrument that should promote and ensure the maximization of human happiness and the full flowering of human potential, generously defined. This is a point of view replicated, one way or another, in the ideas of virtually every utopian thinker and radical political activist. More recently, it has been stimulated by the trend toward impersonality in modern, large-scale, urban societies. It is unlikely that the Institute intellectuals quoted would find congenial the warnings of Iganizo Silone, veteran of the most influential political utopia seeking movement of our times:

> What we call happiness is a personal thing, almost always brief in duration, and well beyond the power of any social order to grant or guarantee. All that can be expected even from the best possible social order is the abolition of such external obstacles as impede man's normal development. (Silone 1968, 38)

Critiques of Capitalism

The portrait of American society presented by the social critics of the Institute is unrelievedly bleak. Hardly any aspect of American life escapes scrutiny and indictment; the criticism is ubiquitous and pervasive.

While it may not be pleasant to be enveloped by such dark and oppressive images of the society one lives in, and to live with the conviction that one is a citizen of one of the most repressive and dehumanized countries history has ever known, a shared attachment to such images may best explain the durability of IPS and its attraction for people united in their deep aversion to American society. People will not devote the best years, indeed decades, of their lives to a cause and a vision unless considerable personal satisfaction is yielded by doing so. A perusal of the writings of those associated with IPS, strongly suggests that their animosity toward American society is the central, consuming passion and preoccupation of their intellectual-professional and probably also personal lives.

It is, then, important to understand the rewards-personal, social, intellectual—that flow to the social critic in American society and how these rewards have helped to perpetrate the adversary culture. Such understanding will shed some new light on the curent forms and meanings of alienation and its subcultural propagation or perpetuation, and on the increasingly tenuous connection between alienation and a genuine marginality as well as the ascendant ties between self-esteem and the exercise of radical social criticism.

None of this is to suggest that the substantive themes generated and sustained by IPS over decades are particularly novel. It is not the originality of the social criticism articulated by IPS that makes it significant but its persistence, comprehensiveness, and wide dissemination, and the combination of such critiques with a variety of political-organizational activities.

Apparently the deepest source of hostility toward the United States is its identification with capitalism, a social system generations of intellectuals have found uncongenial and abhorrent, a tradition the Institute both embraces and seeks to reinvigorate.

Perhaps the single major explanation of this relentless hostility is that capitalism can be held responsible for a wide range of evils, which, allegedly, cannot be remedied as long as this mode of socio-economic organization persists.

According to Professors Martin Carnoy and Henry M. Levin of Stanford University, contributors to the IPS "alternative budget study,"

> The persistence of poverty, unemployment, and differential access to schooling is not the result of the inefficiencies in capitalist development, but the direct product of that development. In order to have a society in which human needs and development are put before the accumulation of capital and the production of goods as ends in themselves, it is a necessary condition to dismantle the capitalist system of production. (Raskin, ed. 1978, 257)

Sentiments displayed by Tom Hayden, among others, further capture the spirit that has animated both past and current critics of capitalism. (His connections to IPS can be traced through "his chief economic theorist Derek Shearer, a fellow of IPS and co-author of *Economic Democracy: The Challenge of the 1980s*" [Bunzel 1983, 441].) Hayden wrote that

> inherent in the process of doing business under capitalism is a marked tendency to put profits above people, to lure the consumer into the highest price possible while conceding the lowest wage possible to the workers. . . . It takes an extraordinary person to succeed in business while being honest and charitable. (Bunzel 1983, 35)

Thus capitalism is not only exploitative, it also deforms the human character, draining it of compassion and empathy by its relentless preoccupation with "profits above people." Similarly, Richard Falk objects to capitalism because "it divides society too much into winners and losers. It is too harsh on the losers" (Falk 1983, 8). As such remarks suggest, the emphasis in recent times and especially since the 1960s has shifted from a predominantly economic critique of capitalism to the spiritual damage it does to people, to a renewed concern with the broad, dehumanizing effects of the "cash nexus."

Again, in the words of Hayden,

> Most of our artists are employed in the creation of mindless commercials, many of our scientists create weaponry, wife beating and violence against women is generally on the rise, pornography is a bigger industry than movies and recording together, racism is still part of the national fabric, crime is rampant and not surprisingly, mental illness is epidemic. (Bunzel 1983, 35)

Gar Alperowitz perceives a relationship between private property and the competitive market on the one hand, and "horrendous problems, including exploitation, inequality, ruthless competition, individual alienation, the destruction of community, expansionism, imperialism" on the other (Lynd and Alperowitz 1973, 55).

There is substantial continuity between the traditional Marxist critiques of capitalism, of the non-Marxist romantics of the nineteenth century, and that adopted by the New Left of the 1960s. Marx was repelled by the depersonalized pursuit of profit, and commented on the ravages brought by the dynamics of capitalism to communal ties and traditional values (Berman 1978). In turn the romantic critics were, in the words of Irving Kristol, "contemptuous of commercial activity . . . regarding it an activity that tends to coarsen and trivialize the human spirit." Artists, writers, and thinkers were also hostile to bourgeois society for not taking them and their ideas more seriously and for enriching the market, "reflect [ing] the appetites and preferences of common men and women" rather than the tastes and values of an enlightened elite they felt themselves to be—an attitude vividly displayed by critics like Marcuse and his many followers who were dedicated to castigating the corruptions and vulgarity of mass culture (Kristol 1983, 32, 22).

Capitalism also stands accused of exploitation and causing much human suffering by depriving people of the opportunity to make a decent living and allowing or actively perpetuating unemployment and poverty. As a mode or production it is criticized for being wasteful and irrational for creating a poor fit between human needs and the forces of production. This theme is powerfully revived in the attacks on the multinationals, perceived as the most visible symbols and causes of the worldwide maldistribution of resources and international inequities. They are responsible, Barnet and other IPS authors believe, for the growing gap between the "haves" of the West and the "have nots" of the Third World (Barnet and Muller 1974). The multinationals are the major instrument of global inequalities which manifest themselves, among other things in "the basic fact that the United States, with six percent of the world's population, uses more than sixty percent of the world's resources for itself, for its own needs, to keep this society going" (Raskin 1969, 18). (These figures have been quoted time and again, in high school social studies programs, as well as graduate seminars, in countless discussions in the media and in political speeches, whenever societal guilt is to be mobilized or displayed. It would be of some interest to know how these world resources have been defined and by whom, and what is the basis of the claim that the U.S. is using 60 percent of them.)

Capitalism has been attacked—in the past as in the present—for depriving people of work satisfaction, for converting labor into meaningless and underpaid drudgery. Indeed, when unemployment is not the target (when there is little of it) the attention of the critics shifts to the meaninglessness of work ("dead end jobs"), or the meaninglessness of its rewards—the emptiness of consumer gratifications, the "tawdriness" of the fruits of (alienated) labor.

Another major charge leveled against capitalism is, of course, that it promotes social inequality. Critics find it especially galling that in a society as rich as America there are poor people. The very richness and the generally high standard of living (reluctantly conceded) add to the intensity of the indictment; a country as wealthy as this one should not tolerate *any* poverty. Moreover, the inequalities are not based on merit, (the critics can tolerate meritorious inequality) but on spurious criteria, privileges of birth, unearned income, or worse, avarice, greed, deceit, lust for possessions.

The critique of capitalism as a critique of inequality is particularly congenial to Americans as products of a culture dedicated to egalitarianism, seeking to reconcile the conflicting values of individual achievement and competition with those of equality and community (see, for example, Lipset 1973.)

Of late the old Marxian theme of "pauperization," has been given new plausibility according to the critics by the tax and welfare reforms of the Reagan administration. They noted a new cycle of polarization between rich and poor, and argue that the middle classes of America are now severely endangered. Barbara Ehrenreich (an IPS Fellow) is among those who entertain a scenario that includes the possibility of the middle classes "disappear [ing] altogether, leaving the country torn, like many third-world societies, between an affluent minority and a horde of the desperately poor" (Ehrenreich 1986, 44). Among the telling symptoms of such polarization she notes the emergence of "two cultures . . . natural fiber vs. synthetic blends; hand-crafted wood cabinets vs. mass produced maple; David's Cookies vs. Mister Donuts" (ibid, 50). Careful to avoid any appearance of glee she has taken the position of detached observer (an approach pioneered by Barnet) regretfully predicting yet another disaster befalling American society.

When all is said and done, the deepest roots of the rejection of capitalism lie not in economic matters but in the spiritual realm. For Western intellectuals, the most unsatisfactory properties of capitalism are moral, spiritual, psychological, and aesthetic, not economic— another circumstance that helps to explain the vigor of its critiques persisting well in the late 20th century, under conditions vastly different from those contemplated by Marx. In the past as in the present, militant and articulate anticapitalism had little to do with "class interest"; it was produced, as Henry de Man put it, not by "the cultural poverty of the proletariat, but by the cultural wealth of instructed members of the bourgeoisie and the aristocracy . . . these doctrines only become intelligible in the light of . . . the spiritual motives which underlie the views of every socialist thinker." Of special interest is the related observation that "socialist doctrine becomes explicable . . . as an antagonistic reaction of cultured bourgeois and aristocrats to the circumstances of their cultural environment" (de Man 1928, 26–27).

What arouses the greatest animosity toward capitalism is that it is not interested in moral regeneration; it accepts human nature as it is. Irving Kristol observed that

> Bourgeois society is without doubt the most prosaic of all possible societies . . . uninterested in . . . transcendence. . . . It is a society organized for the convenience and comfort of common men and women, not for the production of heroic, memorable figures. It is a society interested in making the best of this world, not in any kind of transfiguration, whether through tragedy or piety. . . . [By contrast] Socialism (of whatever kind) is a romantic passion that operates within a rationalistic framework. It aims to construct a human community in which *everyone* places the common good—as defined, necessarily, by an intellectual and moral elite—before his own individual interests and appetites. The intention was not new—there is not a religion in the world that has failed to preach and expound it. What was new was the belief that such self-denial could be realized. (Kristol 1983, 28–29, 33)

Robert Heilbroner, the economist, likewise perceived capitalism as a relentlessly rational-secular force: "Capitalism would be impossible in a sacralized world to which men could relate with awe and veneration, just as such attitudes cannot arise in a society in which exchange value has reduced to a common denominator all use-values" (Heilbroner 1985, 145).

Such critiques of capitalism suggest that the deepest hostility it has inspired in intellectuals and in others frustrated by the meaninglessness of modern life, stems from its profoundly and historically unique irreligious character (see also Schumpeter 1950). By contrast, the appeals of Marxism have been basically religious, especially in our times and among the adversarial intellectuals of Western societies (Kolakowski 1977).

It would, however, be misleading to suggest that the critiques of capitalism levelled by IPS rest exclusively on the intellectual traditions discussed above. In fact, they have been reinvigorated by a new entity: the multinational corporation, the latest alleged embodiment of many of the most unattractive and menacing features of capitalism. Objections to modern capitalism based on "bigness" and bureaucracy are particularly congenial to Americans committed to the values of individualism (alongside their craving for community). The large, impersonal nature of capitalist corporations and multinationals is said to crush individuals as it does poor countries. The global, or multinational corporation, has come to occupy an important position in the Institute demonology and in that of cooperating organizations such as the World Council of Churches. In the words of Jean-Francois Revel, "we have seen a mounting campaign to depict these firms as vultures gorging on the blood of the world, starving it and polluting it." In a document produced by the World Council they were described as "one of the forms of powers which are the greatest obstacle to human development and exert the most pernicious influence upon it" (Revel 1985, 48).

The critique of multinationals makes it possible to attack simultaneously both the domestic institutions and the foreign policies and global impact of the United States. Since two-thirds of the multinationals are U.S. based companies, they can be regarded as largely American institutions although they have a "global reach," to quote Richard Barnet. Their destructive impact, according to Barnet, includes a leveling, homogenizing effect on indigenous cultures and traditions, created, for example, by the inundation of Third World countries with shoddy, mass-produced American consumer goods and television programs. (Another, even worse, example of the malign influence of these corporations has been their alleged campaign to persuade the poor mothers of the Third World to give up wholesome breast-feeding in favor of less nourishing substitutes marketed by multinationals such as Nestlé.)

In the eyes of the critics, the multinationals combine the evils associated with the United States, capitalism, and the Western World as a whole. They also symbolize the exploitative relationship between the rich and wasteful countries of the West and the long suffering, victimized Third World.

"Increasingly," Barnet has written, "global resource systems are being managed by multinational corporations . . . an integrated operation on a planetary scale. Viewed from space, the Global Factory suggests a human organism. The brain is housed in steel-and-glass slabs located in. . . New York, London, Frankfurt, Zurich or Tokyo. The blood is capital, and it is pumped through the system of global banks . . . tax havens in Panama and the Bahamas function as the heart. The hands are steadily moving to the outer rim of civilization" (Barnet 1980, 239).

He also believes that "the multinational corporation, in pursuit of its own interests, constitutes a clear and continuing threat to the interests of millions of people around the world. . . . Corporate planners have become a public menace. . . . They are accountable to no one" (Barnet 1975, Op-ed). Further, "Multinational corporations can evade taxes, speculate against the national currency, despoil resources, frustrate a national employment policy, and governments can do little about it . . . corporations escape into a world market of their own making where no government operates" (Barnet 1980, 305).

Barnet regards multinationals as the gravest threat to material well-being, to the physical environment, and to political democracy in the United States which, (at this stage in the argument), must exist, after all: otherwise it could not be threatened: "it would be naive to think that democracy in America is invulnerable. . . . The excessive power of large corporations over the political and economic life of the country has all but destroyed the system of checks and balances in our society" (Barnet 1975, 24–25). Moreover, "The power to shape our daily lives lies increasingly in the hands of the executives of global corporations" (Barnet and Muller 1975).

The most notable and consistent aspect of Barnet's treatment of the big corporations is the disposition to inflate their power and influence. There is rarely any reference to areas of the world where multinational do *not* operate, are excluded from, or severely restricted in. Moreover, Third World countries today can either expel or seize the assets of such companies, or extort huge compensation for allowing them to operate, circumstances also not alluded to.

The exaggeration of the powers of the multinationals is a form of economic determinism; in Barnet's view, they control the resources of the world, and hence determine the political course of events: "Whoever controls world resources controls the world in a way that mere occupation of territory cannot match" (Barnet 1980, 17). By this logic, the Chevron Oil Company in Angola exercises greater control over Angolan national policies than its Soviet-Cuban mentors who station tens of thousands of troops and military advisors in that country and provide it with weapons. Likewise Soviet military presence in Eastern Europe could be trivialized or compared to that of American companies in Latin America.

Overstating the powers of the multinationals is in part a polemical device designed by Institute authors and adherents to increase apprehension and hostility toward them. Exaggerating the powers of the enemy is an old political weapon.

The Roots of War: American Culture and Capitalism

The exaggeration of the power of capitalist corporations is balanced by minimizing the importance of military force in contemporary global political affairs. This attitude reflects surprisingly limited awareness of the many uses of military force in our times and is prevalent mainly among those who take their own security for granted. As James Schlesinger observed, "It is only in the United States . . . that citizens have held to this curious belief that military power lacks utility. It is the belief of a generation spoiled by an excess, if that's what is is, of security. Only those who have known security all their lives can possibly think that military power is irrelevant" (Schlesinger 1980, 21).

Besides being an expression of a sense of security, belittling military power—especially Soviet military power—has encouraged the trivialization of the Soviet threat and helped to discredit military spending in the United States. Indeed, for IPS, the folly and futility of defense expenditures is a major article of faith and a focal point of its activities. Institute opposition takes many forms, ranging from Waskow's candidly utopian approach ("There shall be no Continental or Commonwealth armed forces") to the far more sophisticated isolationism of authors like Earl Ravenal (and his colleagues Barnet and Klare) who recommend a "noninterventionist foreign policy" based on the drastic, unilateral shrinking of all branches of the American military as "part of an accommodation to the emergence of a new kind of international system with a different distribution of power" (in Raskin, ed. 1978, 152).

As early as 1969 Raskin suggested that there were "two basic choices to which members of Congress and members of the scholarly community must address themselves: "Do they think they can ride the tiger, mediating here, setting some sort of budgetary limits there, or are they prepared to undertake the more difficult tasks of dismantling the national security state?" (Raskin 1969, 19).

If the idea of a Soviet military threat against the United States, or the West, is treated as irrational and fantasmagoric—as Institute authors have regularly done—it becomes more plausible to argue, as IPS authors also do, that American preoccupation with defense has purely domestic causes and serves only questionable domestic political (or economic) purposes (see for example Alan Wolfe, "The Rise and Fall of the 'Soviet Threat'" [Wolfe 1979]).

Indeed, the school of "cold war revisionism"—closely tied to IPS writers such as Gar Alperowitz, Richard Barnet, and Gabriel Kolko—has held that the very concept of "national security" is spurious, and was replaced by "national security state" as a self-evidently derogatory term. They held that the United States has been largely responsible for the cold war and that the Soviet threat has been concocted by the ruling elites seeking to divert attention from domestic problems. According to the Institute doctrine, articulated by Barnet, "the roots of war" are found in "the concentration of power in a national security bureaucracy . . . in our capitalist economy . . . and the business creed that sustains it," and in "the vulnerability of the public to manipulation on national security issues. People do not perceive where their true interests lie and hence are easily swayed by emotional appeals . . . willing to accept uncritically the myth of the national interest" (Friedman 1983, 140–42).

The unattractiveness of military spending can always be readily contrasted with the desirability of spending to improve the quality of life. Thus for example in "Housing: A Socialist Alternative," Chester Hartman and Michael Stone noted that the 58 billion they proposed (in 1978) to spend on better housing was "only 3 percent of the GNP and less than half of the present military budget" (Raskin, ed. 1978, 243).

Opposition to military spending (and the associated denial of the reality of a Soviet threat) serve further objectives as well. Insofar as IPS authors believe that American capitalism is, to a great degree, propped up by military spending and production, reducing such expenditures would contribute to the demise, or at least the weakening, of the system. And since IPS generally finds little justification for the assertion of American power and influence anywhere around the globe, a weaker military establishment would make such assertiveness less likely.

Finally, the disparagement of military power is also related to the idea that in the age of the multinationals and global environmental problems the nation-state itself is of secondary importance, and if that is the case, military force, a major expression of the power of the nation-state, also loses significance. As Barnet sees it, "The lifeboat ethic is undermining the legitimacy of the nation state itself. That process was already well under way before the resource squeeze began. Territorial empires like the United States and the Soviet Union are becoming ungovernable. The traditional function of the nation state, territorial defense, can no longer be performed by any national state however powerful" (Barnet 1980, 305; for an earlier version of the argument see Barnet 1971, op-ed).

Given the economic determinism he embraces, it is not altogether surprising that Barnet seeks to reduce the importance of one of the most conspicuous and consequential developments of our times, namely the proliferation of nation states and the upsurge of the corresponding nationalistic passions and conflicts. More puzzling is his insistence that nation states can no longer defend themselves ("No one knows how to use classic military means to defend national territory and 'national interests' in the nuclear age" [Barnet 1982, 271]) in an era when many conventional wars have been fought (between South and North Korea, India and Pakistan, Israel and its neighbors, Iran and Iraq, Ethiopia and Somalia) and territorial claims settled, one way or another. While from an outsider's point of view such conflicts might have been pointless, for the countries involved they were often vital for their national survival or territorial integrity. Barnet's efforts to deflate the importance of such conflicts and with them that of the nation state, follow directly from his belief in the supreme importance of the global corporations allegedly "seeking to transcend the nation-state" (Barnet 1971, op ed).

The dismissal of the importance of nationalism and the nation state may be further explained by an affinity with the nineteenth century anticipation (shared by both Marxists and liberals) of the withering away of nationalism—along with other doomed, irrational beliefs destined to succumb to other, greater historical forces (Berlin 1972). The claim in turn, that nation states have become undefendable in the nuclear age may be ascribed to what I shall call nuclear-overdeterminism, much in vogue among adversarial intellectuals in the West.

Finally, one may wonder what has prompted Barnet to suggest that *both* the United States and the Soviet Union have become "ungovernable" well before the instability associated with the reforms of Gorbachev. The attribution of a common "ungovernability" may best be explained by Barnet's advocacy of the moral equivalence thesis of which he has been a major exponent (see, for example, Barnet 1977). Postulating a moral equivalence between "Superpowers" entails more than the attribution of moral symmetry and a corresponding reluctance to prefer one over the other. The refusal to take sides and the inability to discern morally significant differences rest on a series of putative structural symmetries. The major characteristic of the moral equivalence thesis is a compulsion to discover similarities where none may exist, such as a shared "ungovernability." It is true enough that the United States with its cultural pluralism, lax social discipline, political permissiveness, and excessive legalism is not easy to govern, although it is far from "ungovernable." On the other hand, a similar characterization of the Soviet Union is far more questionable, given the weakness of its protest movement and the general docility of its population.*

The moral equivalence theory, in spite of its apparent objectivity and detachment, often becomes a new way of criticizing the United States. It is a critical enough proposition by itself that the United States is no better than the Soviet Union, and if the Soviet Union is a deeply flawed social system so is the United States. The favored term of equation, "Superpowers," signifies the unwholesome accumulation of power in the hands of the rulers of both countries and

---

*At any rate that was the case when the IPS writings here discussed were produced.

implies that their preeminent, shared preoccupation is to amass global power. The equation of the two societies can also be used to tone down the critiques of the Soviet Union (if it is no worse than the United States it cannot be *that* bad!)—excepting those who believe that nothing matches the corruptions of the United States.

The tone and style of those subscribing to the moral equivalence thesis also conveys that they are far more critical of and hostile to the United States than the Soviet Union: the critiques of the former tend to be specific, intense, and passionate; those of the Soviet Union perfunctory, superficial, and lacking in the kind of moral indignation and passion that characterizes their comments on the defects of American society. (For a collection of writings critically examining this theory see Roche, ed. 1986.)

Authors like Barnet manage to reconcile the moral equivalence thesis with a wildly exaggerated conception of the powers of the United States (not unlike those of the global corporations). The scrutiny of bloated, and destructive American power is a major preoccupation of Institute analysts.

Even in obviously humiliating circumstances such as the retreat from Vietnam, American power remains envisaged as unscathed and a serious threat. Thus Barnet argued that "the day the last American soldier and airplane leave Southeast Asia the American empire will still be the strongest on earth" (Friedman, ed. 1983, 136). In comparisons with Soviet military power the United States invariably emerges as the stronger, in possession of overwhelming forces and resources, as shown for example by Michael Klare (1981), an IPS specialist on military affairs.

Indeed, the main thrust of IPS writings on foreign affairs, disarmament, and Soviet-American relations is that the American possession of a formidable and excessive arsenal (and the associated false assumptions, misconceptions, and questionable motives) represent *the* major obstacle to disarmament and a lessening of global tensions.

Insistence on the enormity of American power and its potential misuse, is also a useful polemic device. The more powerful the United States appears, the greater its responsibilities, and, in the darker vision, the greater threat it represents to its own citizens and the world at large: "The number one nation is in the strongest position . . . to set the tone for international relations and to create the climate under which the other nations deem it practical, or impractical to organize themselves for peace," says Barnet (Friedman, ed. 1983, 140). In other words, by projecting greater strength upon on it, more can be expected of the United States and the higher the expectations the more opportunities for failing to live up to them and for criticizing it for such failures.

Inflating the power of the United States also endows it with more options, and more choices. It allows it, for instance, to welcome and accommodate itself to Soviet client states in Africa and Asia, even in Central America and the Caribbean (little Nicaragua and little Cuba are no threat to such a big and powerful country). Given its position of allegedly overwhelming strength it can also unilaterally reduce its armaments, humor the Soviet Union (and its insecurity born out of its alleged weakness) and perform other acts of generosity and goodwill. Above all, it never needs to feel threatened by foreign powers. Thus I.F. Stone, a friend of IPS, "told a national television audience on '60 Minutes' that Ronald Reagan . . . 'scares the hell out of me' . . . [but] Col. Quadafi was a provocative 'flea' who should be met with 'patience, restraint, good sense and humor'" (Kincaid 1983, 313).

Overstating the power of the United States and thereby expanding its freedom of choice, while understating the power of its adversaries allows for the application of ethical double standards. It makes it possible to take a severely judgmental stand toward the United States, while reducing or relieving of responsibility other, supposedly weaker political actors. In the Vietnam era this made it possible to condemn harshly the civilian casualties caused by American forces while paying little attention to those resulting from the activities of the Vietcong, portrayed as the ill-equipped David fighting the technological Goliath. Technological weakness conferred moral superiority, while technological strength helped to define the U.S. as the malevolent aggressor-victimizer. In fact, as the outcome of the war made clear, the Vietcong was perfectly well-equipped for the type of warfare it was engaged in.

The attribution of superior strength often becomes an ingredient of a selective determinism grounded in political-ideological preferences which make it possible to endow or deprive political actors of choice and thereby moral responsibility (see also Hollander 1983, 241–251).

Casting a supremely strong United States into a perennial aggressor-victimizer role has been complemented by a partiality toward the perceived victim-underdog nations, in particular those in the Third World which claim socialist credentials. (There have been domestic equivalents, favored underdog groups and movements.) The IPS has, in effect, embraced belief in "the superior virtue of the oppressed," although the designation of the oppressed (or threatened) nations or groups has been quite idiosyncratic, following the contours of an ideologically predetermined moral universe. In fact, one of the more remarkable characteristics of the IPS worldview has been its combination of a highly developed, sharply and consistently critical position toward the United States with a strikingly benign, uncritical sensibility toward many Third World, Asian, and Central American countries and movements.

Bertrand Russell's comments—predating present-day political alignments—help to explain this mentality and place it in a broader historical context:

> One of the persistent delusions of mankind is that some sections of the human race are morally better or worse than others. . . . A rather curious form of this admiration of groups to which the admirer does not belong is the belief in the superior virtues of the oppressed: subject nations, the poor, women and children.

Russell also pointed out that while Alexander Pope idealized the peasant, "For himself, Pope preferred London and his villa at Twickenham" (Russell 1950, 80, 81) an attitude much in evidence among contemporary Western admirers of the Third World and assorted Marxist-Leninist countries.

The visions of the overpowering global strength of the United States often rest on a comparably inflated conception of the strength and unity of its privileged classes. Thus Parenti believes that "Whatever their differences, members of the business community share remarkably like-minded perspectives regarding the virtues of the capitalist order, the evils of alternative systems, and the use of the state to maintain corporate dominance against the demands of working classes at home and abroad" (Parenti 1978, 94).

Not surprisingly, the critical view of the American exercise of power is often accompanied by the attribution of conspiratorial methods and intentions. The committed critic seeks to unearth hidden evil to lend greater force to his revelations. Those associated with IPS frequently adopt this approach. As in the traditional Marxist view of the political process under capitalism, Institute authors regularly look for hidden forces beneath the democratic facade. Most major targets of Institute critiques, whether they are designated as the "power elite" (Mills 1956), the multinationals, the CIA, or other agents of the "national security state," fit some conspiratorial scenario:

> Like the impeachment hearings and the Pentagon Papers, the investigations of the intelligence agencies have provided a glimpse behind the mask of the state. The revelations . . . teach different lessons . . . reviews of the text have shown the shocking range of routine, illegal, destructive acts undertaken by these agencies at home and abroad, which endangered the lives and trampled upon the rights of so many. What can also be drawn from the record is a fairly complete overview of the operating principles of the secret realm of the government. (Borosage in Friedman, ed. 1983, 120)

Even designs of public housing can be associated with conspiratorial intentions, as two Institute specialists on housing aver that "The design and operation of public housing in many cities and the stigma attached to public housing socially and physically have been perpetrated quite deliberately to discredit the concept of publicly developed and owned housing" (Raskin, ed. 1978, 220).

While IPS does not find it difficult to uncover "secret realms" in American political and economic decision-making institutions (and even in the "capitalist control over the distribution of knowledge" [Raskin ed. 1978, 261]), it refrains from attributing conspiratorial design to Soviet activities, including the KGB and its espionage agencies (or terrorist groups hostile to the United States, to NATO, or Israel).

Here, again, one finds exceptions to the moral equivalence approach and its pursuit of symmetries between the superpowers: the Soviet Union is portrayed as the weaker, more restrained, reasonable, and cautious *status quo* power, defensively confronting American arrogance and aggression.

It is the actual exercise and assertion of American power—be it in Vietnam, Grenada, or Central America—that elicits the most viscerally hostile reaction from the social critics associated with IPS. They sense a uniquely aggressive menace in American culture that goes beyond the evils of capitalism. For Tom Hayden, it is a peculiarly American "conquering impulse" which "also damages personal life"

(Hayden 1980, 31). Again, Barnet summarizes what appears to be the prevailing IPS belief on such matters:

> A strategy of peace remains only a pious hope unless it is rooted in institutional change. . . . For more than a generation American society has been organized for war rather than peace. It is still organized for war. . . . What can we conclude from our attempt to trace the roots of war in American society? What kind of institutional changes are necessary? . . . there is no single revolutionary stroke that will cut the roots of war. They are deeply entwined around every institution, including our schools and family life. The number one nation is dedicated to winning. In kindergarten games and high school football contests, in power plays in offices and board rooms of great corporations, in the . . . academic rivalries of universities . . . in the struggles of politics, the overriding objective is to win. The myth of competition and the glory and excitement of victory are fundamental to the American way of life. (Friedman 1983, 138–39)

Competition and competitiveness emerge—as in Raskin's complaints about "channeling" in the schools and other settings of American life—as especially odious and destructive forces which are to be blamed for both the possibility of nuclear catastrophe and the deformation of the personality and social relationships of Americans.

IPS did not discover that Americans are competitive and that American capitalism helps to express and institutionalize such impulses. What is more novel in the IPS perception of and reaction to these phenomena—which it shares with the entire adversary and counterculture born in the 1960s—is the intensity of the rage competitiveness inspires and the exaggeration of its centrality in American life.

One may ask if soccer teams in England or Argentina or Hungary are any less dedicated to winning than the football teams of America? Whether or not the power plays in board rooms (or offices of party bureaucracies) any less serious, or deadly, than in the United States? Is it unusual for political parties and politicians in other societies to seek victory? Don't Marxist-Leninist guerrilla movements want to win? Don't IPS lobbyists want to successfully exert their influence?

Barnet's reproaches seem permeated by a sincere and single-minded belief that the flaws of America are historically and culturally unparalleled. As such they share with much adversarial criticism a curious unawareness of historical-comparative evidence of both the global dimensions of social evils and the limits of institutional perfectibility.

It is a pervasive disappointment with the promises and potentials of America and their incomplete, or nonexistent realization—for which capitalism is held largely responsible—which accounts for the emotional intensity of the social criticism embraced by the Institute and the adversary culture in general. Waskow conveyed this sense of disappointment vividly: "So that is your America. You are 20 years old. Your heroes have been dishonored, killed or attacked. Your society seems unutterably corrupt. And this process has filled the whole of your conscious life. From the time you were 15 until now, your experience as an American has been one of betrayal" (Waskow 1970, 149).

The social critics have no emotional and intellectual energy left to confront and examine the failings of other societies. The recognition that the failings of the United States are far from unique would clash with a determination to designate it as a singular repository of injustice and evil in the world; such a realization would be incompatible, emotionally if not logically, with the intense moral indignation the shortcomings of America inspire.

If irrationality and wastefulness are plentiful in the economic arrangements of other societies, if corporate or federal bureaucracy is more than matched in size, callousness, and inefficiency by those found in socialist and Third World countries, if many police forces are more unrestrained and powerful than the FBI and CIA put together, if the ruling elites of other countries are not less but more interested in staying in power, if the state-controlled mass media elsewhere is an even more purposeful and powerful instrument of political domination and promoter of false consciousness than the commercialized media in America, if bureaucratic impersonality and indifference to human well-being are endemic, if the masses in most countries are excluded from "meaningful" participation in the political process, if most people in most places do not find their work exciting and fulfilling, if urban life and the sense of community is no more vibrant outside the United States, if the lust for power, acquisition and the possession of unworthy material objects is widespread, if human beings do not, for the most part, act caringly and unselfishly toward one another—then what remains of the passionate indictment of America?

When reproached for their neglect of the defects of other societies, and especially those claiming socialist credentials, the critics tend to argue that as Americans they are necessarily more concerned with the defects of their own country than those of others—a position which fails to account for the ferocity with which they attack certain political systems outside the United States, as for example Spain under Franco, the Philippines under Marcos, Chile under Pinochet, Guatemala, El Salvador, South Korea, South Africa, and others.

The real issue is not whether or not a political system is geographically remote from the United States, but whether it is, or is perceived as, allied with, or supported by, the United States and whether its flaws can be linked to capitalism. If so it will unfailingly elicit criticism and moral indignation.

It should also be noted here that many countries escape criticism—and especially those claiming to adhere to some variety of Marxist socialism—because the critics of America apply different standards to them than they do to their own country. As David Horowitz observed, "radical commitments to justice continue to be dominated by a moral and political double standard. The left's indignation seems exclusively reserved for outrages that confirm the Marxist diagnosis of the sickness of capitalist society" (Horowitz 1979, 587). Moreover, Marxist-Leninist regimes produce critiques of the United States and capitalism which are often identical to and always congenial with those emanating from IPS. In addition, the very existence of these social systems helps in some measure to sustain and invigorate the critiques of capitalism in the West since the putatively socialist states can be viewed as counter models, new departures, and laudable initiatives—even when their imperfections are acknowledged, their good intentions are rarely in doubt.

In the final analysis, the mainsprings of the persistence of critiques of capitalism and the United States may be found in the confluence of a tradition of Marxist anti-capitalism and a more general and recent protest against modernity. These critiques have been part of the renaissance of a romantic anti-rationalism that has combined hostility to science and technology with a nostalgic anti-urban, anti-industrial ethos widespread in the West since the 1960s. (Bell 1976)

By the end of the 1980s the importance and influence of the Institute appears to have peaked. According to one source, "interest in IPS waned in Congress" as well as in the media. For example the number of op-ed pieces by IPS fellows in the *New York Times* was halved between 1980 and 1988. Funding has also diminished and "IPS is having trouble making ends meet." There also appears to have been a failure "to nurture a committed second generation" of activist-scholars. Moreover "With global warming, IPS desperately needs new programs" (Boo 1989). That is to say, the collapse and transformation of communist systems did not help the Institute in its pursuit of a "socialist alternative." In fact, a recent pamphlet summarizing its goals and programs proposed that "Our goal is to develop a new set of fundamental ideas for the new century that can move human society beyond the obsolete debates between capitalism and socialism" (Ideas and Practices for Progressive Social Change, 1990). While no longer describing itself as a center of radical scholarship and supporter of some improved version of socialism, much of the domestic social criticism has been retained:

> We believe that American democracy . . . is endangered unless the institutions for making both government and corporations accountable to the people can be strengthened. The democratic values of equality, dignity and social justice have been sacrificed in recent years. Short-term economic growth and aggressive individualism have been celebrated at the expense of the environment and democratic community.

While the passage of time and recent world events have weakened IPS and made some of its objectives obsolete it is likely to remain among the major and predictable voices of the adversary culture in the foreseeable future even if no longer preeminent among them.

References

Advertisement. 1977. "Vietnam: A Time for Healing and Compassion." *New York Times*, January 30

Alperowitz, Gar and Jeff Faux. 1984. *Rebuilding America*. New York: Pantheon

Barnet, Richard J. and Marcus G. Raskin. 1970. *An American Manifesto: What's Wrong with America and What We Can Do About It*. New York: New American Library.

Barnet, Richard J. 1971. "Farewell to the Nation-State." *New York Times*, op-ed, June 19.

Barnet, Richard J. and Ronald E. Muller. 1974. *Global Reach: The Power of the Multinational Corporations*. New York: Simon and Schuster.

Barnet, Richard J. and Ronald E. Muller. 1975. "Planet Earth, a Wholly Owned Subsidiary." *New York Times*, op-ed, January 23.

———. 1975. "Not Just Your Corner Drugstore." *New York Times*, op-ed, June 19.

———. 1975. *The Crisis of the Corporation*. New York: American Management Association.

———. 1977. *The Giants: Russia and America*. New York: Simon and Schuster.

———. 1977. "Less Big-Power Tension, Greater War Danger." *New York Times*, op-ed, December 28.

———. 1980. *The Lean Years: Politics in the Age of Scarcity*. New York: Simon and Schuster.

———. 1982. "The Future of Democracy." *Yale Review*, Fall.

———. 1983. "Challenging the Myths of National Security" in John S. Friedman, ed. *First Harvest: The Institute for Policy Studies*, 1963–1983. New York: Grove Press.

Beginning the Second Decade, 1963–1973. 1974. Washington, D.C.: Institute for Policy Studies.

Bell, Daniel. 1976. *The Cultural Contradictions of Capitalism*. New York: Basic Books.

Berlin, Isaiah. 1972. "Bent Twig: Notes on Nationalism," *Foreign Affairs* October.

Berman, Paul. 1978. "All That Is Solid Melts Into Air." *Dissent*, Winter.

Blumenthal, Sidney. 1986. "The Left Stuff: IPS and the Long Road Back." *Washington Post*, July 3.

Boo, Katherine. 1989. "Left Behind," *Washington City Paper* July 7–13.

Bowles, Sam and Herbert Gintis. 1976. *Schooling In Capitalist America: Educational Reform and the Contradictions of Economic Life*. New York: Basic Books.

Bruce-Briggs, B., ed. 1979. *New Class?* New Brunswick, N.J.: Transaction.

Bunzel, John. 1983. *New Force on the Left: Tom Hayden and the Campaign Against Corporate America*. Stanford: Hoover Institute Press.

Clecak, Peter. 1981. "The 'Movement' and Its Legacy." *Social Research*. Fall.

Dellums, Ronald V. 1978. "The Links Between Struggles for Human Rights in the United States and Third World." Washington, D.C. IPS Pamphlet.

Dickson, Paul. 1971. *Think Tanks*. New York: Atheneum.

Ehrenreich, Barbara. 1986. "Is the Middle Class Doomed?" *New York Times Magazine*, Sept. 7.

Falk, Richard. 1983. Interview in *Prospect*, November.

Farber, Jerry. 1969. *The Student As Nigger*. N. Hollywood, Cal.: Contact Books.

Friedman, John S., ed. 1983. *First Harvest: The Institute for Policy Studies*, 1963–1983. New York: Grove Press.

Gross, Bertram. 1980. *Friendly Fascism: The New Face of Power in America*. New York: M. Evans.

Hartman, Chester, ed. 1983. *America's Housing Crisis*. IPS, Boston: Routledge.

Hayden, Tom. 1980. *The American Future: Visions Beyond Old Frontiers*. Boston: South End Press.

Heilbroner, Robert L. 1985 *The Nature and Logic of Capitalism*. New York: W.W. Norton.

Heritage Report. 1977. "Institute for Policy Studies." May

Hollander, Paul. 1983. *The Many Faces of Socialism*, New Brunswick: Transaction.

———. 1986. "The Survival of the Adversary Culture." *Partisan Review*, No. 3.

———. 1987. "American Intellectuals: Producers and Consumers of Social Criticism." In Alain G. Gagnon, ed., *Intellectuals in Liberal Democracies*. New York: Praeger.

Hook, Sidney. 1987. *Out of Step*. New York: Harper and Row.

Horowitz, David. 1979. "A Radical's Disenchantment." *Nation*, December 8.

Ideas and Practice for Progressive Social Change. 1990. [pamphlet] Washington D.C.: Institute for Policy Studies.

Institute for Policy Studies. 1971. *Memorandum on Seminar on the 1972 Elections*, November 15.

Institute for Policy Studies Report 1983: *The Twentieth Year.*

Isaac, Rael Jean. 1980. "America the Enemy: Profile of a Revolutionary Think Tank." *Midstream*, June/July.

Kelley, David. 1976. "For Socialist Alternatives: A Radical Think Tank Is Working Within the System." *Barron's*, August 23.

Kincaid, Cliff. 1983. "The IPS and the Media: Unholy Alliance." *Human Events*, Special Supplement.

Klare, Michael T. 1981. *Beyond the Vietnam Syndrome: U.S. Interventionism in the 1980s*. Washington, D.C.: Institute for Policy Studies.

Kolakowski, Leszek. 1977. "Marxism: A Summing-Up." *Survey*, Summer.

Kreilkamp, Thomas. 1976. *The Corrosion of the Self*. New York: New York University Press.

Kristol, Irving. 1981. "American Jews and Israel: A Symposium." *Commentary*, February.

Kristol, Irving. 1983. *Reflections of a Neoconservative*. New York: Basic Books.

Lessing, Doris. 1982. "Doris Lessing on Feminism, Communism, and 'Space Fiction.'" *New York Times Magazine*, July 25.

Lipset, Seymour Martin. 1973. *The First New Nation*, New York: Norton.

Lynd, Staughton, and Gar Alperowitz. 1973. *Strategy and Program: Two Essays Toward a New American Socialism*. Boston: Beacon Press.

Man, de Henry. 1928. *The Psychology of Socialism*. London: Allen and Unwin.

Mannheim, Karl. 1936. *Ideology and Utopia*. New York: Harcourt, Brace.

Matusov, Allen J. 1984. *The Unravelling of America: A History of Liberalism in the 1960s*. New York: Harper and Row.

Mills, C. Wright. 1956. *The Power Elite*, New York: Oxford University Press.

Muravchik, Joshua. 1981. "The Think Tank of the Left." *New York Times Magazine*.

———. 1984–85. "'Communophilism' and the Institute for Policy Studies." *World Affairs*, Winter.

Parenti, Michael. 1978. *Power and the Powerless*. New York: St. Martin's Press.

———. 1983. "What If Communists Had Links to Dr King?" *New York Times*, correspondence. November 1.

Piven, Francis Fox and Richard A. Cloward. 1982. *The New Class War*, New York: Pantheon.

Powell, S. Steven. 1987. Covert Cadre: *Inside the Institute for Policy Studies*. Ottawa, Ill.: Green Hill Publishers.

Raskin, Jonah. 1974. *Out of the Whale: Growing Up in the American Left*. New York: Links Books.

Raskin, Marcus G. 1969. "National Security State." *Progressive*, June.

———. 1971. *Being and Doing*. New York: Random House.

———. 1974. *Notes on the Old System*. New York: David McKay.

———. 1975. "A Matter of Values." *Progressive*, October.

————. 1975. "For a Radical Restructuring of the Political System", *New York Times*, op-ed, December 28.

————. ed. 1978. *The Federal Budget and Social Reconstruction*. Washington: Institute for Policy Studies.

————. 1980. "Progressive Liberalism for the '80s." *Nation*, May 17.

————. 1981. "Earlier Republicanism." *New York Times*, op-ed, July 17.

————. 1986. *The Common Good*. New York: Routledge.

Revel, Jean-Francois. 1985. "The Hidden Face of Multinationals." *Encounter*, November.

Roche, Lisa, ed. 1986. *Scorpions in a Bottle: Dangerous Ideas About the United States and the Soviet Union*. Hillsdale, MI: Hillsdale College Press.

Roszak, Theodore. 1969. *The Making of a Counterculture*. Garden City, N.Y.: Doubleday.

Riesman, David. 1986. Interview.

Russell, Bertrand. 1950. *Unpopular Essays*. London: Allen and Unwin.

Russell, Sarah. 1982. "Social Change Was the Theme at Hampshire Commencement." *Daily Hampshire Gazette*, June 1.

Schlesinger, James R. 1980. "American Power and the Survival of the West." *Parameters*, June.

Schumpeter, Joseph. 1950. *Democracy, Capitalism, Socialism*. New York: Harper and Row.

Seligman, Daniel. 1982. "Keeping Up." *Fortune*, June 14.

Shils, Edward. 1956. *The Torment of Secrecy*. Glencoe: Free Press.

————. 1969. "Plentitude and Scarcity." *Encounter*, May.

Silone, Ignazio. 1968. "Re-thinking Progress." *Encounter*, April.

Tolchin, Martin. 1983. "For Blacks, Racism and Progress Mix." *New York Times*, March 11.

Trilling, Lionel. 1965. *Beyond Culture*, New York: Viking Press.

Vidal, Gore. 1983. "Preface" in John S. Friedman, ed., First Harvest, op. cit.

————. 1982. *The Second American Revolution*. New York: Random House.

Waskow, Arthur L. 1970. *Running Riot*. New York: Herder and Herder.

————. 1971. "The 1990 Draft Constitution." *Motive*, March.

————. 1971. "The Liberation of the Intellectual", *Social Policy*, March April.

————. 1971. "Patterns of American Protest." *New York Times*, op-ed, May 4.

Wills, Garry. 1971. "The Thinking of Positive Power." *Esquire*, March.

Wolfe, Alan. 1978. *The Seamy Side of Democracy: Repression in America*. New York: Longman.

————. 1979. *The Rise and Fall of the "Soviet Threat": Domestic Sources of the Cold War Consensus*. Washington, D.C.: IPS.

9

Guide to the Deformation of the Sixties

The retroactive glorification of the 1960s has been with us for some time, gathering momentum through the 1980s. These efforts reflect and reinforce what has become the conventional wisdom of liberal public opinion and especially the mass media and the academic intelligentsia. Thus the 1960s are widely perceived as a period of beneficial social change marked by an unprecedented outburst of idealism among the younger generations. Thanks to their efforts the antiwar, civil rights, feminist, environmental, and antinuclear movements flourished. There were some "excesses" on the fringes of these movements; violent groups such as the Weathermen representing a (minor) blemish on an otherwise glorious chapter of American history. But even these excesses were predetermined by the American social system or culture, provoked by its unresponsiveness, injustices, insanities. Or as the authors of this unusual, antinostalgic volume put it, "Nostalgia artists have made it [the sixties] into a holograph that creates beguiling images of the last good time—a prelapsarian age of good sex, good drugs, and good vibes . . . a time of monumental idealism populated by individuals who wanted nothing more than to give peace a chance; a time of commitment and action when dewy-eyed young people in the throes of moral passion unknown in our own selfish age sought only to remake the world" (14).

By contrast, the more infrequent critical examinations of the same period found among its key characteristics the rise of political extremism, a revival of the no-enemies-on-the-left mentality, (or anti-anticommunism) the outburst of sympathy or outright admiration for left-wing totalitarian dictatorships such as Cuba, China, and Vietnam, a reflexive sympathy with poor, anti-Western, and repressive countries in the Third World seen as victims of the West and capitalism. The authors of this volume rightly note that "sympathy for America's alleged victims developed into an identification with America's real enemies" (145). Anti-intellectualism flourished and inflicted lasting damage on all institutions of learning. The losening or unravelling of social discipline and moral standards has also been associated with the 60s, its hedonism and focus on "self-realization" encouraged by the liberating slogans and rhetoric of the times.

Destructive Generation is one of few critical examinations of the values and movements of the 1960s and it has elicited a remarkable amount of hostility. For the historians of ideas and the students of political psychology the intensity of these attacks is at once morbidly fascinating and thought provoking.

The most obvious explanation of the palpable, emotion-laden animosity may well lie in the common tendency to idealize one's youth, an impulse greatly enhanced by American culture. Most of the hostile reviewers of *Destructive Generation* were young during the 1960s; many were also involved with the movements and ideas of the times. An attack on these ideals and movements is also an attack on their earlier selves, on their personal and political identity and especially on the idea that one must be loyal to one's past and youth and youthful idealism. Thus the attacks are presumably intensified because Collier and Horowitz were among the generation of sixties activists and idealists, indeed they were leading movement figures. If so, their rejection of the past is seen as a classical stab in the back, a betrayal and sell out. Most reviewers scornfully charged them with being turncoats, converts, fanatics, who switched from one set of rigidly held beliefs to another. Particularly unforgivable (and often mentioned in the damning reviews) has been the authors' support of Ronald Reagan.

Since there is historical precedent in the disillusioned soul-searchings of an earlier generation of leftist radicals—the former communists and pro-Soviet fellow travellers (of the 1930s, 1940s and 1950s)—it is instructive to reflect on the difference between the reception the two groups were given.

Disillusionment with Soviet communism was a massive phenomenon that greatly exceeded the corresponding disenchantment with the radicalism of the 1960s. This disillusionment came in several waves and stretched over decades. For some the process began with the purges of the 1930s for others with the Nazi-Soviet Pact of 1939, for the slow learners it was the crushing of the Hungarian Revolution of 1956 or the "Secret" Speech of Khrushchev that finally jolted them into a reassessment of their political loyalties.

Liberal public opinion found it easier to accept the defections from the pro-Soviet communist cause than the corresponding defections from the radical agendas of the 60s. One explanation of this may lie in the difference between the nature of the two types of attachments. Pro-Soviet fellow travelling and association with the American Communist Party was a more isolated and isolating experience; often these attachments were relatively short-lived, especially the fellow travelling. Moreover these loyalties had a foreign, an alien focus: a distant country which encouraged, supported, and manipulated friendly organizations and groups abroad.

By contrast, the attachments and movements of the 60s were entirely homegrown and represented a mass phenomenon which was far from exclusively political. The ties which continue to bind people to the 60s have been more diffuse than were the procommunist causes of the earlier period. Most importantly, the values, beliefs, and attitudes of the 60s persisted not only because of their partly apolitical character but because they have been shared by large numbers of people and because they have found safe havens in supportive institutional settings such as the campuses and some churches.

Thus the ethos of the sixties persists not only because people cherish the memories of youthful enthusiasm, idealism, and selflessness (which increase in retrospect) but also because there are institutional settings and a broad subculture (often called the adversary culture) that preserves, promotes, and propagates these values as sources of personal and group identity. Since these values have solid subcultural support they are less likely to wither or wilt; group solidarity helps to prevent widespread soul-searching or reassessment. When there is a large enough cohort of people who persist in sharing certain beliefs there will not be many who are moved to "second thoughts" especially since such reappraisals, if genuine, are always agonizing and wrenching. It is more comfortable to persist in one's basic beliefs, in certainties acquired at an early age than to face painful readjustments.

Another way to explain the difference is to simply to suggest that in the 1960s and 1970s unlike the 1930s and 1940s there were far more people in the United States estranged from and hostile toward their society and they have retained this disposition well into the 1980s. While many of the specific movements and causes of the sixties which had brought them together vanished the basic attitudes of suspicion or aversion toward American institutions persisted. In particular the conviction that "America was guilty and untrustworthy . . . is perhaps the most enduring legacy of the Sixties" (15). If so one can understand why those willing to vocally and publicly defend these devalued institutions and beliefs—such as the authors of this book—inspire so much hostility.

The authors recognize, as few others had that the sixties nostalgia has more than sentimental implications: "the nostalgia is also a political phenomenon. The growing interest in the Sixties coincides with a renaissance of the radicalism that was the decade's dominant trait and is now being used to jump-start the Next Left" (217). Collier and Horowitz go beyond reminding us of the dark side of the sixties, they pinpoint the specific ways in which it survives and influences the present. They also realize that just because Reagan was twice elected president the American political spectrum did not move to the right, in fact in many respects the opposite happened as so many of the values of the sixties became, in somewhat diluted form, the conventional wisdom of the seventies and eighties. They also direct attention to a generally overlooked political development: the revival and rehabilitation of the Old Left that has been nurtured by the sixties nostalgia and one of its major legacies: anti-anticommunism. Memories of McCarthyism zestfully revived have played a major part in this process as its real or alleged victims "survived to be rehabilitated as martyrs and heroes of an American political 'nightmare' " (170). Even old-line communists dismissed during the sixties as doctrinaire servants of Moscow, "now seemed admirable for exactly the quality that had once seemed so despicable—their obstinate endurance and ruthless loyalty to the Party" (177). More generally, in the aftermath of Vietnam and Watergate, and the collective guilt they both inspired "the specter of 'McCarthyism' was embraced as a metaphor for a guilty past to which America must never return" (180) and it became a "political blunt instrument to beat critics of Leftism into silence," (184), to discredit any form of anticommunism. Of this process and its particular manifestations the authors provide a wealth of examples as for instance the consternation and censoriousness inspired by any reference to the involvement of George Crockett, (a Democratic Congressman from Detroit) with communist causes over a period of forty years. True to his principles, he was the only member of the House who did not join his colleagues condemning the Soviet shooting down of the Korean airliner and who voted against a resolution condemning the Soviet killing of an American officer in East Germany in 1985.

The sixties has also bequeathed to us the unchanging diatribes of Noam Chomsky (scrutinized in these pages) whose view of the United States as the Great Satan continues to receive a respectable hearing on the campuses—an outstanding example of the survival of the sixties in the eighties.

This book chronicles another largely overlooked recent development on the Left, namely the new "popular frontism" and a pretense of liberalism that contrasts so sharply with the undisguised contempt the New Left had displayed for liberals and liberal beliefs. Sensitive to the generational factors in the evolution of various left-wing trend and movements, the authors draw attention to the familial ties between the Old Left of the thirties and forties and their offspring, literal and figurative, in the sixties—the so-called "red diaper babies" (one of the authors, Horowitz was one of them).

The survival of the sixties has found further consequential expression in municipal politics, in the creation of enclaves, usually surrounding or incorporating large campuses, where former activists entrenched themselves, many of them now on the faculties. Among these enclaves—which include Berkeley and Santa Cruz, Calif.; Madison Wisc.; Ann Arbor, Mich.; Burlington, VT.; Amherst, Mass.—Berkeley has been the most instructive and the most extreme. The chapter on Berkeley ("A Tale of Socialism in One City") is perhaps the most memorable since it provides information of developments largely unknown to the American public. It should be required reading for anybody interested in a case study of the tangible survival and institutionalization of the sixties.

Described as a "living museum of insurrection" (187) and "a radical demonstration project—a 'beacon' " (188), the case of Berkeley is also important because it provides a graphic illustration of what happens when lofty ideals are translated into daily practice, when the sixties rhetoric is at last implemented in the "real world." In some ways "the Peoples Republic of Berkeley" replicated characteristic features of "the peoples republics" of countries which sprang up under Soviet or Chinese tutelage and Marxist-Leninist inspiration in various parts of the world. Mercifully, the leaders of Berkeley have been constrained by Berkeley being a part of the state of California and of the United States but within these limits they have gone a long way to emulate their foreign exemplars.

Run by radicals for approximately twenty years, Berkeley's achievements include the ruin of the public school system (which inspired both a white and black exodus from the city and its public schools with "nearly a quarter of . . . [the] black population leaving the city during 1970–80"); and a vastly increased municipal bureaucracy (for example the radical mayor had five full-time aides, while his predecessors managed with one). The accomplishments also included a greatly diminished housing stock (thanks to stringent rent controls and other restrictions on property rights), greatly increased crime and drug abuse, corruption, and grotesque waste of public funds. While increasingly disgruntled residents complain of potholes in the roads, surrealistically, the leaders of the city undertake diplomatic missions and offer a foreign policy of their own. With a budget twice the size of the neighboring city of Hayward, Berkeley, of a similar size, delivers far fewer municipal services.

Among the more humorous examples of sixties idealism gone to bizarre extremes has been the Berkeley Dog Park where unleashed dogs were supposed to "exist harmoniously once separated from their owners' ethic of possessiveness" as a pamphlet put it. Alas, as one chastened promoter of the scheme put it, "Some people were sure that the dogs would prove to be egalitarians. . . . But they aren't. They come here and immediately join the pack which is a strict hierarchy controlled by the top dog . . . they have a great time in the pack, but they aren't really very progressive. It was a hard lesson for some of the radical pet owners . . . to swallow. Not only have we failed to create the New Man in Berkeley. We haven't even created the New Dog" (216).

Idealism turned into power-hunger and intolerance elicited the all too familiar response of a resident that echoes the feelings and experiences of millions in "socialist" countries: "We never just live here in Berkeley. We are always in some sort of struggle, making sure that some scheme . . . isn't going to affect us disastrously. Really we only need one thing in this city—a let-us-alone-law" (214).

The lack of notes weakens this lucid, insightful, and well-written volume. It would have been of interest to know where much of the information came from (sometimes printed matter, sometimes informants). Those suspicious of the authors are likely to question some of their assertions in the absence of documentation. Some of these matters are trivial, some important (e.g., how did the authors know what Bernadine Dohrn did at her parents' retirement home in Florida in 1969, as reported on page 97); other accounts of meetings with prominent activists of the times and of political events deserve documentation. The organization of the book and the reasons for its division into three parts is not entirely clear either. And since some of the chapters had been published before (in modified or identical format) it might also have been of interest for readers, as well as following the proper conventions, to know where and when they had appeared.

Such flaws barely diminish the authenticity and justified moral passion of this volume. It may be the most revealing document that has emerged so far about the dark side of the sixties and the long shadow it continues to cast on the eighties.

10

From Iconoclasm to Conventional Wisdom:
The Sixties in the Eighties

The most remarkable aspect of the transformation of academic culture over the past quarter century has been the thoroughness with which ideas and attitudes that once represented protest, rebellion, iconoclasm, and nonconformity turned into their opposite: widely accepted conventional wisdom, a new form of conformity, values that are taken for granted.

My major theme—and an experience many of us share—is that the adversary culture has survived, and is nowhere more intact than in the academic world. That is to say, the continuities between the 1960s and 1980s in American higher education and campus life remain impressive and substantial although often unrecognized or wishfully denied. Many of our colleagues, as well as those outside the campuses, prefer to believe that the "excesses" of the sixties vanished without a trace, that campus life has returned to what used to be considered normal. And it cannot be denied that generally speaking this has been the case as far as appearances are concerned.

On closer inspection, however, it turns out that there has *not* been such a spectacular swing of the pendulum, as has been widely believed, from "the age of protest" to that of conformity or tranquility, or from fanatical political activism to political apathy. What has been mistaken for such changes has been the sharp decline in the number of protests, demonstrations, and sit-ins on American campuses during the seventies and eighties. Yet despite the apparent tranquility the values and attitudes associated with the sixties have not vanished—quite

199

the contrary, they have become entrenched and institutionalized on most campuses, and especially at elite institutions. The main reason these survivals of the sixties often go unnoticed is precisely that they have become absorbed into the climate of opinion, into what has become the prevailing "mainstream" thinking. They now constitute basic, unquestioned elements of campus culture.

The climate of opinion or ethos being sketched here is reflected in various ways. Officials at Smith College now worry, for example, that opening a croquet court may contribute to the elitist image of the college.[1] A headline in the *Chronicle of Higher Education* reads: "Students Ponder Life Without a Future as Courses on Peace and War Proliferate."[2] Mount Holyoke College stages a teach-in following the 1986 American bombing raid on Libya where the speakers "ranged from those passionately critical [of the bombing] to those . . . only moderately disturbed."[3] Adele Simmons, president of Hampshire College, a durable haven of the adversary culture and radical chic, is appointed president of the MacArthur Foundation, one of the wealthiest in the country.

The New School in New York City begins a full-page advertisement in the *New York Times* with a promise to potential students that "you can see a new film about Castro's Cuba and then join in a discussion led by Saul Landau"[4] (but fails to inform the reader that Landau has been an admirer and ceaseless promoter of Castro ever since he came to power). Another admirer of Castro's Cuba and former organizer of the Venceremos Brigade, Johnetta Cole, is installed as president of Spelman College and awarded an honorary degree by Princeton University.[5] Angela Davis is honored by Dartmouth College as a keynote speaker at the celebration of the fifteenth anniversary of coeducation and is given "a standing ovation after her speech,"[6] while the State University of New York at Binghamton seeks to bestow the Albert Schweitzer Chair in Humanities (with a salary of $105,000 and too many fringe benefits and perks to list here) on Ali A. Mazrui, an admirer of Qaddafi, famous for his television series on Africa castigating the Western world.[7]

An article in the *Chronicle of Higher Education* defends attacks on Western civilization courses and in turn attacks critiques of communist systems on the ground that "it is we—the inventors of conspicuous consumption, the developers of atomic energy, insecticides, and plastic—who are endangering life on this planet."[8]

After a sixties-style sit-in over South African disinvestment ends on the Smith College campus a professor of government rejoices: "Smith is a different kind of campus now. It's a more colorful campus, more like being in the Third World. . . . a really nice feeling."[9]

The University of Michigan at Ann Arbor issues a booklet on "Discrimination and Discriminatory Harassment"[10] which seeks "strictly to prohibit," and encourages to report—to one of nine listed entities—of examples of proscribed behavior that include "a male student . . . remark[ing] in class . . . 'Women just aren't as good in this field as men' thus creating a hostile learning atmosphere for female classmates." Another cited example of potentially serious misbehavior involves a group of hypothetical "students in a residence hall [who, when having a party] . . . invite everyone on the floor except one person . . . they think . . . might be a lesbian." Students are encouraged to make complaints of such "harassment" even if there are no witnesses to the incidents alleged.

In very much the same spirit, the University of Buffalo Law School faculty voted unanimously for a "Statement Regarding Intellectual Freedom, Tolerance and Political Harassment" that says in part that the students' right to free speech within the law school must be limited by "the responsibility to promote equality and justice."[11] It would be interesting to know who will be authorized to define what constitutes equality and justice and just how they are to be promoted. In any event, no totalitarian censor could have put it better.

Such examples, which could be multiplied at much greater length, reflect the institutionalization of attitudes and beliefs of the 1960s which include massive doses of intolerance and revival of the "no-enemies-on-the-Left" outlook.

It is then not surprising that the sixties-style disturbances have diminished significantly: their objectives have been achieved. For example, on most campuses it is no longer necessary for radical groups to disrupt speakers they dislike since such individuals rarely get invited. Administrators, faculty advisors, or student activists ensure that nothing will distract from the dominant left-of-center discourse. On the rare occasion when this tacit contract is breached and speakers with an unconventional viewpoint are invited, they get the sixties treatment.[12] The tacit prohibition of particular individuals is paralleled by taboo topics which are no longer or rarely discussed in public. The decline of free speech on the campuses has been a major legacy of the 1960s and a manifestation of the transformation of academic life.

Another characteristic change in academic culture has been the ascendence of Marxism as a supportive theory in the humanities and social sciences,[13] a particularly perverse development at a time when all over the world social systems inspired and legitimated by Marxism increasingly admit its uselessness either as a guide to practice, or as a source of legitimacy or intellectual stimulation. Marxism has been discredited in every single country where it has been made the basis of the official belief system, but apparently this has not been noted by our academics, or if noted, it does not matter. They are attracted to it mainly because it helps them to articulate, further justify, or make more coherent their aversion to their own society.

The popularity of schools such as "deconstruction" is also among the symptoms of the survival or revival of the adversary mentality. Peter Shaw has aptly identified the roots of their popularity as lying in the means they afford "to undermine the bourgeois perception of reality by attacking the concepts of logic, rationality, objectivity, and above all, reality" in order to strike "a politically revolutionary blow."[14]

Probably the most consequential manifestation of the transformation of academic culture over the past twenty years has been a growing rejection of the Western liberal intellectual tradition—a development which best explains a wide variety of more specific institutional changes that have taken place. To say the least, the radicals of the sixties succeeded in undermining the kind of intellectual consensus which used to make it possible for faculties to decide what books all students should read, what requirements they should take, how they should be evaluated, and on what grounds faculties should be hired, retained, and promoted. Such consensus has been shattered and replaced by an intellectual free-for-all, by academic policies which are most tangibly shaped either by the not too subtle pressure of groups pushing for particular political and ideological agendas, or by a vacuous "open-mindedness" or relativism discussed by Allan Bloom in the *Closing of the American Mind*.

The impact of activist and politicized pressure groups can be most clearly seen in the institutionalization of programs like black studies, women's studies, peace studies, or programs mislabelled as "cultural diversity" studies or "multicultural" studies.

Another development having considerable impact on academic culture has been affirmative action, or the preferential treatment of certain minorities both among faculty and students. These policies—besides increasing the number of students with questionable or minimal qualifications and necessitating various institutional adjustments—provide another example of the displacement of intellectual criteria and the intrusion of the political. For example, at the University of California at Berkeley in 1987 only 40 percent of the entering freshman class were selected on academic grounds alone; the other 60 percent were those in various "protected categories," admitted on the basis of nontraditional criteria, including 12.5 percent who were beneficiaries of affirmative action.[15] With similar inspiration but going several steps further, the *Columbia Law Review* recently decided to "set aside up to five extra places . . . [for which] preference . . . [would] be given to gay, handicapped and poor applicants, as well as women and members of minority groups."[16]

Let us take a closer look at the major premises left over from the sixties which, directly or indirectly, continue to influence academic life, and have come to constitute conventional wisdom. They appear to be the following:

1. American society is unjust and deeply flawed, no better than most and possibly worse than many; therefore universities and colleges are duty-bound to take a critical, opposing stance towards the social system and seek to change it by constantly rejecting the status quo.
2. Racism is deeply ingrained in American society even when it doesn't have any observable manifestations, and even when no discrimination can be established; it is akin to original sin, a virtually permanent, ineradicable blight.
3. The preferential, compensatory treatment of certain minorities is the first duty of society as a whole and academic institutions in particular. In this spirit the National Education Association went on record affirming that "employment policies that treat all people equally regardless of race or sex often are not adequate enough to achieve true integration in employment."[17] Another widely accepted idea is that "all state universities

should reflect the proportional representation of ethnic groups among the state's high school graduates."[18]

Nobody any longer asks why such proportional representation is in the interest of higher education, or of society, or even of the groups and individuals involved. No one asks why such representation should be the singular test of social justice, or whether it is the best means of compensation for past injustices. (Nor is it asked why minority status, rather than class, should be the only or predominant criterion in the pursuit of social justice and preferential treatment, when in fact the varieties of socially or environmentally structured disadvantage are not limited to ethnicity or gender.)

4. Paralleling the domestic mistreatment of minorities, the United States (and/or other political democracies of the West) is largely responsible for the poverty and misery in much of the world (usually called the Third World); hence a compensatory transfer of wealth is in order, a global affirmative action.

5. The United States has not faced any significant military or political threat from abroad since World War II; only our unresolved domestic social problems threaten us; therefore, military expenditures of all kinds are basically superfluous.

6. Anticommunism is one of the most dangerous myths of our time, having led in foreign policy to Vietnam and in domestic policy to McCarthyism. The respectability of far-Left groups and views on the campuses follows from this; the "no-enemy-on-the-Left" mentality has thus become another tacitly accepted part of the conventional wisdom.

7. Much of what used to be seen and taught as Western culture is unworthy of transmission to the younger generations; it is tainted by white, male, patriarchal, racist, sexist, elitist, ethnocentric values. Hence, the curriculum must change to reflect a "cultural diversity" previously denied. (Irving Howe has called this phenomenon "a throwback to the worst of the counterculture.")[19]

The values of the 1960s have persisted in the academic culture for several reasons. Among them is the presence of a large cohort of former radical students and graduate students on the campuses. They acquired proper certification, stayed in academia, and are now largely concentrated in social science and humanities departments.[20] It has not been a secret that the erstwhile activists transformed into academics had every intention of promoting their earlier political agenda as part of the teaching enterprise. As James Scofield and Michael Yates put it, "college teaching itself can be an important radical activity and not simply a way to earn a living." And according to Richard Lewontin, "the primary function of Marxists in the universities [is] to take part in what is, in fact, a class struggle."[21] William Proefriedt advised readers of the *Harvard Educational Review* that "teachers must see to it that their actions link up successfully with the efforts of others toward the creation of a just society,"[22] while a dean of humanities at the University of Arizona revealed to an interviewer that she saw her "scholarship as an extension of [her] political activism."[23]

The popularity of Antonio Gramsci among these academic radicals is easy to explain given his emphasis on the idea that intellectuals have a preeminent role in demolishing capitalist society by changing cultural values. This was a timely and welcome message for all those no longer anxious to engage in acts of civil (or uncivil) disobedience and defiance, preferring their revolutionary activities to be sedentary and more in tune with their age and station in life.

Another explanation for the persistence of countercultural values in the academy is that many campuses and adjacent areas have remained attractive places of residence for the veterans of the insurgencies of the sixties. Former radicals and activists, even when no longer students or faculty members, have stayed around these campuses or college towns creating substantial and durable demographic enclaves of the adversary culture. The influence of these enclaves is often augmented by their control of municipal governance in places like Berkeley, Santa Cruz, and Santa Monica in California; Madison, Wisconsin; Burlington, Vermont; Boulder, Colorado; and Amherst, Massachusetts.[24] As a result, a critical mass of supporters of sixties values has been created in or near what used to be centers of higher learning. Although probably in the minority in relation to the total student and faculty population, these groups set the tone and shape the climate of opinion on the campuses. Such demographic factors help us to understand why, for example, the town of Amherst, Massachusetts, with a predominantly white academic population, voted overwhelmingly for Jesse Jackson in the 1988 presidential primaries.

A third factor in the preservation of the sixties ethos has been an atmosphere that combines nostalgia and memories of intimidation. While most academics, including moderate liberals, willingly renounce "the excesses" of the period, many were and still remain sympathetic to the movement's values, with the retrospective glow intensifying over time. In other words, the sixties can evoke nostalgia for the simple reason that the now middle-aged were then young; moreover, it is tempting, indeed often irresistible, to associate youth with the youthful idealism that supposedly prevailed in the sixties. Such associations nurture support for, or at least acquiescence in, policies which reflect the spirit of those days and represent the institutionalization of many of its beliefs.

A less publicly acknowledged lesson of the sixties has been that campus violence and disruption can be avoided by anticipating or catering to the demands of radical activists. Faculties and administrators, or significant portions of them, have been in a permanent state of intimidation since the sixties, seeking to avoid the bad publicity that goes with calling in the police to maintain order. On the rare occasions when disruptive demonstrators are identified or arrested, the charges are almost invariably dropped, in accord with the prevailing practice of the sixties and early seventies.

Unseemly disruptions can also be avoided by fending off unwanted speakers on the ground that "their safety cannot be guaranteed," as was the case when Smith College changed its mind—under pressure from activists—about having Jeane Kirkpatrick as commencement speaker a few years ago. When a college administration refuses to take responsibility for the safety of an invited speaker,it conveys both its readiness to surrender the campus to the will of a violent minority and its inability or unwillingness to ensure free speech.

It can even be said that college administrators have improved the techniques developed during the sixties to disarm protesters by concessions or promises of concessions. Thus everybody seems happy when administrators make solemn commitments to hire, say, within the next two years, an abundance of black or Chicano teachers of mathematics or physics, despite the fact that almost everybody is equally aware that such people (with the requisite qualifications) simply don't exist in sufficient numbers to satisfy the demands for their representation as "role models" on these faculties. (For example, in the year ending 30 June 1988, a total of four blacks and five Hispanics were awarded Ph.D.'s in mathematics.)[25]

Other aspects of hiring practice have also had their impact on the transformation of American higher education. It is likely, for instance, that during the past twenty years the proportion of academics in the social sciences and humanities who are *not* left-of-center has significantly declined. Supply, self-selection, and informal discrimination may plausibly account for this. Like much ethnic and racial discrimination of the past, political discrimination is also hard to prove or document. We will probably never know how many academics have not been hired, promoted, or given tenure for not having politically acceptable beliefs and attitudes. There is a fair amount of anecdotal evidence to suggest that political values and attitudes do matter in hiring.

Despite their virtual domination of elite institutions, many radicals prefer to believe that they are the underdogs, actual or potential victims, who take great risks in castigating the powers-that-be, and they point to the Reagan presidency as proof of their predicament. They prefer a beleaguered stance for both tactical reasons and because it has long been customary among alienated intellectuals to see themselves as a marginal minority courageously confronting a menacing array of social and political forces. But most of all, they probably prefer assuming this stance because of the moral credit that it confers. Thus, some of them still insist that teacher education programs "represent a significant agency for the reproduction and legitimation of a society characterized by a high degree of social and economic inequality."[26] Others ominously warn that "while the results of the conservative assault on the academy have been profound, in the words of Ronald Reagan, 'You ain't seen nothin' yet.' "[27]

Though one may argue that the academic culture sketched above is out of touch with the mainstream of American life and society, the academic radicals and left-liberals are far from being an endangered species under "massive assault" from any quarter. If, in the words of Irving Kristol, "American universities [are] in exile,"[28] this claim can only be made if we compare them to the values and attitudes of the majority of citizens outside the academic world. If, on the other hand, we compare academia to other elite groups or institutions— mainline churches, the media, foundations, certain professions, etc.—it becomes clear that elite campuses and academics share the attitudes and impulses of the adversary culture with the other elite institutions and groups.[29] While the imprint of the adversary culture is visible enough on the campuses, it remains to be seen how much and how enduring an impact it will have on American culture and society as a whole in the years to come.

Notes

1. "Smith College Croquet Court Elitist?" *Daily Hampshire Gazette*, 7 April 1988.
2. Elizabeth Greene. "Students Ponder Life Without a Future as Courses on Peace and War Poliferate." *Chronicle of Higher Education*, 6 November 1985.
3. Valerie Carlson. "Mount Holyoke Stages 'Teach-In'." *Daily Hampshire Gazette*, 24 April 1986.
4. Advertisement. *New York Times*, 16 January 1989, A9.
5. Glenn Collins. "Spelman College's First 'Sister President'." *New York Times*, 20 July 1987; *Princeton Alumni Weekly*, 13 July 1988, 15.
6. Program. "Coeducation: The Difference Women Make." September 14–19, 1988, published by Dartmouth College; see also, Editorial, *Dartmouth Review*, 28 October 1988.
7. David Rossie. "SUNY bids $500,000 for one prof." *Press and Sun Bulletin*, 28 May 1989.
8. Betty Jeane Craige. "Universities Should Reject Nationalism Disguised as Patriotism." *Chronicle of Higher Education*, 5 October 1988, B3.
9. Athleen Ellington. "Smith Siege Ended." *Daily Hampshire Gazette*, 3 March 1986, 7.
10 This booklet is published by the Affirmative Action Office, Office of the President, University of Michigan, n.d.
11. "Cultural Revolutions." *Chronicles* (July 1987): 5–6.
12. See, for example, Norman Podhoretz, "Academic Tyranny in the Ivy League." *New York Post*, 15 April 1986; John H. Bunzel, "Campus 'Free Speech'," *New York Times*, 13 March 1983; David Brock, "The Big Chill—A Report Card on Campus Censorship," *Policy Review* (Spring 1985): 36–39.
13. For a jubilant account of this development, see Bertell Ollmann and Edward Vernoff, eds., *The Left Academy—Marxist Scholarship on American Campuses* (New York McGraw: Hill, 1982).
14. Peter Shaw. "The Politics of Deconstruction." *Partisan Review* (Spring 1986): 253.
15. John H. Bunzel. "Affirmative-Action Admissions: How it 'Works' at UC Berkeley." *Public Interest* (Fall 1988): 118–19.
16. Stephen Labaton. "Law Review is Entangled in Debate on Bias Plan." *New York Times*, 3 May 1989.
17. Sara Lennox. "Homeward Bound: The Flight from Alienation." *Thought and Action* (Winter 1987): 146; this is the National Education Association's higher education journal.
18. Bunzel, "Affirmative-Action Admissions," 127.
19. Irving Howe. "What Should We Be Teaching?" *Dissent* (Fall 1988): 478–79. In response to a critic who complained that the classics did not address her experience, Howe asked: "Why should they? . . . One (not the only) reason for reading the classics is that they widen and deepen out experience, pulling it out of the all-too-visible limits that any single self is likely to have. Precisely the 'irrelevance' of the classics is what makes them relevant." He also noted that "it ought to be part of any serious university education that students be encouraged to get past the provincialism of the contemporary. They go to college in order to learn something they cannot learn in the streets, on TV, or even at a political rally."

20. See Stephen H. Balch and Herbert I. London, "The Tenured Left," *Commentary* (October 1986): 41–51.
21. Quoted in Guenter Lewy, "Academic Ethics and the Radical Left," *Policy Review* (Winter 1982): 32.
22. William Proefriedt. "Socialist Criticism of Education in the United States: Problems and possibilities." *Harvard Educational Review* (November 1980): 480.
23. Alvin P. Sanoff. " '60s Protestors, '80s Professors." *U.S. News & World Report*, 16 January 1989, 54.
24. Paul Hollander. *The Survival of the Adversary Culture*. New Brunswick, N.J.: Transaction, 1988; see especially 16–18.
25. "The Math Doctorate: A While Male Province." *New York Times*, 27 January 1989.
26. Henry A. Giroux. "Teacher Education and the Ideology of Social Control." *Journal of Education* (Winter 1980): 5.
27. John W. Cole and Gerald F. Reid. "The New Vulnerability of Higher Education," *Thought and Action* (Winter 1986): 39.
28. Irving Kristol. "American Universities in Exile." *Wall Street Journal*, 17 June 1986.
29. See Robert Lichter, Stanley Rothman, and Linda Richter, *The Media Elite*. Washington, D.C.: Adler and Adler, 1986; Stanley Rothman and Robert Lichter, "What Are Moviemakers Made Of?" *Public Opinion* (December–January 1984); Robert Lichter and Stanley Rothman, "What Interests the Public and What Interests Public Interests?" *Public Opinion* (April–May 1983); see also Seymour Martin Lipset, "The Academic Mind at the Top: Political Behavior and Values of Faculty Elites," *Public Opinion Quarterly*, 46 (1982): 143–68.

11

Self-Esteem, Role Models, and Educational Achievement

It was reported in my local newspaper that the associate superintendent of the school system is opposed to grouping the students by ability also known as "tracking," and one teacher defending the system was accused by school administrators of being "elitist" and "classist."[1] Another local paper, called ability grouping an "institutionalized caste system."[2] The associate superintendent of the high school was quoted as saying that grouping "erodes self-esteem of students of lower levels." He observed that since "poor and minority students are disproportionally represented in lower level tracks . . . the issue of ability grouping is really one of equity."[3] Thus at one stroke differences in achievement or performance—and their recognition—were converted into a matter of social injustice. For anyone who doubts that the beliefs of the 1960s have survived and continue to influence standards in education the self-esteem movement is something to ponder.

Placing students in different groups based on ability or performance is indeed a form of evaluation and if it undermines self-esteem so do all other forms of evaluation if they allow rating some people lower than others. If our associate superintendent is worried about the impact of evaluation inherent in grouping he should also campaign for abolishing grades or insist that all students get good grades, or that any information about poor performance be withheld from students.

We need not have especially good memory to recall that the abolition of grades and test scores was high on the agenda of sixties educational reformers, attacked not merely on the grounds proposed

211

above but also because it was proposed that each student performs in uniquely personal ways which no standardized measurement or evaluation can capture.

These trends are not confined to Northampton, Mass. and other enclaves which accommodate many survivors of the adversary culture of the 1960s. According to a recent report "self-esteem is the dominant educational theory" in the country.[4] In New York City the new superintendent of the schools decided that students should not be held back regardless of their performance, in part because doing so injures self-esteem. There is now in existence a National Council for Self-Esteem and a Foundation for Self-Esteem. An examination of teacher education programs around the country led to the finding that "elementary school teachers are being taught to concern themselves with children's feelings of self-worth and not with the worth of hard work or realistically measured achievement."[5]

The state of California actually made self-esteem a public policy issue setting up a commission to study how it could best be promoted and spread to the whole population of the state. The Report produced by this Task Force concluded that "The lack of self-esteem is central to most personal and social ills plaguing our state and nation as we approach the end of the 20th century."[6]

In New York State, self-esteem is being pursued through curriculum reform, by proposals to teach less European history and culture and more non-European history and culture in order to make the children of non-European descent feel better about themselves. Here the assumption appears to be that if (through such curriculum changes) students are assured that their ethnic group has a history rich in accomplishments this will somehow translate into personal pride and academic achievement.

Self-esteem advocacy joins forces with opposition to what became known since the 1960s as "elitism," a term applied to a willingness to make distinctions based on quality, ability, or performance; "elitism" also amounts to a general concern with quality and a belief that talents are not equitably distributed among human beings. It is among the beliefs bequeathed by the sixties that any rigorous, standardized evaluation of students which results in the finding that their performances (or abilities) differ, is destructively elitist and destroys self-esteem. (Similar reasoning has also been applied to job-related tests which uncover large differences in performance between ethnic groups; when this occurs the tests are denounced as "racist" or "culturally biased" as well as irrelevant to job performance and revised until underperforming groups can attain better scores.)

Fears of elitism are illustrated by the misplaced enthusiasm of a teacher who reportedly rejoiced in seeing himself "more as a facilitator than a pinnacle of knowledge"[7] as if it were somehow embarrassing for a teacher to be know more than his students. "Resource person" is another popular term (used by some teachers) designed to reduce the intellectual-cognitive distance between teachers and students and to diminish whatever intellectual authority teachers were supposed to possess.

It was in large measure the onslaught on inequality that led to the aversion to any hierarchy even in the realm of learning and to the reluctance to make value-based distinctions by means of explicit and standardized performance criteria. Similar impulses find expression in the current fad for "celebrating diversity" and multicultural studies which increasingly tend to mean (as far as the curriculum is concerned) that making distinctions between readings and authors are to be avoided except on the currently approved ideological and ethnic grounds designed to reflect ethnic or gender distributions in the reading materials as well as in the student population. "Celebrating diversity" is also a catch-all notion that implicitly enjoins us from judgmental attitudes (moral, intellectual, or aesthetic) and carries the message of ethical and cultural relativity, as for example in suggesting that one form of sexual behavior is no better than any other, or that rap music and classical music have equal artistic merit. Even among its adherents there are limits to enshrining cultural diversity and the associated nonjudgemental attitude. Thus in spite of enthusiasm about "diversity" certain cultural attitudes are severely and unhesitatingly censored. Thus few would argue that apartheid or discouraging women to enter certain occupations are also forms of cultural diversity to be understood and tolerated or that interest in European culture (derogatively labelled as "eurocentrism") is a desirable form of pursuing cultural diversity for those who wish to go beyond the offerings of American culture.

The campaign against "stereotyping" complements the crusade for diversity but here too paradoxes abound. As is well known, the case against stereotyping rests on the idea that stereotypes (ethnic, racial, sexual) are usually negative, and they force the unique individuality of the group member into the mold of distorted group-attributes. It is however not easy to separate stereotyping from making a generalization, from recognizing that certain groups—ethnic, racial, national, occupational—have certain things in common and that some of these shared attributes are not always admirable. One person's stereotype is another's attempts to find a pattern and impose some order on the varieties of human character and behavior. The other problem with the current campaign against stereotyping is that it is highly selective. Some groups are fair game, others are sacrosanct. White males, WASPS, owners or managers of large corporations, employees of the CIA, FBI or the military, the police, the upper classes, and "yuppies" are routinely stereotyped without a murmur of protest.[8]

Notwithstanding the continued influence of the egalitarian beliefs of the sixties teachers know that students differ in motivation, talent, interests, and willingness to work. Does it really help to pretend that this is not the case or to label such commonplace findings elitist or racist? And if the self-esteem argument is taken seriously, would the removal of grouping not be more threatening to the self-esteem of the underachieving students by placing them in close proximity to those who do better? Or should teachers stop calling on students in class who are better prepared or more articulate to avoid invidious comparison, the demonstrations of elitism in the classroom?

The concern with self-esteem as central not only to psychic well-being but also to academic performance is not merely an outcome of the educational reforms of the sixties but is a more broadly based expression of what might be called the egalitarian individualism widespread in our culture. Self-esteem (the universal remedy to every problem) has increasingly been regarded as something to which everybody is entitled in equal amounts regardless of what they do with their life, regardless of what kind of people they are. This of course may also be viewed as a survival of 18th-century Enlightenment beliefs about the (underlying) universal goodness and limitless potential of all human beings.

Adequate levels of self-esteem and the demand for role models have also been closely related; indeed the need for role models (to raise levels of educational-occupational achievement) has been another cornerstone of the currently taken for granted verities. Role models have also been championed as grounds for "affirmative action," that is, preferential treatment or reverse discrimination. Thus it is argued that minorities or women need role models (in schools, colleges, places of work, and in the mass media) they can identify with in order to raise their levels of motivation, aspiration, and achievement. Blacks will not become nuclear physicists or biochemists unless they see around them blacks who succeeded in becoming nuclear physicists and biochemists; women will not become brain surgeons or jet pilots unless well-acquainted with female pilots, and so forth. But if this were the case, black students in schools and colleges with predominantly black teachers would perform better than in schools which have a mixed or predominantly white teaching personnel as would women who had women teachers. I am unaware of any findings suggesting that this is the case. (As far as curriculum reform is concerned, even remote historical role models, great heroes of the past, are supposed to provide such services.)

Whether or not students have role models and high levels of self-esteem are among several factors which have a bearing on their motivation and academic performance.[9] But even if they have a putative role model it does not follow that they will model themselves on such a person, that they can or wish to identify with him or her. Will black students do better at math because they have a black math teacher? Surely this will also have something to do with the qualifications of the teacher, with the interest of students in learning math and their parents' attitude about these matters and those of other potential role models in their environment. (But even if it were true that such role model teachers do wonders, the fact remains that there are not enough black math teachers to go around, not enough science, language, history teachers, either at the high school or college level.[10]

In one of the schools in my part of the world where ability-level grouping was completely abandoned (Northfield Pioneer Valley Regional) the assistant principal was enthusiastic about the policy while admitting that "the results are not all measurable. . . . Can you measure self-esteem, leadership ability, the feeling that 'I can do whatever

I want?' "[11] He did not seem to entertain the possibility that such beliefs of omnipotence may rest on shaky foundations or wonder if
schools should encourage illusions as to what a person is capable of.
There is evidence to suggest that there may be huge gaps between
self-evaluation and self-esteem on the one hand, and actual accomplishment on the other. Research by Harold Stevenson found that

> When asked to rate such characteristics as ability in mathematics, brightness and
> scholastic performance, American children gave themselves high ratings, while
> Japanese students gave themselves the lowest. . . . When asked how well they
> would do in mathematics in high school 58% of American fifth graders expected
> to be above average or among the best. . . . These percentages were much higher
> than those of their Japanese or Chinese peers, among whom only 26% and 29%,
> respectively, were this optimistic.[12]

Other studies, too, show that the self-esteem levels of high school
students in this country are high. The University of Michigan Institute for Social Research found that over three quarters of high school
seniors in 1988 declared to be entirely satisfied with themselves and
judged themselves persons of worth. These were the same young
people only 26 percent of whom was capable of writing a literate letter, one in twenty of whom could read at a level required for college
work and a third did not know that the Mississippi flowed into the
Gulf of Mexico.[13]

Nobody would deny that self-esteem is a good thing to have and
an important part of emotional health (unless of course it is delusional in relation to its basis.) The larger unresolved issue is whether
or not it promotes learning, or scholastic achievement. As the findings quoted above indicate it is far from clear that underachievers in
school have low self-esteem; they are certainly capable of wildly mis-
judging their performance; their self-esteem may also have a totally
different foundation than grades, or the mastery of school materials
or praise by a teacher. In fact a study of twelfth graders in Michigan
showed little difference in levels of self-esteem between blacks and
whites.[14] Moreover performance in school, in whatever way measured, may be totally irrelevant for the self-esteem of many students
which may rest on physical strength, looks, sexual attractiveness,

athletic prowess, defiance of adult authority, criminal mischief, or possession of certain consumer goods.

Further explanations of the irrelevance of academic achievement for self-esteem among many black students were suggested by a study of two anthropologists who found that "Many black students may perform poorly in high school because of a shared sense that academic success in a sellout to the white world." Academic learning and success was a form of "acting white" which also included "speaking standard English, listening to so-called white music, going to the opera or ballet, studying in the library, going to the Smithsonian Institution, doing volunteer work, camping or hiking, putting or airs and being on time."[15]

The major source of self-esteem for most people is the love and attention they get as children from their parents and other members of their families. To be sure success in school or at work and being loved later in life by other people also nourish self-esteem.

The question remains, is it the task of schools to try to implant or foster self-esteem rather than find the most effective ways to teach? If there was a well-established procedure for inculcating self-esteem outside the family and past early childhood it should be entrusted to the schools. But nobody has yet invented it. In the meantime pretending that there are no substantial differences between levels of student achievement and aptitude may imbue those upholding such beliefs with a sense of virtue or righteousness but it will neither raise self esteem nor improve education.

Notes

1. Jody Ericson. "No tracking, says panel." *Daily Hampshire Gazette* (DHG below) Northampton, Mass. 11 May, 1990; Jody Ericson: "Disagreement delays decision on tracking," DHG 27 April 1990.
2. "Student Caste System," *Advocate*, 14 May 1990, p.4.
3. Ibid.
4. John Leo "The trouble with self-esteem," *U.S. News & World Report*, 2 April 1990.
5. Rita Kramer, cited in Chester E. Finn, Jr., "Narcissus Goes to School," *Commentary*, June 1990, p.41.
6. Finn, op.cit., p.40.
7. Advocate, op. cit.

8. See also Robert Weissberg, "Safe-Bashing," *Academic Questions*, Winter 1989–90.

9. Stephen P. Powers, David J. Rothman, and Stanley Rothman, "The Myth of Low Black Self-Esteem." *The World and I*, March 1990.

10. For example, Don Wycliff. "Blacks' Advance Slow in Science Careers" *New York Times*, 8 June 1990; also "The Math Doctorate: A White Male Province," *New York Times*, 27 January 1989.

11. *Advocate*, op. cit.

12. Finn, op. cit., p. 42.

13. Finn, op. cit., p. 43.

14. Ibid.

15. Seth Mydans. "Black Identity vs. Success and Seeming 'White,'" *New York Times*, 25 April 1990.

12

George F. Kennan:
Critic of Western Decadence

George F. Kennan is well known as a historian, diplomat, student of American-Soviet relations, and a major architect of U.S. foreign policy after World War II. He is far less known as a social philosopher, critic of American society and culture, detractor of modernity and romantic nature lover. Still less is known of his private life and beliefs and about the complexities and paradoxes of his personality, outlook, and public roles except perhaps by those familiar with his *Memoirs* (1925–1950 and 1950–1963).

Yet Kennan is a most unusual and complex figure, impressive and thought-provoking in more ways than is generally realized. He is an American from Wisconsin, fluent in several foreign languages, who spent much of his youth and the prime of his life abroad. A life-long critic of many aspects of American culture and estranged from American society, he invested much of his life in faithfully representing the interests of the United States abroad. An intensely private man, he devoted decades of his best years to public affairs and life; a rugged individualist, he longed for community and mourned its decline; a man yearning for stability and a settled life, he spent much of his life travelling; he preferred his own company, yet chose a career that imposed upon him the necessity of endless mingling with people whose company he did not desire; he was at once a member of the foreign policy establishment and its lifelong critic; an exceptionally dutiful and conscientious public servant who, it seems, hardly ever ceased to wonder about the purpose and fruits of his labors. Publicly acclaimed, showered with honors, he nonetheless felt, much of his life, an unappreciated loner and outsider; a favorite of American and Western European liberals, yet a genuine conservative in his principal values and attachments.

The volume here reviewed goes a long way to bring balance to the neglected aspects of the life and beliefs of George Kennan. It also provides absorbing, often poetic accounts of his many travels and sundry incidents in his life. This collection of diary excerpts spans sixty years, from 1927 to 1988; it ranges over much of Europe, its major cities as well as places off the beaten track; it records trips to Africa, India, and China undertaken both as a member of the foreign service and as private citizen or as sought-after academic speaker. No one who reads the book could fail to be impressed by the depth and complexity of the mind and character of its author and by his contributions to a better understanding of our times.

Perhaps the least appreciated trait of Kennan's personality and outlook is a gloomy assessment of modernity and high regard for tradition and the past which also help to explain his aversion to many aspects of contemporary American life and culture. Already in his twenties, writing in 1927 as vice-consul in Hamburg he wrote: "Reading *Buddenbrooks* . . . I cannot help but regret that I did not live fifty or a hundred years sooner. . . . We know too many cities to be able to grow into any of them . . . our arrivals and departures . . . are to common . . . we have too many friends to have any friendships, too many books to know any of them well. . . . I should have liked to have lived in the days when a visit was a matter of months . . . when foreign countries were still foreign . . . when there were still wars worth fighting and gods worth worshipping."

Similar nostalgic ideas recur in 1978 on the pastoral island of Gotland (off the Swedish coast): "While I knew that such a one as I might eventually die of loneliness and boredom in this rural setting . . . I could not help reflecting that just so, in just such a simple room, without electricity and heated only by wood stoves, is the way I would have liked to live. Compared to that, the present age, with all its noise, its overpopulation, and its mad wastage of energy strikes me as a nightmare."

In 1938 he frets in the shadow of the splendid architecture of Prague: "The world had taken final farewell, it seemed, of nearly everything these monuments represented. Gone were the unifying faith and national tolerance of the Middle Ages. . . . A sterner age was upon us." In 1940 in Holland he expresses admiration for the "fidelity to habit and tradition" he encounters. Even his complicated attitudes toward the Soviet Union can best be explained by such sentiments and values. Consider the following observations of the Russian countryside: "two women were working in a small potato field . . . [they] had broad faces, brown muscular arms. . . . They laughed and joked as they worked . . . it was clear that they enjoyed the feeling of the sun on their bodies and the dark earth, cool and sandy, under their bare feet."

A picture of a Moscow suburb observed in 1952 is equally revealing:

> I know . . . of no human environment more warmly and agreeably pulsating with activity, contentment and sociability than a contemporary Moscow suburban dacha area on a nice spring morning. . . . Everything takes place in a genial intimacy and informality: hammers ring, roosters crow, goats tug at their tether, barefoot women hoe vigorously . . . small boys play excitedly in the little streams and ponds, family parties sit at crude tables . . . under the young fruit trees. The great good earth of Mother Russia, long ignored in favor of the childish industrial fetishes of the earlier Communist period, seems once more to exude her benevolent and maternal warmth over man and beast.

Even illiteracy acquires a romantic hue, as in his reference to the observations of a Russian woman which "had all the pungency and charm of the mental world of those who had never known the printed word." The poverty in India strikes him as tolerable in a world as yet uncorrupted by modernity: "No great sign, anywhere, of unhappiness. There is poverty, of course; but all is sociable, intelligible, and workable. . . . Life is not all that complicated. One can usually help one's self. . . . One is, for the most part, not at the mercy of great unseen forces, mechanical and technological."

He contrasts favorably a Russian amusement park or Bavarian beer hall with the impersonality of human interaction in this country—a parade of cars carrying dating teenagers in a small Wisconsin town prompts these reflections in 1938:

> What was in England an evil of the upper classes seemed to have become the vice of the entire populace. It was the sad climax of individualism, the blind-alley of a generation which has forgotten how to think or live collectively. . . .

I could not help but feel that one ought to welcome almost any social cataclysm . . . that would carry away something of this stuffy individualism and force human beings to seek their happiness and their salvation in their relationship to society as a whole rather than in the interests of themselves and the little group of intimate acquaintances.

The critiques of American customs and ways of living are colored by a peculiar elitism (and a dislike of the "the greed, the pretense and the narrowness of the lower-middle-class environment"). It is not that Kennan dislikes the common man in general, only his American embodiments, being so far removed from what he regards as the earthy, authentic qualities of ordinary people elsewhere. He writes of California and Californians:

Here it is easy to see that when man is given . . . freedom from both political restraint and want, the effect is to render him childlike . . . fun-loving, quick to laughter and enthusiasm, unanalytical, unintellectual . . . given to . . . seizures of aggressiveness, driven constantly to protect his status in the group by an eager conformism. . . . In this sense Southern California, together with all that tendency of American life which it typifies, is childhood without the promise of maturity.

Further observations about California highlight his unease with many aspects of life in America:

California reminds me of the popular American Protestant concept of heaven: there is always a . . . flow of new arrivals . . . people spend a good deal of their time congratulating each other over the fact that they are there; discontent would be unthinkable. . . . California is outwardly one-dimensional in the emotional sense . . . one wonders whether such a thing as anguish exists at all—whether . . . there is any anguish in love, or whether this too, is experienced . . . with the same cheerful casualness that seems to dominate all the other phenomena of existence. . . . These people . . . ask no questions . . . they waste no energy . . . on the effort to understand life . . . their consciences are not troubled by the rumblings of what transpires beyond their horizon.

There is clearly truth to these observations, even to the stereotypes of Americans as naive, childlike, innocent, lacking a sense of the tragic, etc. Kennan, not the first to comment on these qualities, describes them forcefully and wittily. The question one is tempted to raise is whether any of these attitudes are peculiar to these free and affluent Americans? Would Russian peasants or Italian small town dwellers be troubled by "rumblings beyond the horizon" or display a greater determination to plumb the mysteries of life? Here as elsewhere Kennan appears to expect more of Americans than others.

On the other hand, he is certainly able to rise to criticism when contemplating the ravages of modernization in Europe as well ("this new Europe—this materialistic, impersonal, semi-Americanized . . . Europe") and what he sees as the moral and psychological costs of the welfare state. He perceives the young German and Scandinavian tourists as "occupants, all of them, of the intellectual and spiritual vacuum which the European welfare state produces, comfortable enough now . . . with their cubicles of flats, their TV . . . but victims of a deeper sort of drugging."

It is this "deeper sort of drugging," this spiritual malaise, that is at the center of his critique of modernity and of American society. As he looks around on a Sunday morning "in a wretched motel," waiting for commencement ceremonies at an unnamed American university, he is distressed by the "asphalted desolation," by "this wasteland." As with other critics of American culture, Kennan feels that "All is unnatural; all experience vicarious; all activity passive and uncreative."

Here as in some other places one is reminded of two other critics of America in our times, neither readily associated with Kennan: Solzhenitsyn and Marcuse. With Solzhenitsyn, Kennan shares a belief in the redeeming value of tradition and a pre-urban world, an old-fashioned puritanism and contempt for the prevailing materialism and hedonism of the West. (For instance, Kennan has reservations about co-education because while "it would be easier, softer, more comfortable with women around," he was not sure if it would benefit the intellect. After all, he notes, "the great environments of the flowering of the spirit had been not the sunlit gardens of California or Florida, but rather the dark, cold, rainy ones—the ones that involved deprivation, personal discomfort, loneliness and boredom.") Kennan, however, has none of the self-righteousness, intolerance, and prophetic anger of Solzhenitsyn.

With Marcuse he shares an aesthetic revulsion toward the vulgarities of the common man and his America, but Kennan towers above Marcuse in general wisdom, tolerance and humaneness. Unlike Marcuse, he writes lucidly and his knowledge of the world is not wholly abstract and theoretical. It is hard to imagine Marcuse squeezing into third-class train compartments, conversing with Russian peasants, mingling with Scandinavian fishermen, or exploring on foot the seedier neighborhoods of European cities.

Kennan sees himself misplaced not so much in America but more generally in the contemporary world, "an expatriate in time rather than in place." Elsewhere he wrote: "The Western world must today be populated in a very great part by people like myself who have out-lived their own intellectual and emotional environment." These feel-ings were recorded in 1959 when he was in his mid-fifties, hardly an old man, at the height of his intellectual powers (one may surmise also in excellent physical health since many years later he would still sail his own boat in stormy Scandinavian waters). Moreover, he was hardly treated as someone who outlived his intellectual usefulness, being sought after as a font of wisdom and a voice of reason.

Much of Kennan's unhappiness with America has a large aesthetic component. His great love of nature is—as is often the case—another reflection of estrangement from his society and fellow human beings. Perhaps his professional incarnation as diplomat and academic histo-rian could not fully accommodate his talents and yearnings, his romantic sensibilities and artistic impulses. At the same time, it is also clear that his forced retirement from the Foreign Service in 1953 was a bitter occasion that enhanced the feeling of not being ap-preciated by his country, by the powers-that-be. This rupture in his career also helps to explain why late in life he is so touched by the appreciation and warmth of Gorbachev on their meeting in Washington in 1987: "I reflected that if you cannot have this sort of recognition from your own government . . . it is nice to have it at least from the one-time adversary."

One cannot read these often moving reflections without being struck by a developed capacity for gloom and distress, by a seeming predisposition to loneliness, by the outlook (if not the role) of the outsider and especially a great sensitivity to loss. Not everybody be-comes so profoundly dispirited by the downtown sections of Ameri-can cities, bleak as they are. He wrote in Chicago in 1951: "So I shuffled back to the hotel, in the depression born of hunger plus an overpowering sense of lack of confidence in my surroundings; and a small inward voice said, gleefully and melodramatically, 'You have despaired of yourself; now despair of your country.'" On another visit to the heartlands in 1956, he looks at his fellow passengers and the monotonous landscape outside and is seized again with foreboding: "For a moment I saw this age . . . as my father might see it from the grave: blind, willful, doomed and not very interesting. I am living in the world my father despaired of, and rightly so."

Perhaps what stays above all with the reader is a (justifiably) tragic view of life, of the human condition, "the blind and helpless way in which each generation of us . . . staggers through life." Fragmentary as some of these musings are, they address—beyond the colorful depiction of distant lands and their inhabitants and the great events of contemporary history—the most essential and insoluble concerns of human existence.

13

An End to the Political Pilgrimage?

Political Pilgrims was first published in 1981 by Oxford University Press in New York. It was widely and, for the most part, favorably reviewed though numerous reservations were also voiced. Well over a hundred reviews appeared not only in the United States, but also in Great Britain, Canada, Australia, Hong Kong, India, Holland, Denmark, Sweden, Finland, Germany, Switzerland, Italy, and France. After Oxford University Press sold out its hardcover edition, Harper and Row published a paperback in 1983 and the University Press of America a second paperback edition in 1990.

A Spanish translation of the book was published in two separate volumes in Madrid by Editorial Playor in 1986 and 1987 respectively, and an Italian edition by the Mulino Publishing Company in Bologna in 1988 (The Italian edition was enriched by the addition of a new chapter by an Italian scholar, Loreto Di Nucci, on "The Political Pilgrimages of Italian Intellectuals. . . ."

While the book received more attention than most academic or semi-academic volumes, its impact was circumscribed. Comparing, for example, the attention the book received to that lavished upon another recent and more demanding academic volume (*The Decline of Great Powers*), by Paul Kennedy, is illuminating. The latter elicited a lengthy article in the *New York Times Magazine*, many talk-show appearances by Kennedy, and thorough coverage in relevant publications. Obviously Kennedy's suggestion that excessive military spending will hasten the decline of the United States (as it had of other great powers) struck a far more responsive cord than my cautionary tale of intellectual gullibility and Utopia-seeking.

Despite the fairly large number of reviews, *Political Pilgrims* was ignored by many important American journals and magazines including the *New York Review of Books, The New Yorker, Atlantic, Harpers, The Nation, Dissent,* the *Wall Street Journal,* and others. Talk-show hosts, with the exception of William F. Buckley, were not interested. The most hostile and dismissive reviews came from the professional journals of the two academic disciplines I have been most closely associated with (either by virtue of my training or because of the nature of my published work): *Contemporary Sociology* (the review journal of the American Sociological Association) and the *American Political Science Review,* the journal of the American Political Science Association.

All in all, it would be fair to say that the book had an ambivalently favorable, or mixed reception. Most reviewers quite readily accepted its historical account, namely that many Western intellectuals, distinguished and less distinguished, were deceived and self-deceived about various Communist countries. Visiting the countries (being "on-the-spot"), made matters worse, not better. On the other hand, reviewers seemed to be irritated by the suggestion that the susceptibility of the intellectuals was directly proportional to their estrangement from their own society. Heightened criticism of the United States (or other Western countries) could be combined with near total suspension of critical faculties while on the conducted tours and under the influence of political preferences and predispositions.

What of the phenomenon a decade later? Are political pilgrimages only a matter of historical interest or have they survived? If so, in what form? Some reference to this question has been made in the preface to the paperback edition. History, however, has not stood still and further reflections are in order in light of relatively recent developments in what used to be called the "Socialist Commonwealth," or the Soviet bloc. There are good reasons for a new look not merely at the pilgrimage itself, but at the attitude that underlies it.

The most striking political-intellectual phenomenon of the last few years is the growing imbalance between ideological uncertainty and turmoil inside the Communist bloc, *and* the persistence of certain Western political attitudes among those who have traditionally been drawn to political tourism. I referred to this phenomenon recently as "the survival of the adversary culture."[1] In *Political Pilgrims* I argued at length that it has always been the adversarial attitude—the estranged sensibility—that moved the pilgrims to look for glorious alternatives to their own flawed society. These attitudes have survived intact while developments in the socialist countries made it increasingly difficult to perceive them as alternatives to Western corruption and decline. The impulse to embark on new pilgrimages is still there but the number of available destinations had become much smaller.

By the mid-1980s the pace of change—especially the volume of self-critical disclosures—within the Communist bloc greatly increased. Most importantly, from the standpoint of potential pilgrims, internal scrutiny and soul-searching, now officially authorized, has sharpened. As a result, neither in China nor anywhere in the Eastern bloc, including the Soviet Union, was much left of the outward assurance and self-congratulatory disposition that had earlier impressed visitors in search of political rectitude, sense of purpose, and collectivized transcendence.

The new openness meant that critiques of these systems, earlier suppressed, could now be voiced and widely disseminated both in the official media and in new semi-official sources. These new revelations made mockery of what used to be the major appeal of these systems. By the mid-1980s, not even the most determined or visionary pilgrim (or potential pilgrim) could find the sense of purpose, warm social bonds, social justice, egalitarianism, let alone the spectacular material progress that had in the past exercised such a powerful attraction.

It was no longer merely the poor record of these societies regarding civil liberties and free expression that made idealization difficult. The new Gorbachev-era revelations made clear that these systems faced serious domestic crises and their claims of great material progress—formerly the justification for the lack of personal freedom— were unfounded. Social problems thought to be peculiar to capitalism abounded: crime, alcoholism, corruption, pollution, poor public health, disintegrations of family, shortages of food and basic commodities, declining living standards, and old-fashioned poverty—the socialist countries had them all and they were getting worse not better.[2] Under state socialism, alienation held in its grip not only idealistic intellectuals with high expectations (as is more commonly the case in the West), but the masses of ordinary people as well. A new sense of stagnation and decline, even decomposition, not a sense of purpose or optimism, became the hallmark of these countries.

While Western intellectuals continued to lament the ravages and injustices of capitalism, socialist systems increasingly acknowledged the failures of the state control of the economy, massive inefficiency and the lack of productivity, and inability to meet human needs. Their leaders cautiously sought to reintroduce private enterprise.

There was great irony in all this. In the West, Marxism continued to bask in the reverence of academic intellectuals. In the countries where it has been the centerpiece of the official value system, a guide to practice and major source of legitimacy, Marxism became a discredited doctrine not only for the masses (who never embraced or understood it), but even for the intelligentsia.

For the most part the estranged, adversarial intellectuals and quasi-intellectuals in the West averted their eyes from these developments, from the resounding moral and material failures of these socialist countries. They were especially disinclined to detect any connection between the ideas and ideals of Marxism-Leninism and the sorry states of the societies that sought to implement these ideas.

The persistence of Marxist belief in the West can most readily be ascribed to the institutionalization of the values of the protest movements of the 1960s giving rise to the adversary culture.[3] The survival of these political and cultural values is hard to miss. Witness the candidacy of Jesse Jackson in both the 1984 and 1988 presidential campaigns and the support he received not only among blacks, but among the white, liberal-left strata of the population (especially the academic community). Support for Jackson in these circles was proof of belonging to the right-thinking, enlightened sections of American society; of being an upholder of a critical worldview and a "caring" attitude.

Another example of the influence of the adversary culture has been the successful frustration of the efforts of the Reagan administration to sustain the anti-Communist guerrillas of Nicaragua.

A third indication of the spread of the adversarial outlook has been the triumph of the moral-equivalence school in public discourse: the belief that there are no moral distinctions worth making between the

American and Soviet political systems and that both deserve to be viewed with equal cynicism (on closer inspection the upholders of this theory turned out to be far more critical of the United States than of the Soviet Union).

A fourth, tangible manifestation of the persistence of these attitudes may be found in the continued growth and entrenchment of demographic-municipal enclaves of the adversary culture, towns dominated by radical-left groups, usually campus towns such as Berkeley, Santa Cruz, and Santa Monica in California; Ann Arbor, Michigan; Madison, Wisconsin; Burlington, Vermont; and Amherst, Massachusettes, etc.

The recent movement to reform the curriculum in the colleges and universities so as to enhance its "non-Western" elements may also be a reflection of the mind-set discussed here. "Multicultural" courses and curricula generally consists of materials conveying criticism of Western values and institutions from a Marxist, Third-World, or militant-feminist perspective. While all this was already available in many courses, the new programs make it mandatory for everybody to study.[4]

How did these developments affect the political pilgrimage? While the Western pilgrims to the Soviet Union dwindled after World War II, in the last few years a new generation of Westerners has visited the Soviet Union in growing numbers. In the 1980s, it has been primarily the longing for peace and the hope that human contacts at the grassroots level will help to avert a nuclear holocaust, rather than the pursuit of political Utopia that brought well-meaning Westerners, and especially Americans, to the Soviet Union. (Others, in smaller numbers, went in pursuit of lucrative business, but revealingly trade was often justified less as a profit-making activity than as a device for promoting peace and understanding.) Whether such hopes were more realistic than those that inspired the earlier generation of pilgrims is debatable.

China, since the death of Mao, lost much of its political attraction as stories of its embrace of capitalism flooded the American media. Sympathizers could no longer thrill at its high-minded totalitarian morality or the egalitarian fervor of the Cultural Revolution.[5]

While Communist Vietnam (formerly North Vietnam) had its champions during the war and played host to many prominent Western, especially American, visitors, it never attracted large numbers of pilgrims, remaining quite inaccessible due to distance and political controls. (The phenomenon of the boat people also made it more difficult to be publicly supportive of the Vietnamese regime.) Occasional Western delegations in the 1980s were given the usual treatment. Among them an American church group (composed of members of the Church World Service and United Methodist Committee on Relief) was profoundly impressed by a model "reeducation camp,"[6] under circumstances reminiscent of the well-organized visits to Soviet, Chinese, Cuban, and Nicaraguan model prisons.

Cuba under Castro has retained a fair amount of support in the "adversarial" circles, though it has remained one of the most repressive, intolerant, militaristic, and economically mismanaged of Communist systems. It has also been a country 10 percent of its population preferred to leave (often under difficult and risky conditions) for reasons that were both economic and political. Such matters were overlooked by the sympathizers, perhaps in part precisely because the Cuban regime, personified by Castro, never lost its outward self-assurance and never failed to claim moral superiority over the United States and other capitalist systems. Presumably Castro's charisma and durability played a part in keeping the loyalties of foreign admirers: here was an original revolutionary hero, still at the helm and unwilling to dilute the revolutionary purity and idealism of this system by concessions either to "bourgeois freedoms" or capitalistic greed.

Thus, it never became quite acceptable to express moral indignation toward Cuba among American or Western European intellectuals on the left. As Reinaldo Arenas, the exiled Cuban writer, observed, "It is not fashionable to attack Fidel Castro; that would not be progressive. . . . It is difficult [in the West] to get ahead as an enemy of a regime like Cuba. . . . I encounter this in academic circles everywhere. At Harvard I was asked not to talk about politics during a lecture. In the meantime communist writers like Cintio Vitier and Miguel Barnet were given free reign to talk of nothing else."[7]

Jesse Jackson is among the friends of Cuba. As journalist Fred Barnes has noted, his attitude toward Cuba is "similar to Shirley MacLaine's toward China in the 1970s, or the Webbs' toward the Soviet Union in the 1930s. . . . Jackson visits the schools on the Island of Youth and finds them 'creative'. In truth they are the essence of totalitarianism, where Cuban children are leached of what a pro-Castro American tells me are their 'backward attitudes.'"[8] On his visit to Cuba Jackson also toured a renovated prison and inspected prisoners who were made to play baseball (in new baseball uniforms for the occasion).[9]

Church delegations were prominent among the last-ditch supporters of Church. A spokesman for some Methodists saw "a country where the great majority of people believe that they are the masters and beneficiaries of a new society. . . . Cubans are characterized by . . . a burning desire for the rest of humanity to gain the freedom that Cubans have so recently won."[10] Methodist bishops were persuaded that in Cuba people are imprisoned who oppose policies designed to remove inequalities. They found these grounds for imprisonment far superior to those in countries like Chile or Brazil where—they averred—those in favor of social justice are sent to jail.[11]

A National Council of Churches study guide praised the Cuban educational system: "Permeating Cuban educational practice is the concept that a new type of society will develop a new type of human being . . . [who] regards work at the creative center of life and is bound to others by solidarity, comradeship, and love."[12] Another publication of the National Council of Churches concluded that "at home Cubans have found a new dignity. . . . Internationally, the island nation . . . has been adopted as a symbol of revolutionary hope and courage by the Third World." Further south, the archbishop of São Paulo assured Castro on the thirtieth anniversary of the revolution that he was "present daily in [his] prayers," and that "Christian faith discovers in the achievements of the revolution signs of the Kingdom of God."[13]

The enduring support of Cuba also found expression in the sympathetic (though not uncritical) report of a delegation organized by the Institute for Policy Studies to assess prison conditions there. The participants "encountered a very strong sense of mission in most prison officials. They expressed great faith in their system and . . . seemed determined to work increasingly on their plan for reeducation and for incorporation of the penal population into work and free society . . . The regular prison facilities we saw were all clean and hygienic, and we heard no serious complaints in this regard. We heard no complaints about the use of instruments of torture, . . .

neither did we find any policy of extrajudicial executions or disappearances."[14] Such statements call to mind the Webbs in the Soviet Union during the 1930s, who noted that "the [prison] administration is well-spoken of and is now as free from physical cruelty as any prison in any country is ever likely to be." Debra Evenson, a professor at the law school of DePaul University in Chicago, could not stomach even such restrained criticism of Cuban prisons as was presented (in the *New York Review of Books*) by Aryeh Neier, and in a vigorous rejoinder assured readers of their superiority over American prisons.[15]

These exchanges and the prison report appeared just a few months before the Americas Watch Committee report, which offered renewed evidence of the human rights violations and overall repressiveness of the Cuban system.[16]

No matter how devoted the remaining supporters of Cuba have been, by the 1980s, the major setting of the pilgrimages and political tours shifted to Nicaragua. (To be sure, those supportive of Cuba were also sympathetic toward Nicaragua, and vice versa.) Political tourism may better describe the new phenomenon since visits to Nicaragua have been for the most part highly standardized group tours, rather than journeys of discovery by single, distinguished individuals accompanied by an entourage of guides and interpreters—a type of travel more properly described as a pilgrimage.

A new feature of the visits to Nicaragua is volunteering for various projects such as picking coffee beans or miscellaneous construction. (This has few precedents in the Soviet Union or China and was modelled on the Venceremos Brigade in Cuba, which brought in sympathizers to cut sugar cane.) Some Americans and Westerners also live more or less permanently in Nicaragua, while others are content to spend a few weeks on various projects.

An estimated 1500 Americans are "living and working in Nicaragua. . . . Since the Sandinistas came to power in 1979, about 40,000 Americans have gone to Nicaragua for humanitarian or political work."[17] The motives of the participants was summed up by a member of a women's brigade intent on building a school: "Going to Nicaragua is a direct act of conscience in opposition to our government's aggression and in solidarity with the Nicaraguan people.[18] The attraction to Nicaragua was also associated with a "renewal of belief in the possibility of a revolution not foreordained to be the cat's-paw of either superpower rivalry or homegrown despotism."[19] In other words, Nicaragua was the new antidote to the loss of illusions following the 1960s.

In a single year, according to a Nicaraguan government official, 100,000 foreigners visited Nicaragua, of whom 40 percent were Americans. As the article quoting these figures pointed out, most of them did not come "to see natural beauty, but to get a look at the Sandinista revolution. Most of them . . . are connected with churches, unions, and universities; groups generally sympathetic to the Sandinistas."[20]

Sympathy toward the Nicaraguan Marxist-Leninist government had other manifestations as well. The Boston City Council proclaimed November 3, 1988, "Ernesto Cardenal Day" in honor of the Sandinista minister of culture, also a poet and priest.[21] Burlington, Vermont and Berkeley, California became sister cities of Managua. Across the nation support groups, especially those connected with churches, collected substantial amounts of money and supplies. In 1987 a national campaign aimed at collecting $60 million on top of another $40 million already raised in 1986.[22] At the anti-inauguration concert held in Washington, D.C., protesting the Bush presidency, Kris Kristofferson sang an ode to the Sandinistas that included the lines, "You have lived up to your name. . . . May your spirit never die! Hold a candle to the darkness! You're the keeper of the flame!"[23]

Daniel Ortega, on his visit to New York City, was honored at a reception at the Riverside Church (then presided over by the Reverend William Sloan Coffin, himself a pilgrim to both North Vietnam and Nicaragua, basked in the admiration of the assembled celebrities, who included Morley Safer, Betty Friedan, Eugene McCarthy, Bianca Jagger, and Bernadine Dohrn, the former Weather Underground activist. Ortega also addressed the congregation of the Park Slope Methodist Church in Brooklyn.[24]

The misconceptions of, and the praise for the Nicaraguan political system and its representatives were impressive both on account of their repetitiveness, and because of the extraordinary resemblance they bore to earlier praises of other Communist systems, chronicled in this book. There was a willful, cheerful determination to overlook both the conflicting evidence of the nature of the political system and the lessons of history readily available by 1980. The reader of this book will undoubtedly observe that the tours of Nicaragua and the accounts written of them have reproduced with an almost improbable fidelity every illusion, idealization, projection and misperception that has been displayed in the earlier travelogues of the 1930's, 60s, or 70s.

Salman Rushdie, the now very famous British writer, (courtesy of the Ayatollah Khomeni of Iran) made no secret of his favorable predisposition toward Nicaragua stimulated by his antipathy toward the policies of the United States: "When the Reagan administration began its war against Nicaragua, I recognized a deeper affinity with that small country. . . . I did not go as a wholly neutral observer. I was not a blank slate." Indeed he was not. His visit to Nicaragua had all the hallmarks of the earlier trips of other famous Western intellectuals described in this volume. He was taken on a splendidly organized conducted tour that featured both sumptuous feasts (the "delicacies" included turtle meat "Which had been unexpectedly dense and rich, like a cross between beef and venison") and humble but all the more hospitable peasant meals, colorful fiestas, poetry readings, peasant cooperatives and speedboat rides in picturesque lagoons. The top leaders were always available and often kept him company on his tours of inspection; they turned out to be congenial intellectuals, more than that, fellow writers and poets whose only concern was to uplift the poor and retain the independence of the country. He "couldn't think of a Western politician who could have spoken so intimately" to a crowd and could not imagine Reagan or Thatcher "agreeing to submit themselves to a monthly grilling by members of the public" while failing to notice that these open and spontaneous leaders had no intention of ever leaving office, intending to carry out the mandate of history that fell upon them. Nor did he seem to have noticed the divergence between their life styles and those of the masses they sought to serve although he noticed (for instance) the "wonderfully kept tropical gardens" of foreign minister Miguel d'Escoto that was his "other great love", besides his collection of Nicaraguan art.

Rushdie confessed that "For the first time in my life . . . I had come across the government I could support." He also found

Nicaragua's constitution "amount[ing] to a Bill of Rights that I I couldn't have minded having on the statute book in Britain." Most importantly the country and its way of life was unlike the contemptible "West stuffed with money, power and things"[25]; instead there was a sense of purpose and community. There was also poverty and not a lot of material progress but it could be blamed on the past, the United States and the contras. Censorship caused him fleeting unease but that too was due to the hard times. Most importantly the system was dedicated to social justice and the people were simple and authentic. As a reviewer summed it up "Mr. Rushdie appears to have set out on his pilgrimage, first to affirm his belief in what he would like Nicaragua to be, and by extension what he himself sorely feels he has failed to practice in his own life."[26] He was only one among a huge number of pilgrims and political tourists ready to discover and praise the new socialist virtues of Nicaragua.

According to Alice Walker, the American writer, Nicaragua "is a writer's paradise."[27] For a professor of philosophy at the University of Massachusetts at Amherst (and a frequent visitor) the Nicaraguan government was "honestly committed to the poor and could be a model to other Latin American countries . . . "[28] A writer in the *Village Voice* reported that visitors to Nicaragua experience "a renewal of faith . . . what Nicaragua gives back to the Internationals [the volunteer workers] is hope . . . "[29] A retired Presbyterian minister from Atlanta found that the Sandinistas "have done some things that as a Christian I value very highly. They conducted one of the most sensational literacy campaigns in history . . . it is consistent with Christian values to spread health care to rural areas. They have given land to peasants. As a Christian I applaud that."[30] Even *Vanity Fair* found much to praise in Nicaragua including its first family. Rosario Murillo, spouse of Daniel Ortega was said to possess "the charm of a revolution peopled by the young, the brave and the good looking . . . " (the reader may juxtapose this observation to those of Julian Huxley who paid similar tribute to the "fine physique" of the Russian people he observed: apparently all "solid, robust, healthy" and approximating the Greek Ideal of bodily perfection. But there was more than charm to Ms. Murillo—"the dreamy poetess who oversees her fiefdom with an unyielding eye; the egalitarian revolutionary who revels in Ralph Lauren, the First Lady of a modest little country . . . " She was also characterised as "halfway between La Pasionaria [the Spanish Stalinist communist of the 1930s] and Bianca Jagger."[31]

Recent political tourists were just as certain as those of earlier generations that the citizens of the countries they held in high esteem cheerfully accepted all hardships in the joyous expectation of a better future and because of their appreciation of the good intentions of their leaders. A Labor Member of the British parliament wrote, "the Nicaraguans accept all these hardships . . . because . . . most citizens realise that their government is doing its best in exceptionally difficult circumstances, that hardships and shortages are fairly shared."[32] How did Mr. Kaufman know? As others before him, presumably he too relied on the information he was provided by his hosts who undoubtedly spared him of comparisons between *their* diet, housing, and means of transportation and those of the general population.

These curious perceptions of life in Nicaragua had much to do with the determination of the visitors (as was the case in the pilgrimages past) to accent the positive. A director of a theological seminary in California advised that it was desirable to try" to discard our U.S. ideological lenses . . . and enter into networks of trust." He apparently was successful since he concluded that "Nicaragua has achieved more freedom, justice and grass roots democracy than any of its neighbors (with the exception of Costa Rica) has achieved in five hundred years."[33]

The churches were in the forefront of the support for Nicaragua and in organizing tour groups. In particular the Quakers, and their activist arm, the American Friends Service Committee, (their offshoot, the Witness for Peace), the National Council of Churches as whole and the Methodists in particular, the Catholic Maryknoll and the Sojourners (a leftist evangelical group) were the most dedicated to these efforts.

If the Reagan presidency (and the distaste it inspired in the left-of-center citizenry) helped nurture the sympathy toward Nicaragua presumably the Bush presidency will continue to have a similar, though perhaps milder effect of the same kind. Continued disenchantment with domestic conditions is likely to remain the major source of the susceptibility toward political systems that make impressive idealistic claims and also gain the goodwill of the domestic social critics for being critical of the United States.

It remains to be seen what if any long term effect of the cessation of the guerilla war in Nicaragua may have on the sympathizers and supporters. While in progress it provided the most satisfactory explanations (and excuses) of both the dire economic conditions and the political repression that prevailed. (After all, war was raging so the authorities were justified in restricting civil liberties. As to the economy, it was destroyed by contra sabotage and drained by the diversion of resources to the war effort.) Since the fighting stopped economic conditions continued to decline precipitously and civil rights barely improved either—conditions which may yet have some impact on the continued idealization of the system. The end of the guerilla war has also made it more difficult to blame the United States for its interference in Nicaraguan affairs and by the same token absolve the Nicaraguan authorities of responsibility for the conditions in the country.

These reflections seem to imply that the favorable attitudes toward Nicaragua have important rational components and when those weaken the admiration will subside. Unfortunately the record of past pilgrimages casts doubt on such speculations. For example, the fervent support for the Soviet system peaked at a time when the country lived under its worst totalitarian conditions, with Stalin's terror in full swing, the show trials in progress and millions starving. Likewise the veneration of communist China was most intense during Mao's insane campaigns, including the Cultural Revolution which exacted a huge price, human as well as material. In neither case were objective conditions a significant factor in shaping attitudes toward the countries and their political systems.

It may be predicted that if the Sandinistas' appeal becomes tarnished with the passage of time, or the craving for novelty overpowers old loyalties, there will be other political systems or movements to be idealised (on similar grounds), possibly the radical-leftist guerillas in El Salvador, in or out of power. Already they have attracted a vocal and well organized following that includes Hollywood actors such as Edward Asner who hopes that they will win power and who has it on good authority that "the rebel forces are now the most effective institution in El Salvador committed to health delivery."[34]

The continued outpouring of favorable sentiment toward the authorities in Nicaragua (and assorted anti-Western guerilla movements elsewhere) suggests that time has stood still within the adversary culture—the complex of beliefs, attitudes and values which entail suspicion, aversion, or hostility toward American society, its major values and institutions. Its adherents have not reexamined their ideals and pondered their alienation in the light of the changes taking place in the socialist world in the 1980s and especially since 1985, when Gorbachev came into power. They have managed to ignore not only the rising tide of revelations about the general malfunctioning of these systems and their intractable social problems but also the truly systemic failings of socialist economies.

Yet there is a limit to both self-deception and the impact of the skillful, organised deception Marxist-Leninist systems practised (see "political hospitality" below) for the benefit of those predisposed to admire them.

It has taken several decades for the facts to sink in about the nature of the Soviet system among those estranged from Western societies. It may take even longer for the more general, and (for them) far more disturbing idea to sink in that political systems inspired by Marxism-Leninism are incapable of realizing the dreams of the Western seekers of justice, social harmony and personal fulfillment.

Postscript, November 1990

Since I wrote the above time did not stand still, if anything the pace of change in communist systems quickened. Indeed several of them are no longer communist systems: Eastern Europe has been transformed, no longer part of the Soviet bloc; Germany has become unified, or rather incorporated into what used to be West Germany; Marxism-Leninism and the rule of the Communist Party in the Soviet Union has become thoroughly delegitimated and the constituent republics moved toward autonomy; the Marxist-Leninist government in Nicaragua was voted out of office in February 1990; Angola and Mozambique are in the process of discarding their Soviet-style institutions and official ideology; the June 1989 massacre of students in China dealt a final blow not only to democratization but to any lingering illusions about the attractions of communist China. Even Albania allowed a few thousand dissidents to leave and made some moves toward liberalization. Vietnam has loosened economic though not political controls. Only Cuba and North Korea (and beleagured Ethiopia) hang on grimly to their totalitarian heritage.

Such developments obviously had an impact on political tourism. Foremost, the developments in Nicaragua—the last bastion of leftist hopes during the 1980s—undercut the phenomenon here discussed. Almost at one stroke Nicaragua ceased to be a popular destination of the critics of the United States[35] and no new country or political system has taken its place.

For the moment the political pilgrimage is on hold. To be sure the Marxist-Leninist guerillas in El Salvador remain popular with the American Left but the areas they control are too small and dangerous to visit. It is my belief that the next major contender for the status of a promising socialist system that could inspire a new wave of pilgrimages could be South Africa *if*, the African National Congress succeeds in gaining control. If that were to happen the politically alienated would have a new country and political system to support. It would have two great attractions: it would be a government run by blacks and pursuing socialist ideals of some type.

It is hard to think at this point in time of other potential destinations, unless by some fluke one of the formerly communist countries in Eastern Europe would return to a left-of-center government, or, in an even more unlikely scenario, the Soviet Union fell apart and one of its former republics moved in such a direction. A left-of-center Arab country would be another attractive destination for the political tourists if it put forward the appropriate socialist rhetoric in combination with the denunciation of the West, authenticated by the emphasis on the obligatory Third World victim status. In the meantime such potential political tourists can sympathize with the PLO.

The developments over the past two years do not alter the basic proposition made earlier in this essay: there remains a striking discrepancy between the turmoil and disintegration within the communist or formerly communist states and the persistence of political estrangement among Western intellectuals and other elite groups and their camp followers. The decay of communism failed to set into motion any major reassessment of the political attitudes and sympathies of Western social critics, and occasioned little soul-searching on account of their profound misjudgments of "existing socialist systems." This reluctance to confront the implications of the moral and material bankruptcy of communist systems (and of the ideals which inspired them) is more pronounced in the United States than Western Europe.[36]

It may be concluded that the impulses which gave rise to the pilgrimages survive even at a time when there are no acceptable destinations for the potential pilgrims.

Notes

1. Paul Hollander. *The Survival of the Adversary Culture: Social Criticism and Political Escapism in American Society.* New Brunswick: Transaction Books, 1988.
2. For a sampling of the Soviet coverage of some of these problems see T. Anthony Jones, ed. "Social Deviance and Social Problems." *Soviet Sociology,* 1989, vol. 27., no. 4.
3. For a discussion of the origins of the concept see Hollander cited pp. 10–13.
4. For example Thomas Short. " 'Diversity' and 'Breaking the Disciplines'." *Academic Questions,* Summer 1988.
5. But if China no longer stimulated rhapsodic reports nor was the general public necessarily well informed about the continuation of its repressive policies. Huge gaps of information remained as for instance about the violence in Tibet on March 5, 1988 when " . . . hundreds of Chinese police had rampaged through these sacred corridors [of Jokang Temple, the "holiest shrine of contemporary Chinese Buddhism"] clubbing and shooting to death thirty monks in retaliation for an unarmed, pro-independence demonstration. Hundreds of monks and lay Tibetans . . . were arrested and taken away to local prisons in Lhasa where they endured days of savage beatings . . . " J. Michael Luhan: "How the Chinese Rule Tibet." *Dissent,* Winter 1989, p.21.
6. "Joint Statement by Dr Cleary and Ms. Meinertz" quoted in *Time for Candor: Mainline Churches and Radical Social Witness.* Institute for Religion and Democracy, Washington, DC 1983, pp. 63–67.
7. Octavio Roca. "An Exile's Home Away from Home." *Insight,* 10 October, 1988 p. 61.
8. Fred Barnes. "The Jackson Tour." *New Republic,* 30 July, 1984, p.21.
9. See for example S. L. Nall. "Prisoners Say Cubans Fooled Jackson on Jail." *Washington Times,* 2 July, 1984.
10. Rusty Davenport. "Cuba: A Land of Contrast". *Common Ground,* Summer 1981; quoted in *A Time for Candor* cited p. 85.
11. *Time for Candor* cited p. 81.
12. Quoted in Joshua Muravchik. "Pliant Protestants." *New Republic,* 13 June, 1983.
13. *Time For Candor* cited, p. 90; Alan Riding. "Brazil Cardinal's Praise of Castro Stirs Protest." *New York Times,* 5 February, 1989, p. 20.

14. "Cuban Prisons: A Preliminary Report." Institute for Policy Studies, *Social Justice*, Summer 1988, p. 58, 59.

15. Debra Evenson. " 'In Cuban Prisons': An Exchange" *New York Review of Books*, 29 September, 1988.

16. Joseph B. Treaster. "Rights Group Reports Continued Abuses in Cuba" *New York Times*, 29 January, 1988.

17. Cheryl Sullivan. "U.S. Volunteers head for Nicaragua." *Christian Science Monitor*, 2 June, 1987 pp. 3–4.

18. Margaret Lobenstein. "Brigada Companeras builds hope." *Valley Womens' Voice*, February 1987.

19. Tom Carson. "The Long Way Back." *Village Voice*, 12 May, 1987 p. 5, 7.

20. Marjorie Miller. "Nicaragua's Tourism Up Despite War." *Los Angeles Times*, 12 March, 1986.

21. "Sandinista Holiday." *New Republic*, 21 November, 1988.

22. Sullivan op. cit, p.3.

23. Alex Heard. "Inaugural Anthropology." *New Republic*, 13, February, 1989 p. 14.

24. Jim Motavalli. "Ortega Takes Manhattan." *Valley Advocate*, 6 November, 1985; "Sandinista Makes His Case On A Brooklyn Church Visit", *New York Times*, July 28.

25. Salman Rushdie. *The Jaguar Smile: A Nicaraguan Journey.* New York: Viking, 1987, pp. 12, 32, 36, 63, 70, 96, 119, 170.

26. James LeMoyne. "Three Weeks in Managua." *New York Times Book Review*, 18 March, 1987.

27. Harriet Rohmer. "Managua's First Book Fair." *Publisher's Weekly*, 4 September, 1987 p. 19.

28. John Bretlinger. "Needed: a clear impression." *The Collegian*, November 7, 1985.

29. Carson, op. cit., p. 28.

30. Steven Donziger. "The Nicaragua Connection." *Atlanta*, February 1988, p. 99.

31. Lloyd Grove. "Rosario's Revolution." *Vanity Fair*, July 1986 p. 58, 98.

32. Gerald Kaufman. "A makeshift toast to Nicaragua Libre." *New Statesmen*, 11 September, 1987, p. 16.

33. Ross F. Kinsler. "Observing Nicaragua Through Different Lenses." *Monday Morning* (a magazine for Presbyterian ministers) 10 March, 1986, p. 16, 17.

34. "TV actors attack U.S. over Salvadorian policy" (Associated Press), *Daily Hampshire Gazette*, 16 February, 1982, p. 11.

35. See for example: Chris Hedges. "Sandinistas' U.S. Friends: Case of Dashed Ideas", *New York Times*, 21 July, 1990. The article noted, among other things that "The morale of those men and women [who used to go to Nicaragua— P.H.] has suffered . . . and irreversible blow . . . . Although Americans could continue their humanitarian programs there, the Sandinistas' loss of power has removed much of the utopian appeal of their work." This was said with reference to both those who went to Nicaragua as volunteer workers on various construction projects or to assist with agricultural work, and those who went on the political sightseeing tours.

36. See also Seymour Martin Lipset. "The Death of the Third Way." *National interest*, Summer 1990.

14

Resisting the Lessons of History, or, How the Adversary Culture Responded to the Disintegration of Communism?

I.

The rapid and unexpected unravelling of communist states in Eastern Europe and elsewhere was the great and unexpected historical development of the late 1980s and it attracted much well-deserved attention. By contrast there has been little reflection over the Western reactions to these events and especially little said about the reaction of those who for decades regularly cautioned us against the evils or folly of anticommunism. For them these events had, or should have had, a special significance as they offered a further, perhaps, final opportunity to reevaluate their views of communism and anticommunism and to reexamine the relationship between theory and practice and the prospects of the various existing embodiments of socialism. These embodiments—let it be said at the outset—while a far cry from the ideals of Marx, were not totally unrelated to them, either.[1]

I am not suggesting that the importance of how Western leftists (or the adversary culture[2]) reacted to these events is comparable to what actually happened in these countries; nonetheless, for the student of political movements and behavior these reactions are also of interest and importance. The manner in which adversarial groups and critics responded to the collapse of communism informs us not merely about their character and political psychology but also about more general

245

and enduring patterns of political behavior; in particular these responses reveal the strategies individuals and groups adopt to protect
threatened political committments and ideological beliefs.

The response of American intellectuals and quasi-intellectuals[3] of
leftist-adversarial persuasion is of special interest as it contrasts in
some ways with those on the left elsewhere. This divergence may be
part of a broader trend Lipset noted recently and connected with the
peculiar part played by Marxism in American intellectual and political life:

> In the United States . . . the involvement of intellectuals (and their camp follow-
> ers) with Marxism has been more personal and less institutional, more abstract
> and involving little in the way of "praxis" . . . the attachment [to Marxism] has
> been inspired and sustained more by a desire to be anti-establishment, to be ad-
> versarial towards bourgeois and national values, than by concern to implement
> specific political and social programs. In these circumstances increasing evidence
> that Marxism does not deliver, that regimes and policies associated with it are dis-
> astrous failures, is largely irrelevant.[4]

It is important to stress here that for decades prior to the collapse
of communism in Eastern Europe and its spectacular decay in the
Soviet Union there was a wealth of information that made clear that
these were profoundly inhumane as well as inefficient systems of
government. The *moral significance* of their collapse lies not in offering new evidence of their failings but in providing conclusive proof
of their total lack of legitimacy and the depth of hostility they inspired among those who were their putative beneficiaries. In point of
fact the critiques of these systems mounted by those who lived under
them have been far more virulent and impassioned than anything
Western "cold warriors" or "professional anticommunists" had ever
dreamed of or dared to say. Moreover, as Owen Harries observed,
"the account of the Soviet system now being given by its own
spokesmen is very close to what conservatives always believed—and
were dismissed as biased and obsessive for believing."[5] In other
words the collapse and internal rejection of communist states in Eastern Europe (and Nicaragua) demonstrated that the anticommunist assessment and critique of these systems in the West was neither
groundless, nor irrational, nor in the least exaggerated. Anticommunist critics of Marxist-Leninist systems erred only in one respect:

they did not anticipate their abrupt disintegration and the concomitant (or antecedent) loss of nerve of their leaders.

While the substance of the revelations unleashed by the reestablishment of free expression in these states has been familiar for a long time, two aspects of these developments were cause for some surprise. The first, that the collapse of communist authority, both in the Soviet Union and Eastern Europe occurred at all and at this particular time—contrary to Western expectations and theories. It may be recalled that it was the long-standing conventional wisdom in the West and especially the United States, that only as the Soviet economy and living standards improve, would political liberalization be possible. As it turned out it was the pressure of growing economic difficulties that forced Gorbachev to (begin to) democratize the Soviet system and release the satellites from the grip of the Brezhnev doctrine—this at any rate is the new conventional wisdom.

The second novelty, for most Americans, has been the abundance of new evidence indicating that not only were Soviet-type societies lacking in "Western-style" freedoms and legitimacy but they were also riddled with the familiar social problems of the capitalist West (more of this below).

But perhaps the greatest significance one can attach to these developments is further evidence—if more was needed—that Marxism and its derivatives do not lend themselves to successful social engineering, or more painless modernization, let alone to the creation of non-alienated, selfless, harmonious, communitarian human beings released from the shackles of the division of labor, competitiveness, profit, and power-hunger. The trajectory of the evolution of these systems and the attitudes and policies of those in control of them have also shown that those initially inspired by Marxist ideas ended up by making the retention of power their major concern rather than the liberation of the masses from the assorted privations they faced.

Especially startling (for some) might have been the revelation that these "existing socialist systems" while lacking the political freedoms and high living standards found in Western capitalist societies, also had their full share of problems often thought to be peculiar to capitalism: crime of every variety, family instability, the neglect of the old, cynicism among the young, environmental degradation, corruption of huge proportions, lack of work satisfaction, crass materialism—all the vices of capitalism without its benefits. If all this came about in the name of, inspired by, or in conjunction with the attempted realization of the ideals of Marxism, then something was profoundly wrong with the theory and not just the practice—the most painful issue for Western Marxists to confront. For good reason did many of them increasingly retreat to the theory, seeking to overlook its attempted applications.

Thus the most thought-provoking and disconcerting lesson of the collapse of communist systems for Western leftists has been (or should have been) that not only did they possess distinctively unpleasant characteristics of their own but they also shared most inequities and corruptions found under capitalism which the remedies proposed by their official theory failed to cure.

II

To better understand the responses in the adversary culture to the crisis of communism we must take a look at its origins and evolution since the 1960s. From the beginning of that period Western social critics and the Western left have been in a somewhat anomalous position. On the one hand, during the 60's the ranks of social critics greatly expanded and a mass movement of sorts emerged embracing all those dissatisfied—on the most varied grounds—with American society and culture. While the movements of that period have largely vanished, they left behind a well-entrenched subculture, a set of internalized beliefs and mindsets exerting continued and substantial influence on major social institutions such as education, the churches, the media, publishing, and the Democratic Party.

At the same time these movements, once also called the New Left, were amorphous and ideologically unfocused and unclear both regarding their long-range objectives and the best ways to attain them. They no longer were firmly committed to specifics of Marxism-Leninism (although greatly attracted to its major message: that Western-capitalist societies were evil and doomed); these adversarial groups disassociated themselves from traditional embodiments of leftist loyalties such as the communist parties and the Soviet Union but replaced them with communist systems in the Third World: China under Mao, Cuba under Castro, and communist Vietnam. When the attraction and reputation of these countries also waned for a variety of good reasons, revolutionary Nicaragua came along in 1979 to offer a new haven for the free-floating political longings in search of a new physical setting, where hopes for an authentic socialist system could be realized. The attractions of Nicaragua endured for a decade until dealt a blow by the elections of 1990 which unexpectedly ousted the leftist government.

Thus except for Nicaragua (until February 1990) the American Left has been for some time without existing socialist systems to admire, support, and contrast to the corruptions of their own country. There remained, nonetheless, a vocal and influential minority of the population that persisted in rejecting the prevailing social-economic system even when deprived of foreign counter-models to emulate or revere. These groups have been unflinching in their aversion to capitalism and professed commitment to ideals of socialism they continued to hope will one day be realized somewhere.

While Eastern Europe along with the Soviet Union has long been written off as inauthentically socialist, its failures did not attract much attention or elicit much indignation among the groups here discussed; they dealt with these systems (dependencies of the Soviet Union) in the framework of the moral equivalence theory they adopted and was popular during this period (1960s to the 1980s). Theoretically, both superpowers were equally bad, but the Soviet Union usually escaped searching criticism while the United States was held responsible for threats to world peace, the misery of Third World masses, and the assorted evils of global capitalism. In the adversarial circles the typical view of the Soviet Union has been that regrettably enough it did not turn out to be a model socialist system (for which in large measure the West and the arms race were responsible), but on the other hand it provided its people with basic material security: there was no unemployment, not rampant inequalities, medical services and education were free. Whatever was wrong with the Soviet and similar systems, at least they were not capitalist, which was an important ethical advantage from the point of view of the groups here discussed. As an English writer observed of these benefit-of-doubt attitudes: "Deep down in the heart of all socialists was and still is a sneaking admiration for the communist experiment in Russia, a lingering regret at its failure and a refusal ever to think of the Russian empire as evil."[6] Little was known or said, in these circles about Soviet (and East European) social problems, including simple poverty, a word studiously avoided even in discussions of shortages in these countries. There was also a tacit assumption that the Soviet system (and its dependencies) enjoyed broad legitimacy among the masses, who in any event, had little interest in bourgeois freedoms but appreciated the material security these systems supposedly provided.

It was also assumed in the adversary culture that the defects of these systems could not be quite as severe as described by the cold warriors, professional anticommunists, and other reactionaries obsessed with the faults of communism. Revisionist historians for a long time made it their task to blame the United States for the Cold War; more recently some of their colleagues began to discover that even Stalin's crimes were exaggerated.[7] In turn the resurgent peace movement through the 1980s discouraged criticism of the Soviet Union on the ground that the cause of peace would be better served by overlooking differences and stressing similarities (between the Soviet Union and Western democracies) and arguing that critiques of the Soviet Union would perpetuate hostile stereotypes, and, besides who are we to criticize the Soviet Union? As Tom Wicker once wrote: "Where is the moral superiority that affords the U. S. Government and people the right to judge others as moral inferiors?"[8]

What difference the recent developments in Eastern Europe and the Soviet Union were to make to these attitudes? At first glance it would seem that the collapse of communism in Eastern Europe and its publicly admitted failures in the Soviet Union need not have been problems for members of the adversary culture for the reason noted above: the Soviet Union and Eastern Europe for the past quarter century played no important part in the political loyalties, dreams, and inspiration of American leftists. Yet on closer inspection matters turned out to be somewhat different; the adversary culture, for the most part, could not ignore these events; sensing, but not fully acknowledging their importance, it developed several defensive strategies to deal with them. Each included a reflexive affirmation of unrelenting hostility toward capitalism and the American social order

and insistence that events in Eastern Europe had no relevance whatsoever to the evil they were habitually denouncing. It may indeed be
possible that such hostility increased rather then diminished notwithstanding the obliteration of virtually every single existing alternative to the abhorred system. Kenneth Minogue, an English political
scientist observed that "as radicals have lost plausible utopias of one
kind or another—from the Soviet Union to Cuba—they have become
more ferociously intolerant of the society in which they live."[9]

III

Several distinct patterns have emerged in the responses of the adversary culture to the collapse of communism. The most popular has
been the insistence that these developments are irrelevant to the evils
of the Western world and in no way should they be allowed to influence the ideas and activities embraced by these groups and individuals. A variant of this response has been the reinvigoration of the
moral equivalence theory, the new variant making use of glasnost to
indict capitalism (and the United States) in the light of the latest
Soviet achievements.

Second, it came to be asserted that these systems had nothing
whatsoever to do with true Marxism hence their collapse proves nothing about its weakness; in fact with the disappearance of these systems it will now be possible to reclaim the good name of Marxism
and vindicate its propositions.

Third, (and still more unconvincingly) it has also been suggested
that Eastern Europeans themselves are either already anticapitalist or
will reject capitalism in due course and build true socialism. (Sometimes their capitalist leanings are ruefully acknowledged but dismissed as a transitory manifestation of false consciousness.)

Fourth, the decay of communism is said to prove the folly of
American foreign and military policies which rested on the exaggeration of the threat and power of these systems.

Finally, among the most radical groups, the liberalization in the
Soviet Union and the changes in Eastern Europe were met with undisguised outrage and disappointment. "Gorbachev's plans are more
and more bourgeois as opposed to anything Communist" was the
view of a representative of the Revolutionary Communist Party in

Berkeley, California; the chairwoman of the Communist Party of the U.S. in Northern California was displeased with Gorbachev's willingness to meet Reagan, the "ultra-right, racist, sexist member of the ruling class." She also averred that socialism was not failing "just correcting its mistakes."[10]

Perhaps the most remarkable thing about these responses has been the freely and frequently expressed apprehension, indeed alarm, that the demise of communist systems will be used to legitimate capitalism, or American social institutions, and the corresponding insistence that the discrediting and decline of communism had no bearing on the sins of capitalism. Paul Sweezy hopefully proclaimed in *The Nation* that

> As far as global capitalism is concerned, its internal contradictions will hardly be effected one way or another . . . these contradictions, as in the past continue to multiply and intensify, with all indications pointing to the maturing of one or more serious crises in the not-so-distant future.[11]

In a similar spirit, Janice Love, a United Methodist Church member of the World Council of Churches warned that "because of the events in the USSR and Eastern Europe, there appears to be a new-found triumphalism about capitalism that I find uncritical, unwarranted and chauvinistic."[12] The 202nd General Assembly of the Presbyterian Church (USA) in June 1990 "expressed 'sorrow and repentance' that our government and churches 'in perpetuating the cold war may have added to burdens of persons living in Central and Eastern Europe.' A background paper criticized 'the triumphalistic, self-righteous, self-congratulatory presumptions' of those who rejoice at the demise of communist dictatorships."[13] A professor of sociology from Illinois was irritated with "all the self-righteous, sanctimonious celebration of the 'victory' of capitalism over Communism precipitated by the upheavals in Eastern Europe." She was not content to remind her readers of the evils of capitalism but also of the accomplishments of these unhappily declining systems:

> These governments . . . constructed massive social service delivery systems that eliminated illiteracy, petty street crime, prostitution and a myriad of other social cancers. . . . Though disadvantaged in consumer gadgetry, their populations are well educated and healthy.[14]

While these assertions would undoubtedly come as a surprise to most residents of Eastern Europe they do reflect residual beliefs which used to be even more widespread in the adversary culture and helped to neutralize whatever critical sentiments existed toward these systems.

More typically, reflections on the left about the collapse of communist systems stressed less their virtues than the similarities between their newly discovered (or admitted) vices and those prevailing under capitalism. Thus somewhat unexpectedly, the collapse of communism, and its unequivocal and public repudation by millions who had lived under it, has reinvigorated and enriched the moral equivalence thesis. While earlier it was used primarily in Soviet-American comparisons, now it was applied more broadly to "East" and "West." Todd Gitlin commenting on the new developments wrote that

East-West confrontation apparently reduced all choices to one either/or choice: Light vs. Dark, Freedom vs. Slavery, Godliness vs. Atheism, Capitalism vs. Socialism, Democracy vs. Dictatorship. . . . Virtue and paranoia fused to make us the Good Guys. Our cars, kitchens, families, schools, synagogues and churches were all defended in the name of our goodness. . . . For more than forty years . . . it was virtually impossible to talk about America without talking about its enemies.[15]

The burden of these remarks is that there was something harmful and irrational in thinking that the United States was preferable or superior to the Soviet Union and other similar systems, and there was something similarly irrational and delusional about a worldview that sharply contrasted democracy to distatorship; moreover, the vices of communism were cynically used to conceal the flaws of our own systems; thus, it remains unclear if one system was better than the other.

Reassertions of moral equivalence were to be found not only in the musings of academics but also in the popular media. A columnist in *USA Today* wrote:

While Central and Eastern Europeans are embracing democracy . . . citizens of the USA . . . are dropping out and failing to participate in ever increasing numbers. . . . From the point of view of these folks democracy and its trappings, from conventions and elections to the referendum and recall, look like a really big improvement. . . . But give it a little time . . . and it will gradually begin to look less and less like utopia. Just give the democratic politicians time, as their new Central and Eastern European constituents will find out . . . and they'll find ways to make themselves into commissars of a sort in their own right. . . . By then, perhaps the people of Central and Eastern Europe will have learned about democracy what we began learning about it decades ago—that the fact that a man can vote to change his master every few years doesn't mean he isn't a slave.[16]

Often these reflections—aimed at putting events in Eastern Europe into the proper perspective, began with (or at) the Berlin Wall and then moved rapidly to the evils of American society as in the case of the comedian, Jackie Mason commenting on these matters in a *New York Times* op-ed piece. His tour of American inequities included McCarthyism, the denial of rights to women and homosexuals, the uselessness of free expression ("if we can't leave the house to buy a newspaper"), the burdens of leading "an unpopular life style" and of course, "poverty, inequality and discrimination." He expressed hope that "perhaps Mikhail Gorbachev would do for us what he did for East Germany. Maybe he could make us aware of the fact that we too could unburden ourselves from our own forms of oppression. He might remind us that we could be a free country once again."[17]

For another writer the demolition of the Berlin Wall inspired reflections about the sorrows caused by "more subtle, elusive walls," including "the wall of doubt that takes over from within" and interferes with self-realization in America. The author who had a graduate degree and worked for a New York law firm also complained of her insufficient salary, limited career choices, anticipations of divorce (in case she got married), difficulties of child care (in case she had children) and waxed particularly indignant over her lack of funds to buy a house in California where she would have preferred to live.[18] While some may be tempted to dismiss such complaints as idiosyncratic and unrepresentative, the *New York Times* deemed them worthy of publication presumably on the assumption that these sentiments captured deeper and widespread discontents of our time, as they may well have. By contrast the president of NBC television was saddened over the failure of present day American youth to complain and protest—as he compared them with those of Eastern Europe—and he feared that they may turn out to be as apathetic as the generation of the 1950s.[19]

Tom Wicker began an article by quoting a Czech citizen celebrating his newly won freedoms in Prague but immediately moved on to a listing of the afflictions of American society including violent crimes and accidents, drunkenness, drug abuse, and other misbehaviors which occurred on New Year's Eve in New York City. He concluded: "Freedom is . . . not a panacea; and that Communism failed does not make the Western alternative perfect, or even satisfying for millions of those who live under it."[20] In another piece he applied the same perspective to foreign affairs: "Why not draw the lesson of Eastern Europe . . . and leave the Sandinistas to the Nicaraguan people? Or would that be too 'new' a world for the U.S. still bent, as in Panama, and as always, on dominating its so-called 'backyard'?"[21] In the same spirit a *New Yorker* editorial advised that given the decline of the Cold War the United States might as well let events take their course in El Salvador.[22] The U.S. invasion of Panama designed to remove and capture Noriega was a welcome opportunity for Saul Landau (one of the most faithful supporters and propagandist of Castro in the United States) not merely to decry "Imperialism, Bush-Style" but to conclude that "Mikhail Gorbachev has removed the Soviet enemy as a monster worth fighting, yet our political leaders refuse to look inside, and yearn instead for the distraction of the perpetual foreign devil."[23]

Glasnost and the changes in Eastern Europe were also put to more specific uses in service of particular causes. Yet another editorial writer in the *New York Times* began with the East European's delving into past political crimes only to introduce the suggestion that the "Cold War's [American] victims Deserve a Memorial" and "America shields its secret government" and refuses to reveal the innocent victims of nuclear tests and other environmental atrocities. He concluded by quoting Vaclav Havel, making it quite clear that he found his remarks about the Czech communist system fully applicable to the United States:

"The previous regime, armed with a proud and intolerant ideology, reduced people into means of production. . . . Out of talented and responsible people . . . it made cogs of some great, monstrous . . . machine."[27]

An article by Daniel Singer in *The Nation* that began with the changing political map of Europe went on to conclude that the Western left should get on with its job. It must attack the very foundation of our own system . . . its incapacity to conceive of growth for any purpose other than profit, with the attendant environmental destruction; its commercialization of art, culture and even human relationships; its exploitation of the Third World and its perpetuation of social, sexual and racial inequities.[28]

Elsewhere Mr. Singer was led from his survey of developments in Eastern Europe to the conclusion that "our task is to spread the conviction that a radical change of society in all its aspects is on our own historical agenda. In the long run, the collapse of the Stalinist model should help us in this search for a socialist alternative."[29] It was a view similar to that of Paul Robeson Jr. who summed up these developments by noting that "This is death of Stalinism and birth of Marxism."[30]

It should be clear by now that the spectacular repudiation of communism in Eastern Europe did not extinguish among many American intellectuals the longing for "a socialist alternative," nor did it lead to serious reflection about the relationship between the discredited practices and the unattained and still revered ideals. To be sure, increasingly "the socialist alternative" meant not so much a specific blueprint but rather, an open-ended quest for a better world and a generalised attack on human meanness. Irving Howe (not to be associated with the *Nation* authors) was among those who thought "that this might be a good time to reassert socialist convictions—not ideologies, not rigid programs, not exhortations, but the animating values that have inspired the socialist idea."[31] He was among those who, like Michael Walzer, took the position that "Communism has given socialism a bad name."[32] To be sure this was a position more legitimately taken by those, such as Howe and Walzer, who were always critical of Soviet-type societies (as well as Third World dictatorships claiming socialist credentials), and whose critical impulses were not paralysed by the anti-anticommunism widespread among liberal intellectuals since the late 1960s. They differed from the adversarial critics who had for decades viewed the communist states with indulgence or indifference (or mild and perfunctory criticism), but decided upon their collapse to further distance themselves from these "failed experiments."

Sheldon Wolin, a political philosopher at Princeton University, pondering the changes in Eastern Europe found occasion not only to renew his critique of American society but also to praise these communist systems for their egalitarianism:

> In the past decade the perception and sensibilities of many Americans have been Reaganized, shaped by counterrevolutionary concerns regarding welfare, race relations, health care, ecology, government regulation of business . . . the rights of minorities and women. . . . [By contrast] Even acknowledging gross distortions, Communist regimes have been the only ones that professed, and to some degreee achieved, a commitment to equality.[33]

The most remarkable (and grotesque) attempt to disassociate the repudiation of these systems from the repudiation of Marxism has been made in an editorial of *The Nation* that explained the migration of East Germans into West Germany:

> The exodus of . . . East Germans . . . cannot be interpreted, as some Western commentators would have it, as an abandonment of the teachings of Karl Marx . . . the country to which they are traveling . . . is not Thatcher's Britain or apres-Reagan America . . . The new emigrants have chosen capitalism with a human face [i.e., West Germany] . . . And so the newcomers have gone from Stalin back to Marx.[34]

We will never know if it occurred to the editorial writer that speaking the same language and being offered help and citizenship might have played a part in their choice and that West Germany was rather close while neither Britain nor the United States extended hospitality.

Some academic Marxists, as for example Sam Bowles of the University of Massachusetts at Amherst and Philip Green of Smith College, chose to solve the problem by proclaiming relief at the events in Eastern Europe insisting that "for the first time in history there is a chance of a true socialist and democratic state, one based on the writings of Karl Marx." They also averred that "Eastern Europe now will lead the way to creating the first truly socialist nations. . . . The soil in Eastern Europe is prime for true socialism to take root."[35]

This was also the view of Norman Birnbaum, another durable social critic and academic Marxist, who coupled the insistence that "socialism is far from dead" with the proposition "to recast socialism in a contemporary idiom."[36] Increasingly this recasting enterprise and the attempt to prove the continued relevance of Marxism has taken the form of upholding and emphasizing the most generalized and watered-down versions and propositions of Marxism which affirm every conceivable human right and oppose every widely abhorred political or economic practice, or personality trait (e.g., greed, selfishness, dishonesty, etc.) The attitude of these academic Marxists in the United States was reminiscent of that of the late Raymond Williams, the English literary Marxist: "He knew the chief historical predictions of Marxism had been falsified by events, and clung all the harder, for that reason, to its conceptual framework."[37]

If we recall that there was a time when numerous American intellectuals had succeeded in convincing themselves that the Soviet Union under Stalin and China under Mao represented the fulfillment of the dreams of Marx, then perhaps the belief that East Europeans long for Marxist socialism and Eastern Europe is uniquely prepared by history for such a socialism, will strike us less amazing. (It may be noted here that East Germans wasted little time changing the name of Karl Marx City back to its original, Chemnitz; that Czech students called their newly won freedom from studying the clasics of Marxism "a dream come true"[38] and that in their first free elections both in East Germany and Hungary even mildly leftist social democrats were badly beaten and right-of-center parties voted in, as was also the case in Slovenia and Croatia.)

The durable affection for Marxism in the West is also illustrated by the report that "tourists and pilgrims of the left are flocking in greater numbers to the Marx gravesite in Highgate Cemetery." One among them correctly observed, "We come here for hope . . . for inspiration"[39]—sentiments which lend further support (if more is needed) to the conclusions of Raymond Aron and Leszek Kolakowski (among others) who decades ago brought attention to the religious functions and dimensions of Marxist thought.

Among the more bizarre responses to the collapse of communism the new fantasies of revolutionary change in the United States must be mentioned. *The Village Voice* began a section entitled "Perestroika, USA—Can It Happen Here?" with the following adversarial pipedream:

Summer 1993. America is in the 25th month of the . . . Great Depression II. George Bush . . . was carried off by a heart attack. . . . The Federal Deposit Insurance corporation declared bankruptcy . . . President Quayle . . . has his hands full. In the second year of a massive drought induced by the greenhouse effect, America has become a food importer . . . prices are skyrocketing. Gasoline rationing has immobilized the American workforce. . . . Armies of the unemployed . . . trudged the polluted streets in search of nonexistent jobs. . . . President Quayle ordered troops to fire on food rioters at Christmas . . . General strikes have immobolized cities from coast to coast . . . America is in the streets.[40]

Its author called this "an optimistic fantasy." As he explained: "With whole peoples on the march these days from the Danube to the Don, America's relative passivity and quiescence make a stark and disillusioning contrast."[41] It was, needless to say, his unstated premise that Americans had just as good, if not better, reasons to march and protest as the East Europeans. Another writer in the same *Village Voice* suggested, still more wishfully, that the East European revolutions struck fear into "our own bureaucrats. . . . Revolution is contagious."[42]

Thus focusing renewed attention on the shortcomings of the United States was at the heart of the adversarial reactions to the collapse of communism. This usually took the form of contrasting the newly revealed evils of communism with the corresponding defects of American culture and society. It has also been argued by Christopher Lasch, (among others), that the very opposition to communism had deformed American society:

The cold war inflicted much deeper wounds on American society. Preoccupation with external affairs led to the neglect of domestic reforms, even basic services. The development of secret police organizations, the erosion of civil liberties, the stifling of political debate . . . the concentration of decision-making in the executive branch . . . the lying that has come to be accepted as routine in American politics—all these things derive . . . from the cold war. . . . Thanks to its willingness to support corrupt and repressive regimes . . . the North American colossus is now widely regarded as a colonial power whose verbal championship of freedom, democracy and social reform cannot be taken any more seriously than that of the Soviet Union.[43]

Another reaction to the decomposition of communism—not incompatible with the others noted above—has been to try to ignore it altogether and persist in familiar preoccupations such as boycotting Salvadoran coffee beans, divestment in South Africa, or advocating "multicultural" studies in colleges. It has also been popular to burrow deeper into academic Marxism, concentrate on more esoteric critiques of American society and capitalism and devise new ways for their delegitimation. For example at a conference on matters literary at the University of Utah in 1990 topics included "the erotic politics of the female body," "postmodern terrorism," post-colonial body politics, "postmodern feminism and Madonna." Those who "once occupied buildings and marched on Washington . . . these days are more apt to use the arcane and specialized language of literary criticism to expose . . . the evils of 'late' capitalism." At the same conference, in a rare reference to Eastern Europe, a speaker warned that it "must fend off the capitalist threat."[44] Such attitudes reflect the unshaken conviction—still prevalent in the adversary culture—that no country or political system can surpass the corruption and injustice found in American society and history.

IV

As the unexpected electoral defeat of the Sandinistas (in February 1990) followed the rejection of communism in Eastern Europe disaffected American social critics had their hands full seeking to explain these matters in an emotionally satisfying and ideologically acceptable manner. Evidence of the unpopularity of the communist authorities in Nicaragua expressed in their electoral defeat was particularly painful as this system was designated as the last remaining (or first emerging?) authentic socialist country by the critics of capitalism and the United States.[45] Here was a system, they insisted, that was free of the errors made in Eastern Europe and one which supposedly sought to distance itself from the Soviet model and its bureaucratic shortcomings and was enjoying the ardent support of the masses. For these supporters (as for most media experts) electoral defeat was unthinkable.

Insofar as communist Nicaragua was closer to the hearts of the adversary culture than any country in Eastern Europe, more explaining had to be done and the more important it was to hold the United States responsible for the discouraging developments.

An article in *The Nation* published shortly before the election noted that "the Sandinistas have no credible opposition," and that "As the campaign moved . . . into 1990 it became increasingly obvious that they couldn't lose." The only question left to ponder was "How the

Bush Administration will greet a Sandinista victory."[46] Another *Nation* correspondent wrote: "Daniel Ortega will be re-elected . . . and his ruling Sandinista National Liberation Front is likely to win a majority . . . That's not left-wing wishful thinking . . . the political opposition . . . is morally and ideologically corrupt . . . [it] does not offer credible alternative to the FSLN."[47] A "Quaker and journalist" attacked *The New Republic* for allowing itself criticism of the Nicaraguan regime and for entertaining the possibility of its electoral defeat. He wrote:

> Your thinking that anybody but Daniel Ortega will win . . . is like believing that Americans would have voted for a British candidate for the American presidency after George Washington . . . had won the American revolution. Everywhere in Nicaragua . . . you will see signs, "They shall not pass!". "There will be no surrender!"[48]

A bitter *Nation* editorial formulated what became the main theme of the efforts to delegitimate the result of the election and hold the United States responsible for the outcome:

> The defeat of Ortega by Violeta . . . Chamorro shows that the imperial monarchs of Washington still have more weapons at their disposal . . . than we . . . had suspected. . . . A few Nicaraguans will again enjoy the freedom of the shopping mall. . . . Nicaraguan voters have done what they have been bludgeoned, starved, and blockaded into doing.[49]

The defeat of the Sandinistas was thus explained by a combination of immense American pressures and sometimes by the false consciousness of the masses who preferred the promise of American largesse to the austere purity of the revolution. It was also popular among the American supporters to suggest that the preferences expressed in the elections were irrelevant to the true feelings of the electorate. An observer of the elections, sympathetic toward the Sandinistas, said: "They voted with their pocketbooks . . . but their hearts are still with the revolution . . . [the results] should not be mistaken as a vote against the Sandinistas or the goals of the revolution."[50] Likewise among the "internacionalistas"—Americans and other Westerners living in Nicaragua—it was an article of faith that "despite the results of the . . . vote, the Sandinistas and not Mrs. Chamorro represent the Nicaraguan people."[51] This conclusion was presumably based either on the belief that the people did not vote their true convictions but compromised or acquiesced (in the hope of ending the civil war and improving their standard of living), or on a view that the Sandinistas represent the people in some deeper, more essential way that transcends the prosaic and crude measurements of public opinion elections provide.

Of all the interpretations of the election results only one was rigorously excluded: that the leftist rulers were voted out of office (on the first occasion when this was possible, and despite their virtual monopoly on the mass media and other means of electioneering) because the voters rejected both their performance and their rhetoric.

V

Why has the adversary culture been so determined to avert its eyes from the meaning of the events of 1989 and 1990? Why the convoluted rationalizations and evasions, the reluctance or outright refusal to confront the moral, intellectual, or political lessons involved?

The contrast between the reactions that followed the collapse of an earlier "evil empire," that of the Nazis, and those that accompanied the recent disintegration of the Soviet empire adds a historical dimension to the puzzle. Peregrine Worsthorne, an English author addressed this question:

> After the collapse of Hitler's Third Reich everybody who had ever said or written a good word about . . . Nazism, suffered unrelenting obloquy. . . . Nor was it only people whose reputations were destroyed. A whole range of previously respectable *ideas* was also so tainted . . . as not to be mentioned in polite society— race, nation, authority, obedience. Thus was the slate cleared of anything remotely smacking of right-wing ideology. . . . But having done such an exemplary job in anathematising right-wing thinking after the fall of the evil Hitler empire, why is not civilised opinion doing a similar intellectual cleansing job on left-wing thinking after the fall of the evil communist empire? The contrast in reactions is truly remarkable. All the old Marxist gurus are still in their academic chairs . . . with the young encouraged to sit at their feet. . . . Nobody seems to think worse of famous people who until recently were on excellent terms with the East European communist tyrants, or who thought that communism was the hope of mankind.[52]

It may be added that despite all the revelations of the past half century and the number of victims exceeding those of Hitler, Stalin's holocaust never attracted the same moral attention as Hitler's and never inspired the same revulsion and condemnation in the West. There have been several reasons for this including the uniqueness of the Nazi methods of extermination, the lack of photographic documentation of the Soviet camps, the lingering sympathy for the "Soviet experiment" and the Western efforts to coexist peacefully and without recrimination.

As far as the adversary culture is concerned the simplest explanation of its unwillingness of confront the significance of the recent developments is that they provided definitive proof of the illegitimacy, unpopularity, and inefficiency of communist systems and thereby fully vindicated the anticommunist outlook the adversary culture has been at pains to discredit and ridicule for over a quarter century.

Further explanations of the attitidues documented in this article may be suggested. Deeply held beliefs provide direction and meaning to the lives of people. This is especially the case when these beliefs are shared, in both private and public, in more or less cohesive groups or subcultures. It is always disagreeable or outright painful to radically revise or abandon such beliefs and the incentives to do so, especially when they are widely held, are minimal. Such abandonment results both in inner conflict and ostracism by the group and the loss of communal bonds. This applies as much to political as to religious beliefs which make life meaningful in more obvious and explicit ways. An English writer recently compared these processes of revising political beliefs (and the resistance to doing so) to the "anguished writhings of those whose intellectual belief in traditional revealed religion was shaken, but who could not shed its thrall emotionally."[53] American universities are full of people beholden to such emotional ties to a theory, a worldview, and attendant self-conception resting on such political-theoretical commitments. Marxian socialism has been virtually the only comprehensive and intellectually respectable belief system available in contemporary Western societies outside conventional religion. While interest in the specifics of Marxism declined, its ethical and quasi-religious appeals have persisted. Correspondingly, socialism came to be treated as a set of ideas and attitudes, adoption of which placed the individual on the side of justice, decency, compassion, and high moral values. Marxism in particular appealed, and continues to appeal, to intellectuals (or quasi-intellectuals) as it combines an apparent social scientific rigor with moral passion. In Leszek Kolakowski's classic formulation

Marxism has been the greatest fantasy of our century . . . a dream offering the prospect of a society of perfect unity, in which all human aspirations would be fulfilled and all values reconciled. . . . The influence that Marxism has achieved, far from being the result or proof of its scientific character, is almost entirely due to its prophetic, fantastic, and irrational elements. . . . Almost all the prophecies of Marx and his followers have already proved false, but this does not disburb the spiritual certainty of the faithful.[54]

It is precisely this spiritual certainty, or some semblance of it, that the adversarial community—as other believers at other times—seeks to preserve. It is a natural and basic human tendency to hold on to such political-emotional investments as long as possible. The adversarial beliefs gained strength and durability from becoming sources of self-esteem for those for whom the role of the righteous social critic, bearing witness to the injustices of his society, has become an integral part of personal identity. This sense of righteousness and the capacity for moral indignation—however selectively standardized and stereotyped it has become—are hallmarks of a mindset that needed some practical or theoretical alternative to the hopeless corruption of his own society. When the actual alternatives failed, at least the theoretical ones had to be salvaged—some version of Marxism and the possibility of its eventual realization. The new evidence of the failures of existing socialist systems could be brushed aside as no more than an irritating diversion from the truly important task of denouncing capitalism and Western culture.

The current lack of soul-searching in the adversary culture—that contrasts with the intense self-scrutiny and self-criticism of many former partisans of the Soviet Union in the 1940s and 1950s—may be further understood by the differences between the social basis and impact of the old and new leftism. The old, procommunist, pro-Soviet left even in its heyday (which did not last long) was far more isolated and limited in its cultural reach and social-political influence than the adversary culture which emerged from the New Left of the 1960s. The political-cultural disaffection of the 1960s that persisted throughout the 1980s, has been far more massive and durable and involved large portions of our intelligentsia and the educated middle classes and their children. Most of the activists of the sixties have never been in the mood to engage in serious self-criticism, to rethink their values, politics, ideals.[55] They resisted such temptation (if there was any), because they sought to be faithful to the values of their youth, (a matter of apolitical nostalgia), and subscribed to the myth of the sixties as one of the most idealistic and noble period history has ever known. But more importantly there was strength in numbers. The adversarial values of the sixties were upheld, to different degrees, by hundreds of thousands, if not millions of people. They provided assurance, mutual support, and a certain generational solidarity especially when their adherents congregated in relatively cohesive academic settings and adjacent enclaves. The adversarial beliefs of the 1960s—including anti-anticommunism—were preserved because its upholders were not isolated, because large numbers of people adopted them, many of them subsequently entering elite positions in academia, the media, and the churches thereby adding new authority to these beliefs.

While it is hardly a new discovery that personal needs influence political attitudes, the responses of the adversary culture to the crisis of communism provide a new wealth of information about these connections and the intellectual and psychological resources which are mobilized to prevent or minimize injury to a cherished worldview. Thus even as societies undergo long overdue transformation, such changes are met by defensive interpretation to fend off threat to deeply held values which have given a certain meaning to life.

Notes

1. While this is not the place to address at any length this enormous topic it may be noted at least that the gap between theory and practice in these systems was far from total and that some key ideas of Marx were actually realized although not the benefits they were supposed to yield. Thus the means of production were nationalized and private enterprise terminated; central planning was introduced; massive attempts were made to rid people of their religious beliefs; these systems were also profoundly contemptuous of peasants and their hunger for land. Finally, the streak of personal intolerance characteristic of Marx also found expression in widely institutionalized political intolerance.
2. The concept of "adversary culture" is discussed in some detail in this author's

The Survival of the Adversary Culture, New Brunswick: Transaction, 1988. I use the term to refer to taken for granted (hence cultural) beliefs and attitudes, (and their organizational-institutional expressions), centered on a reflexive hostility toward the dominant social, political, and economic institutions of the United States, Western culture, and a virulent anti-capitalism; these attitudes have also been associated with what used to be called "the New Left," "The Movement," and the spirit of the 1960s.

3. By quasi-intellectual I mean something similar to Lipset's "camp follower" (see below); people with some higher education who share the social-critical impulse of intellectuals without their creativity or originality and full-time preoccupation with ideas.

4. Seymour Martin Lipset. "The Death of the Third Way—Everywhere But Here, That Is." *National Interest*, Summer, 1990, p. 36.

5. Owen Harries. "Credit Ratings." *Ibid.*, p. 112.

6. Peregrine Worsthorne, "Why no shame on the left?" *Sunday Telegraph* 24 December 1989.

7. For a review of this type of revisionism see Peter Kenez, "Stalinism as Humdrum Politics." *Russian Review*, October, 1986.

8. Tom Wicker, "Bush and the New Moralism About China," *New York Times*, 15 December 1989.

9. Kenneth Minogue, "Societies Collapse, Faiths Linger On." *Encounter*, March, 1990, p. 4.

10. Lonn Johnston, "Leftists Scoff at 'Bourgeois' Itinerary." *San Francisco Chronical.* 2 June 1990, p. A8.

11. Paul M. Sweezy, "Is This Then The End of Socialism?" *Nation*, 26 February 1990, p. 278.

12. *Newsletter*, United Methodist News Service, 13 November 1989, p. 3.

13. Alan Wisdom, "The General Assembly: Moving Toward Moderation?" *Mainstream*, Newsletter of Presbyterians for Democracy and Religious Freedom, Summer, 1990, p. 214.

14. Harriet E. Gross, "Don't Count Communism Out Yet." *New York Times*, correspondence, 7 January 1990.

15. Todd Gitlin, "After the European Revolutions—A Jump-Start to History?" *Tikkun*, March–April 1990, p. 28.

16. Jeff Riggenbach, "Dropouts are right; system doesn't work." *USA Today*, 4 July 1990.

17. Jackie Mason, "America, Land of the Unfree," *New York Times*, op-ed, 23 March 1990.

18. Lucinda Rector, "Some Walls, Like Mine, Don't Fall," *New York Times*, op-ed, 1 December 1989.

19. George Will, "Liberals can't deal with new East Bloc," *Daily Hampshire Gazette*, 11 December 1989.

20. Tom Wicker, "Freedom For What?" *New York Times*, 5 January 1990.

21. Tom Wicker, "The New 'Sooners,'" *New York Times*, 2 January 1990.

22. "Notes and Comment," *New Yorker*, 5 February 1990.

23. Saul Landau, "Imperialism, Bush-Style," *New York Times*, op-ed, 22 December 1989.

24. William H. Honan, "Endowment Embattled Over Academic Freedon," *New York Times*, 17 December 1989.

25. Donatella Lorch, "A Controversial Mural Is Damaged With Paint," *New York Times*, 23 December 1989.
26. Anthony Lewis, "But We Close Our Eyes," *New York Times*, 20 February 1990.
27. Eugene Rochberg-Halton, "Cold War's Victims Deserve a Memorial," *New York Times*, op-ed, 10 March 1990.
28. Daniel Singer, "Europe In The Post-Yalta Era," *Nation*, 11 December 1989, p. 720.
29. Daniel Singer, "Revolutionary Nostalgia," *Nation*, 20 November 1989, p. 600.
30. Donald Baer, "Leftists in the Wilderness," *U.S. News* and *World Report*, 19 March 1990, p. 27.
31. Irving Howe, "Notes From The Left," *Dissent*, Summer 1990, p. 301.
32. Michael Walzer, "A Credo For This Moment," *Dissent*, Spring 1990, p. 160.
33. Sheldon Wolin, "Beyond Marxism And Monetarism," *Nation*, 19 March 1990, p. 373.
34. "Borderline Marxists," *Nation*, 2 October 1989, p. 333.
35. Robet Grabar, "Marxists in area predict better time for socialism," *Daily Hampshire Gazette*, 8 February 1989, p. 11.
36. Norman Birnbaum, "Hope's End or Hope's Beginning? 1968—And After," *Salmaqundi*, Winter 1989, p. 150, 152.
37. George Watson, "Memoir—The Return of the Sage," *Encounter*, January-February 1990, p. 54.
38. Associated Press, "Germans Let Marx Wither," *New York Times*, 25 April 1990; Brenda Fowler. "New Courses and Even Votes At Czechoslovak Universities." *New York Times*, 31 March 1990.
39. Tom Kuntz, "In Highgate Cemetery, Marx is Safe on a Pedestal," *New York Times*, 14 March 1990.
40. Doug Ireland, "Perestroika, USA—Can It Happen Here?" *Village Voice*, 19 December 1989, p. 22.
41. Ibid.
42. Ellen Willis, "To Emma With Love," *Village Voice*, 19 December 1989, p. 32.
43. Christopher Lasch, "The Costs of Our Cold War Victory," *New York Times*, op-ed, 13 July 1989; for a rejoinder see A.M. Rosenthal, "Warning to Lamenters." *New York Times*, op-ed, 15 July 1990.
44. Richard Bernstein, "Academic Left Finds the Far Reaches of Post-modernism," *New York Times*, 8 April 1990.
45. Paul Hollander, 1988, op. cit., pp. 233–265.
46. Larry Bensky, "Campaigning with the Sandinistas," *Nation*, 5 March 1990, pp. 302–05.
47. Tony Jenkins, "The Unmaking of Dona Violeta," *Nation*, 26 February 1990, p. 268.
48. Jerry Copeland, *New Republic*, correspondence, 26 March 1990.
49. "Spoils of War," *Nation* 19 March 1990, pp. 367–68.
50. Dylan Sanders, "Observers begrudgingly endorse sanctity of vote," *Daily Hampshire Gazette*, 6 March 1990, p. 9.
51. Larry Rohter, "Sandinistas' Foreign Legion Is Faithful in Defeat," *New York Times*, 13 March 1990.
52. Worsthorn, op. cit.
53. Geoffrey Wheatcroft, "Old Believers," *Encounter*, March 1990, p. 48.

54. Leszek Kolakowski, *Main Currents of Marxism*, vol. 3. New York: Oxford University Press, 1978, pp. 252–26.

55. For some exceptions see John H. Bunzel, ed., *Political Passages*, New York: Free Press 1988; and Peter Collier and David Horowitz, *Destructive Generation*, New York: Summit Books, 1989.

15

Sidney Hook: Critic of the Critics

I only knew Sidney for a relatively short period of time: since the beginning of this decade; I think it was in 1981 or 1982 that we first met. I was familiar with many of his writings since graduate school and admired him and his work well before I met him. In my ripe middle age he became something of a role model for me, let me just say model, or exemplar since I suspect he would have some reservations about the concept of role model, and the uses to which it has been put of late. Perhaps it would be more accurate to say that he became a kind of counter-model, the opposite or antithesis of everything I found unappealing in American intellectual and academic life.

He is certainly one of the most remarkable people I have known and one of the few who made a difference to their times. I feel fortunate for having known him even for a relatively short time, late in his life. I spoke to him over the phone for the last time about ten days before his operation early this summer and I did not think that it would be my last conversation with him.

Our acquaintance began by my writing to him about shared intellectual-political concerns and my drawing his attention to something I wrote that I thought might interest him. It did and he immediately responded in his characteristic and orderly handwriting. A visit to South Wardsboro followed and such visits became regular events each following summer, in fact high points of my summers. Anne's company and hospitality added to the enjoyment of these visits as did the beauty of the setting. For a nature lover, born in the city of Budapest and resident of Massachusetts for over a quarter century, this corner of Vermont, indeed much of the state, became and has remained a place of endless attraction. The association of the place and the person enhanced one another. I also appreciated the paradox of Sidney's rural incarnation as seasonal resident of the isolated cottage on the Vermont mountainside although he was in some ways the quintessential city person and New Yorker.

Besides these visits Sidney and I also kept in touch through correspondence, the phone, exchanging manuscripts, often sharing our dismay over the state of the world, and trends in this country or specific events.

Unhappy as he was sometimes with what was going on in the world and in this country, Sidney's belief in some basic human decency and rationality never deserted him. This was one of his qualities I found most amazing and inspiring. Unlike most intellectuals in our times he truly believed in reason and in the possibility that reasoned argument and information can change and improve people's minds and lives—an attitude many pay lip service to but few act upon. Somehow Sidney transcended the damage Marx and Freud have (unwittingly) inflicted on our beliefs in human rationality as well as the impact of historical events of this century which called into question such rationality.

Sidney also stood out among his fellow intellectuals by remaining untouched by the fads, fashions, trends, and pretenses which flowered so luxuriantly in contemporary intellectual settings, especially the academy. As far as I could tell he was totally and blissfully incapable of self-deception. And he also managed, astonishingly enough, to avoid becoming a cynic although his long life, knowledge, and experiences fully entitled him to become one. (I suppose very recent developments in the Soviet Union and parts of Eastern Europe offer some vindication of his basic optimism.)

Much as I admired his ideas and values there are certain personal qualities I would like to dwell on now, in these brief remarks. What I found most appealing and impressive about Sidney was his total and effortless unpretentiousness—again, a rare quality among intellectuals and especially among well-known and influential intellectuals, indeed among any group of people with an established reputation. He wrote and spoke and argued in a simple language; never was there any hint of pomposity and jargon, never any need to inflate himself by being obscure and convoluted. In his style and manner he sometimes reminded me of Harry Truman, I hope he would not mind the comparison. He too was simple, forceful, sometimes refreshingly abrasive and pugnacious, utterly unpretentious, possessed of a sense of humor, common sense and good sense. He managed somehow to uphold values insistently without being becoming self-righteous.

Much has been said in his lifetime and since his death about his courage and I cannot resist mentioning it either. Sidney was never afraid of taking unpopular stands and in the atmosphere of the 1960s, and in the ethos it left behind, this attitude could not be taken for granted. When most academics cowered, appeased, rationalized, or flattered, Sidney was among the handful who spoke his mind, confronting the waves of nonsense, fanaticism and intolerance that swept this country, the campuses, and the intellectual world; he took unpopular stands and did not bask in the rewards of the stereotyped and standardized social criticism which, over the last quarter century became the conventional wisdom in many intellectual and political circles, culminating in the reflexive rejection of this country, its social system and values. His outspokenness was truly exceptional and it earned him the animosity of people whose respect he would not have enjoyed in any event.

Let me say at last that he has been and will remain for me a source of optimism about human nature, about the possibility of being both a person preoccupied with complex ideas and problems and an accessible and unpretentious human being. His life offers a lesson in how to combine and unite the private and public roles in a simple, effortless, and authentic way.

He exemplified a solid and essential decency difficult to define but not difficult to recognize and appreciate. He showed that it is possible to make certain ideals central to one's life without becoming a fanatic, an ideologue, or dogmatist, a person who forgets real human beings in the course of his (alleged) devotion to the good of mankind. Particular human beings mattered to Sidney; he cared about his neighbors and his neighbors—in New York, Palo Alto, and South Wardsboro—cared about him.

16

New Antiwar Movement, Old Social Criticism

Several months before the war with Iraq began, a new peace or antiwar movement emerged and began energetically to organize in the fall of 1990. Its policies, slogans, and organizational core tell us a great deal about what has and what has not changed in this society during the past quarter century. It is of particular interest to compare the new peace movement to its predecessors, notably the Vietnam anti-war movement and the corresponding movements opposed to American intervention in Central America during the 1980s. This procedure is all the more appropriate since activists in the new peace movement are fond of comparing the current U.S. intervention in the Persian Gulf to the American involvement in the Vietnam war (which in turn was often compared to the American involvement in Central America). In fact, memories of the Vietnam war are the major legitimating themes of the current peace movement.

The war with Iraq (and its anticipation) produced two major peace movements. One is the Coalition to Stop U.S. Intervention in the Middle East and its spokesmen freely acknowledge its association with what is called the Marxist-Leninist Workers World Party. (The latter was described as "a group that distinguished itself by being the only Trotskyist splinter to whole-heartedly endorse the Soviet invasion of Hungary in 1956." It also supported the massacre of students in Tiananmen Square in 1989.[1] The Coalition refuses to criticize Saddam Hussein and his government and does not favor economic sanctions against Iraq either. The Administrative Committee of the Coalition includes Ramsey Clark; the National Association of Black

Lawyers; Blacks Vets for Social Justice; Ben Dupuy of the Committee Against Repression in Haiti; Adeed Abed of the Jerusalem Cultural Center; Saleh Fawaz of the Palestine Aid Society; Preston Wilcox, professor and Harlem community leader; Teresa Gutierrez of the Independent Commission of Panama; Dr. Elias Guerero of ACT-UP; Karen Gellen of *The Guardian*, among other groups and individuals.[2] As the presence of such groups and organizations suggests, the Coalition has a strong Third World focus. *A Guardian* editorial stated: "The anti-war movement must unite on the basis of respect and equality for Third World people. Our movement has to include anti-racism as a primary focus." The same editorial also warned:

> We must also guard against sectarianism and red-baiting. Marxist-Leninists are a legitimate part of our movement. No one should balk at working with an anti-war group because some of its leadership is Marxist-Leninist. We should recognize the important contributions that communists have played in peace and social justice movements.[3]

The January 19 march on the Coalition in Washington, D.C. was headlined in *The Guardian* as follows: "Stop Bush's War Now! Fight Racism and Poverty at home! Money for jobs, healthcare, housing, education and AIDS. . . . Bring the U.S. Troops Home!"[4]

The Coalition, as its constituent groups suggest, also has a strong pro-Palestinan and anti-Israeli thrust; according to one source, "their actual objectives are to get America out of the Middle East and to help set up a Palestinian state. Many of the protesters also have the attendant goal of crippling or destroying Israel."[5]

If the Coalition is the more radical of the two peace movements, how should we characterize the other one, The National Campaign for Peace in the Middle East?

An advertisement announcing its march and rally in San Francisco on January 26 was entitled: "No War in the Middle East! Bring the Troops Home Now! Money for Human Needs, Not War!"

The organizational and individual endorsements of the *Campaign* listed in the same advertisement included

> The American Friends Service Committee, Art Against Apartheid, Christic Institute, Church Women United, Clergy & Laity Concerned, Committee for a Democratic Palestine, Fellowship of Reconciliation, General Union of Palestinian Stu-

dents, Gray Panthers, Greenpeace, Lesbian/Gay Labor Alliance, Middle East Justice Network, National Alliance of Third World Journalists, National Lawyers Guild, National Organization of Women, National Pledge of Resistance, National Rainbow Coalition, National SANE/FREEZE, Nicaragua National Network, Riverside Church New York City, Socialist Party USA, Socialist Workers Party, Out Now, Palestine Aid, The Guardian, Women Strike for Peace, United Muslims of America, Young Communist League, Young Socialist Alliance, Vietnam Veterans Against the War, Eqbal Ahmed, Noam Chomsky, Alexander Cockburn, Barry Commoner, Ossie Davis, Daniel Ellsberg, Arthur Kinoy, William Kunstler, Jack O'Dell, Grace Paley, Toshi and Pete Seeger, Studs Terkel, Howard Zinn and over 400 additional local coalitions, national organizations and individuals.[6]

While the Campaign appeared to have a broader constituency, and was willing to criticize Saddam Hussein, its supporters included an impressive collection of groups, organizations, and individuals who have, over the past quarter century distinguished themselves by their relentless critiques of American society.

If we compare these organizations and their pronouncements with those opposed to U.S. participation in the Vietnam war it becomes clear that the concern with peace (now as at earlier times) is inseparable from a preoccupation with and condemnation of various flaws of American society not all of which are connected to issues of peace and war. It may be recalled that for the antiwar protester of yesteryear the American involvement in Vietnam was a symbol of everything that was wrong not merely with U.S. foreign policy but American society itself. Susan Sontag summed up that attitude remarking that "Vietnam offered the key to a systematic criticism of America." Many similar observations were made at the time.[7] The new antiwar or peace movement discussed below also has agendas which go beyond the issues of peace and war—its ostensible concern.

Before examining more closely the similarities between the anti-Iraqi war movement and its two predecessors there is another issue that needs to be addressed, namely the claim of the current peace movements that U.S. intervention in the Gulf closely resembles corresponding involvement in Vietnam with all its disastrous consequences.

Let me simply list the differences between the Vietnam war and the Gulf war.

1. Unlike in Vietnam, in the Persian Gulf there has been no semblance of a civil war, or guerilla war.
2. In the current conflict the U.S. is supported by the U.N. and by the

troops of other nations (in this regard as in some others, the current war is more reminiscent of Korea than Vietnam).

3. In Kuwait there was a clear-cut aggression with conventional troops moving across a national border (as in Korea) a fact not in dispute; (in Vietnam, Northern intervention was covert, as least until the last stages of the war).

4. Iraq, unlike the Vietcong guerillas, does not have a supportive neighboring country (equivalent of North Vietnam) where its troops can regroup, rest, seek refuge, get supplies from and so on.

5. Iraq—unlike North Vietnam and the Vietcong and in spite of the socialist designation of the Ba'ath party—does not claim socialist, or Marxist-Leninist credentials and does not enjoy the benefits and prestige which such claims confer—at least among many potential peace activists often found at the left of the political spectrum.

6. It is far more difficult to admire Saddam Hussein (and his system) and to perceive him as a benevolent, widely respected, altruistic leader than was the case with Ho Chi Minh (not that he necessarily merited the reverence lavished on him by Western sympathizers).

    Saddam Hussein stands out among contemporary Third World dictators as the head of a police state of totalitarian efficiency; he also accumulated huge quantities of conventional, chemical, and biological weapons and sought nuclear ones; used poison gas on civilian populations of both his own (Kurds) and the enemy (Iran). He also initiated war with Iran which lasted for eight years and cost at least a million lives; he developed a personality cult that compares favorably with the cults of Hitler, Stalin, Mao, Kim Il Sung, and Castro.

7. This is a war fought by a volunteer army on the part of the United States, not draftees.

8. The geography is vastly different making guerilla operations difficult and aerial bombardment more effective.

9. Unlike Vietnam, Iraq is isolated and does not receive military or other supplies due to the U.N. imposed blockade.

10. Also unlike Vietnam, Iraq does not enjoy the support of any major power (compare Soviet, Soviet bloc, and Chinese support of North Vietnam). What support Iraq has comes from a few terrorist groups and unorganized Arab masses in different parts of the Arab world and it is far from clear how strong or consequential this support is, or will remain, given the volatility of such mass movements.

There is one similarity between Iraq and what used to be North Vietnam and what became communist Vietnam: both are garrison states, highly militarized societies fielding huge armies even in peacetime.

Michael Walzer writing before the outbreak of the war summed up some of these differences and especially their moral aspects:

> The Vietnamese case was very different. . . . That was an unjust war. Here by contrast we would be fighting against the Iraqi state and its leader for the sake of another country's political survival. . . . From the standpoint of morality, it is hard to imagine a better cause or a more appropriate enemy. . . . To resist aggression on one's own behalf and to come to the aid of the victim of aggression: these are the classic just causes of warfare. . . . The aggressor, as Clausewitz wrote, is a man of peace; he wants nothing more than to march into a neighboring country unresisted. It is the victim and the victim's friends who must choose to fight . . . it is very bad to make a deal with an aggressor at the expense of the victim.[8]

If the actual conflicts have little in common the response to them on the part of the antiwar movements each stimulated has far more similarities, to which I will now turn.

None of these peace movements (inspired by either Vietnam, Central America, or the Gulf war) had (or have) a consistent pacifist orientation; that is to say, they were not, for the most part, opposed to the use of force under all conditions. Most of their activists and leaders had no difficulty to find occasions when the use of force was acceptable, as a "last resort," or when the party they supported "had no choice" in their opinion, when not turning to the means of violence meant acquiescing in "structural violence" or the "greater violence of the status quo," when violence was perceived as "liberating" and correcting deep-seated social injustices.[9]

Vietnam era war protestors had little to say about Vietcong or North Vietnamese atrocities. Protestors of U.S. involvement in Central America were not in the habit of chiding the Salvadorian communist guerillas for blowing up buses packed with civilians or executing civil servants; nor did they rebuke the Marxist leaders of Nicaragua for relying on political repression that, they were assured, was purely defensive. Not many peace activists could be spotted picketing the Soviet embassy in Washington while the Soviet Union slaughtered in a leisurely way over a million Afghan civilians. In general, the violence of Third World guerillas was given every benefit of doubt (unless they were anti-communist, as in Afghanistan, Nicaragua, Angola, and Mozambique). Peace activists did not become energized by the brutal and destructive war between Iraq and

Iran either. Most recently Ramsey Clark eloquently deplored the sufferings of civilians in Basra and elsewhere in Iraq caused by aerial
bombardment but displayed no moral indignation over the treatment
of the civilian population of Kuwait by the Iraqi army.

On the domestic front activists of the antiwar movement of the
Vietnam era could "understand" those protesting the injustices of
American society and U.S. foreign policy by occasionally blowing up
a few buildings or taking potshots at policemen; if they criticized
groups like the Weathermen or Black Panthers or Black Liberation
Army it was more for tactical than moral reasons. The ardent social
critics of the sixties and seventies (who also were antiwar activists)
rarely counselled patience and restraint to such groups.[10]

More recently peace activists had nothing to say about the use of
civilian hostages as human shields at military targets in Iraq, nor was
there any outpouring of moral outrage when the Iraqi government announced that it would make the same use of POWs. Nor did Iraq's
targeting of civilian areas in Israel and Saudi Arabia with Scud missiles inspire any discernible protest or indignation in the ranks of the
new peace movement.

It may be concluded that a key attribute the new peace movement
shares with its predecessors is an exclusive preoccupation with the
use of force by the United States or it allies.

Another striking similarity between the antiwar movements past
and present is to be found in the participants themselves: many of the
"activists" of the Vietnam era are once more in the front ranks of the
new peace movement, (as the partial listing provided earlier also
shows) exhilarated and energized by the new conflict and the fresh
opportunities it provides for generalized social protest. According to
Todd Gitlin, a sixties activist, "the antiwar effort reflects the number
of anti-Vietnam War campaigners who now hold positions of power
in mainstream institutions"[11]

It should also be noted here that since the end of the war in
Nicaragua there was no major issue, foreign or domestic, that could
mobilize widespread protest and political activism. The war with
Iraq, much as many of the antiwar protesters may regret its human
and economic costs, has provided a new and apparently welcome opportunity to renew many of the familiar critiques of American society

and U.S. foreign policy. This impression is supported by the excitement, the joyous eagerness and readiness with which the activists threw themselves into the new round of vigils, marches, rallies, protests, and picketing—attitudes suggesting that these activities are not altogether lacking in enjoyment. A survey found that of those participating in the 26 January 1991 Washington, D.C. rally, nine out of ten had previously attended a protest demonstration for some political or social issue.[12]

This is not to say that all prominent antiwar activists of the sixties support the new antiwar movement. Notable exceptions include Sam Brown, organizer of the 1969 Vietnam moratorium who rejected the parallels with Vietnam. "Every time I hear a parallel to Vietnam I blanch. I see the movement people gearing up, the same familiar faces and I want to say: 'Hold on, hold on.' It is a wholly different situation that needs to be analyzed on its own merits."[13] Paul Berman another former sixties activist and social critic also broke ranks with his former comrades in arms. He wrote: "The gist of the anti-Vietnam War argument looms up. There is the idea that the far away enemy, creepy though this time, would pose no threat to us if only we gave him time to ponder or left him alone. And there is the idea that America is itself a trouble-making country and can wreak nothing but harm."[14]

The social composition of the two (or three) antiwar movements compared here also appears similar: intellectuals, quasi-intellectuals, people residing in academic settings or enclaves, former anti-nuclear activists, social studies teachers, social workers, feminists, AIDS activists—all those who feel dissatisfied with life in this country on the most varied grounds and are in the habit of protesting in a more or less permanent state of moral indignation, convinced that a lot of things are wrong with this society *in addition* to waging war against Iraq—a conviction that permeated the antiwar movements of the sixties as well. On the other hand it seems that the age composition of the current peace movements is somewhat different and less youthful: the proportion of the middle aged appears higher at the present time than was the case in the 1960s and early 1970s. According to one report, 58 percent of the marchers were thirty-one or older in Washington, D.C. on January 26.[15] The survey of the Washington marchers also showed that 81 percent described themselves as liberal (half of those "very liberal").

Not only do the peace movements discussed here resemble one another in their readiness to champion causes other than peace, specific targets of their criticism are also highly similar. Above all these movements are linked by the axiomatic belief that the U.S. is incapable of conducting a just war, that whatever cause or side it supports, is, almost by definition, the wrong one.

In the words of a *Nation* editorial, the U.S. government is, "the party of death," "thirst[ing] for conquest."[16] It is also widely asserted that cheap oil is the major reason for the war, (as in the slogan "no blood for oil"), or the profit of multinational corporations, the benefit of the military-industrial complex, the recklessness of the ruling elites, (or George Bush's fear of being perceived as a wimp); or the lack of a decent environmental and energy policy. Many activists believe that the war erupted because ours is an aggressive, trigger-happy culture.

The attributes of the adversary are rarely mentioned and citing them is usually dismissed as "self-righteous" fingerpointing at "totalitarian aspects" which in no way justify "a policy of madness built on the arrogance of power" (in the words of a professor of humanities)[17]—reproaches which echo almost verbatim those of the 1960s.

Samuel Bowles an academic social critic whose political credentials also go back to the sixties found the war with Iraq not only the latest confirmation of the incorrigibly imperialist character of the U.S. but also an occasion for developing a new doomsday scenario:

In the years following the Gulf War, will the U.S. government come to treat the rest of the world as just so many Grenadas and Panamas? Will it be America's world for the taking? And should this reassertion of U.S. supremacy come to pass what will it do . . . to us? First, an attempt to reassert U.S. military power on a global scale seems inevitable: too many powerful groups in the U.S.—the Pentagon, weapons contractors, conservative politicians in both parties—will benefit . . . in the short run, even if it proves disastrous for most of us in the long run. . . . Second, the costs of policing the world—whether it be in interest of cheap oil or high oil company profits, or to promote the ideology of free enterprise—will place a crushing burden on the U.S. economy.

He foresaw a world "which your tax dollars will make safe for IBM, Exxon and GM" but one which will see "the U.S. economy crumble," American society stamped by "growing economic inequality and declining educational opportunity . . . [and] escalating social tension," where only the security industry will flourish: "the ranks of private and public sector guards, police, prison wardens, makers of security devices and handguns will burgeon." He concluded (one may suspect not without some satisfaction) that "The economic signs on the roadway to renewed U.S. imperialism point to disaster" and "Americans will have a hard time accepting the tightening circle of economic decline and environmental decay which continued military muscle flexing will require."[18]

Another apocalyptic scenario was entertained in a *Nation* editorial:

> For two decades a kind of domestic cold war, brutal but not usually bloody, has been waged by the powers that be against those new powers that would be. . . . The corporate campaign against unions and workers gathered steam and success. While politicians' efforts to limit the assimilation of blacks into mainstream economic structures have redoubled in the Reagan-Bush years. Repression of liberated sexual culture is in full swing. . . . The left is floundering, weak and isolated. The hot war must now be seen as an extension of the cold version, a battle to suppress and reverse consciousness as well as a campaign to eliminate challenges to the most powerful sectors of society.[19]

Michael Klare, formerly of the Institute of Policy Studies and currently on the faculty of Hampshire College in Amherst, Massachusetts, sketched another cheerless prospect with grim relish:

> To pay for these overseas adventures, American citizens can expect diminished medical care, reduced food assistance and a deteriorating housing supply. Many Americans will resist these new demands and deprivations. Protests will abound—and thus the other major consequence of Pax Americana II: increased repression, jingoism, intolerance at home . . . draft evaders and tax resisters will be hunted down. . . . We will become a garrison society, like the one George Orwell envisioned in 1984.[20]

As some of these predictions suggest, the war in the Gulf tapped the rich reservoir of apocalyptic thinking which in the 1960s and early 1970s gleefully anticipated imminent fascist-style repression, a veritable police state.

The opposition to the war with Iraq also reflects a form of isolationism based on the conviction that a deeply flawed social system such as ours must not be allowed to influence others, especially through force, that this world would be a far better place if the U.S. exercised as little influence as possible. The current critics of the war, like their predecessors, also repeat ceaselessly that nothing but the unresolved domestic problems can threaten American society.

An observation I made some years ago about the Vietnam antiwar movement applies to the current peace movement, or large sections of it:

> The moral indignation unleashed by the war tapped deeper reservoirs of discontent and hostility toward the established institutions and dominant values of American society . . . there was more to the antiwar protest than revulsion against the use of napalm or the relocation of peasants into "strategic hamlets." The major objection to the war coincided with deeply felt objections to the nature of American society and the attendant protest against the assertion of its political will and military power.[21]

Colman McCarthy's comments in *The Washington Post* (written before the war with Iraq began) are characteristic of the mindset I am trying to describe not the least in its unstated premise that a conflict involving the U.S. and another country has nothing whatsoever to do with the other country but is a matter rooted entirely and exclusively in American attitudes and policies and pathologies:

> [American] college students have been conditioned to quick-fix violence. There is a problem in Grenada? Bomb it. . . . in Libya? Bomb it. In Panama? Bomb it. In the persian Gulf? Get the bombs ready. . . . Organizers of campus antiwar protests . . . can begin to wake up their individual campuses by reminding their schoolmates that opposition to U.S. militarism first means opposition to what the nukes, bombs, armies are protecting—"vital interests" which means vital excesses.[22]

At the present time, as in the sixties and eighties on the corresponding occasions, the grounds for U.S. involvement provided by the government are reflexively dismissed by the peace activists; just as there was no merit in fighting a totalitarian movement and government in Indochina, there is no merit in fighting a noncommunist totalitarian dictator who has been both a threat to his own people and neighbors and commands impressive and lethal military resources including chemical and biological weapons.

Then as now those supporting the war, including members of the military forces, are seen by peace activists as suffering from false consciousness or mindless patriotism. My local paper quoted an antiwar activist as saying: "I believe we are in the minority. . . . But I think the majority is not well informed."[23] Another account of a peace demonstration quoted a counter demonstrator who said: "They (the peace protestors) were screaming at us. . . . They called us uneducated warmongers."[24]

Today as in the past the peace movement has a paradoxical interest in the conflict becoming more bloody as reflected in the endless, almost obligatory references to the body bags in which dead soldiers are shipped home: " 'At this point we are a minority because casualties haven't started to build up' said Margaret Hummel, a 50 year old community organizer from Underhill, Vt. 'I think this will all change when we start bringing them home in human pouch containers."[25] The conclusion is inescapable: if the peace movement is to become more influential and widely supported it needs vindication in the form of many more body bags coming home. It is difficult to arouse intense moral indignation over the aerial bombardment and destruction of missiles, nuclear reactors, chemical and biological weapons factories, or even by the bombardment of the Iraqi Republican Guards (elite troops comparable to the Waffen SS). So the peace movement in order to flourish and capitalize on moral indignation needs a war that exacts a high human cost especially in American lives.

It will require less space to comment on the *differences* between the anti-Gulf war movement and its predecessors. The major difference is that Iraq, its leader, and political system are more difficult to admire and idealize than was the case with the Vietcong, the North Vietnamese, the Nicaraguan communists, or the guerillas in El Salvador. Iraq cannot benefit from the alleged socialist credentials of other countries which impressed many peace activists in the past. It is my impression that people in recent protest demonstrations have not marched with Iraqi flags or portraits of Saddam Hussein, unlike the

60s when they marched with Vietcong flags, chants, and Ho Chi Minh portraits. Furthermore, as distinct from the case of Nicaragua, visited by perhaps a quarter million American sympathizers during the 1980s, few American "idealists" and social critics (Ramsey Clark and Jessie Jackson excepted) have shown interest in visiting Iraq although this may change should Iraq offer especially attractive samplings of alleged American brutalities and succeed in appearing as another virtuous victim or Third World underdog in the eyes of the protesters.

The difficulty of projecting upon Iraq various appealing qualities makes the task of the current peace movement harder. It is always easier emotionally, psychologically, to demonize one side (the U.S.) if the other one can be held up and contrasted as the embodiment of virtue, or progress, or social justice. The old maxim, "my enemy's enemy is my friend" is more difficult to apply in this conflict. (Although I have seen an article on Saddam Hussein in the Third World section of the student newspaper on my campus, depicting him as a great anti-imperialist fighter and liberator of the Arab masses. We may also recall that he made an excellent impression on a visiting U.S. congressional delegation last year.)

I may be underestimating human ingenuity and resourcefulness; there may yet be a positive redefinition of Saddam Hussein and his system as progressive and humane, its excesses understandable in the light of the historical circumstances and the colonial legacy, and the intrigues of the West and especially the United States. (This line of argument however may not be easy to pursue since prior to his occupation of Kuwait virtually all major Western countries traded with him and helped him to create his huge military machine. Nor is the oil wealth of Iraq a typical attribute of an underdog country.) Perhaps the newly popular doctrine of cultural diversity could be employed to rehabilitate Saddam Hussein: for example, it may be argued that if he has a predilection for changing members of his cabinet or high command by having them shot, (or worse) this may simply be a particular, culturally sanctioned approach to conflict resolution, or a non-Western way to improve administrative effiency, or handle political competition in a culture we do not understand and must not approach in a judgmental, ethnocentric spirit and seek to impose upon it our Western values.

I also predict that the moral equivalence thesis (which was used to deny any moral superiority to the U.S. when compared to the Soviet Union) will find application in comparisons of American and Iraqi misdeeds. After all, how can we to make high-minded pronouncements about Iraqi domestic affairs given the number of homeless in our country, or the persistence of racism, sexism, or homophobia, or insufficient funds for AIDS research? And those critical of Saddam Hussein for his methods of dealing with his critics had better remember McCarthyism and the Hollywood Purges. As to the Iraq's deliberate pollution of the entire Gulf with oil, let us remember the Exxon Valdez and above all, our greed for oil, which is the root cause of all these problems . . .

Another difference between the current and past peace/protest movements is that in the current conflict a "pathological" or "obsessive" anticommunism on the part of the U.S. cannot be used as the explanation of American involvement (as was the case in Vietnam and Central America) since the Iraqi regime is not communist or Marxist-Leninist (although it seems to share with such systems techniques of political control and social mobilization, propaganda, indoctrination, and intimidation).

It is too early to predict the impact of the new peace movement which will depend far more on the nature of the war than on the nature of the movement. Even if there seem to be similarities between this movement and its predecessors, history does not repeat itself completely; the Gulf war is not like the Vietnam war and the conflicts in Central America. I doubt that the new peace movement will have an impact similar to its predecessors because it operates in a different domestic social-political context and global environment. That times have changed may also be illustrated by the juxtaposition of the converging views of two authors we would not expect to share important beliefs.

Michael Walzer already quoted observed:

War as a "last resort" is an endlessly receding possibility, invoked mostly by people who would prefer never to resist aggression with force. . . . Values like a country's independence or the defeat of aggression cannot be expressed mathematically. They will always lose out to the body count, though there are times when, if we are to preserve any decency at all, we must be prepared to count (and discount) human bodies.[26]

And Norman Podhoretz, also before the outbreak of the war wrote,

Once upon a time, before the end of the cold war, we were told that we must not use force because it might escalate into nuclear holocaust. Now we are being told by the new peace party, with its constant harping on "body bags" that we must not use force because someone might get hurt. If this attitude should prevail, the U.S. would have proved itself unwilling to undertake military action even when the reasons for doing so were politically and morally compelling. . . . Among the . . . questions to be answered by the Persian Gulf crisis, then, is whether anything really has changed since Vietnam, or whether our defeat in that war has left us . . . forever unmanned by the idea (which Nietzche saw the mark of a slave) that nothing is worth fighting and dying for.[27]

Few would dispute that most peace activists, today as at other times, believe that nothing is worth fighting for, at any rate not for Americans living under the current system of government, in their wasteful, corrupt, and unjust society. At the same time it is also clear that most Americans do not subscribe to this belief, and that despite everything that happened in the last few decades, most Americans believe that there are things worth fighting for and risking one's lives for. It is something of a mystery how such archaic beliefs survived in a modern, secular, consumer, and individualistic society with an influential adversary culture—beliefs no less puzzling (under these circumstances) than the convictions of those who cannot bring themselves to grant that this country can engage in a just war.

Notes

1. David Horowitz. "The 'Peace' Movement." *A Second Thoughts Paper* presented at a conference organized by the Standing Committee of the American Bar Association on Law and National Security in Washington, D.C. on January 31, 1991; Jacob Weisberg: "Means of Dissent," *New Republic* February 25, 1991.
2. *Guardian*, 12 December, 1990.
3. *Guardian*, 21 November, 1990.
4. *Guardian*, 12 December, 1990.
5. Max Friedman. "Who's Who Anti-War," *Forward*, October 26, 1990.
6. *Guardian*, 23 January, 1991.
7. "The Antiwar Movement and the Critiques of American Society." In Paul Hollander: *The Survival of the Adversary Culture*, New Brunswick: Transaction 1988.

8. Michael Walzer, "Perplexed." *New Republic*, 28 January, 1991, p. 13.

9. Guenter Lewy thoroughly chronicled and documented these attitudes in *Peace & Revolution: The Moral Crisis of American Pacifism*, Grand Rapids: Erdman, 1988.

10. Daniel Berrigan, the famous and fiery social critic and Vietnam era antiwar protester exemplified these attitudes as he excelled in justifying the type of violence he approved of. See for example William van Etten Casey and Philip Nobile eds.: *The Berrigans*, New York: Avon, 1971, p. 211; also Daniel Berrigan and Robert Coles: *The Geography of Faith: Conversations Between Daniel Berrigan and Robert Coles*, New York: Bantam, 1972, p. 76, 84. Blase Bonpane (also a priest) is another author who offered passionate justification for the violence he believed to be necessary for attaining social justice. Like other individuals of similar conviction he could rationalize almost any act of violence by comparing it to the always greater violence and injustice the United States was supposed to be guilty of. For example: " . . . every precaution is necessary to avoid innocent victims. But many 'terrorist' acts must be seen as acts of war, and we have to be ready to compare what the terrorists have done with what our government has done." Blase Bonpane: *Guerillas of Peace: Liberation Theology and the Central American Revolution*, Boston: South End Press, 1985, p. 114.

11. Michael deCourcy Hinds. "Drawing in Vietnam Legacy, Antiwar Effort Buds Quickly," *New York Times*, 11 January, 1991.

12. Richard Morin. "Marchers in DC Liberal, Educated, Survey Finds." *Washington Post*, 27 January, 1991; see also Daniel Wattenberg, "Making Noise, Not War," *Insight*, 11 February, 1991.

13. Jane Gross. "The Vietnam Generation Surrenders Its Certainty." *New York Times*, 15 January, 1991.

14. Paul Berman. "Protesters Are Fighting the Last War." *New York Times*, op-ed, 31 January, 1991.

15. Morin, op cit.

16. "Choose Peace" [editorial], *Nation*, 24 December, 1990, p. 1.

17. Francis Shor. Letter, *New York Times*, 20 January, 1991.

18. Samuel Bowles. "U.S. Imperialism Triumphant? Domestic Economic and Social Consequences." Text of address at teach-in, University of Massachusetts at Amherst, 28 January, 1991.

19. "The War State" [editorial], *Nation*, 11 February, 1991, p. 148.

20. Michael T. Klare, "Pax Americana II," *Nation*, 11 February, 1991, p. 149.

21. See Hollander, op cit. p. 118.

22. Colman McCarthy, "Campus Cries for Global Peace," *Washington Post*, 25 November, 1990.

23. Brenda Elias. "Valley People at DC Rally," *Daily Hampshire Gazette*, 28 January, 1991.

24. Bruce Watson and Phyllis Lehrer. "Protests and support as fighting starts up," *Amherst Bulletin*, 23 January, 1991.

25. Peter Applebome. "Day of Protest Is the Biggest Yet." *New York Times*, 27 January, 1991; see also Weisberg, op cit., p. 20.

26. Walzer, op cit., p. 14.

27. Norman Podhoretz, "Enter the Peace Party," *Commentary*, January 1991, p. 21.

Epilogue
Intellectuals in The East and West

The controversies sparked by Paul Johnson's recent book, *Intellectuals*, are among the indications that the essential attributes and proper public roles of intellectuals remain in dispute. Intriguing questions are still unsettled regarding the manner in which intellectuals integrate, or fail to, their private lives and preoccupations with their public roles and pursuits.

A comparison of intellectuals in the East and West may help to shed some light on these matters and illuminate the key characteristics of intellectuals as they appear in different incarnations in different parts of the world in which the private and public realm and their relationship to one another have also been defined in profoundly different ways.

There is no great mystery about the two concepts, East and West. The latter refers to the small number of stable, liberal, pluralistic, and capitalist societies and their political cultures (found mostly in Western Europe and North America); the East applies to those widely dispersed societies which until recently sought to legitimate themselves by some version of Marxism-Leninism, were dominated by a one-party system, and had a predominantly state-controlled economy.

It may be recalled that Johnson's book was highly critical of intellectuals. His "sample" consisted largely of famous Western intellectuals no longer with us—Rousseau, Shelley, Marx, Ibsen, Tolstoy, Hemingway, Brecht, Bertrand Russell, Sartre, Edmund Wilson, Victor Gollancz, and Lillian Hellman—each given a chapter. A final

chapter included discussions of Orwell, Evelyn Waugh, Cyril Con-
nolly, Norman Mailer, Kenneth Tynan, Rainer Maria Fassbinder,
James Baldwin, and Noam Chomsky. No explanation was offered as
to why and how these particular figures were selected. As his choices
indicate, Johnson made no attempt to compare intellectuals living in
Western and non-Western societies and he offered no suggestions as
to how those two groups might differ from one another.

Johnson's criticism of intellectuals rests on several related propositions. He argued that intellectuals, such as those selected for his
book, are unattractive human beings as far as their personal relationships and qualities are concerned, that they rarely practice what they
preach, and that their ideals are unrealistic and prove destructive
whenever their realization is attempted. He also seemed to suggest
that intellectuals often seek to divert themselves from their personal
problems by preoccupation with social evils, that their social-critical
temper is a reflection, or projection of their troubled personalities.
The author made it quite clear that he regarded the figures chosen as
typical and used them to generalize freely about intellectuals.

It is tempting to dismiss Johnson's views both on the ground of his
peculiar sample and the familiarity of his basic idea, namely that
seemingly idealistic intellectuals, especially in their iconoclastic,
nonconformist mode, are a neurotic lot, lacking in common sense
and sound judgment, that they are either impractical dreamers or
dangerous fanatics.

Such well-worn stereotypes notwithstanding, it is a legitimate un-
dertaking—rarely attempted in a serious and systematic manner—to
examine how intellectuals handle the relationship between the private
and the public, the personal and the social spheres. It need not be a
form of dubious "psychologizing" to scrutinize the connections between the personality and the direction of intellectual effort and the
moral-political agenda promoted. Although there are many variations
in these relationships (that is, between the private and the public
sphere) that are not readily accessible to cursory observation, little is
gained by pretending that the two spheres do not interact and have no
significant impact on one another.

Johnson's book, while flawed in some ways, raises or leads to interesting questions about the intellectual as a social and personality
type, about the psychological underpinnings of the intellectual's so-

cial-cultural role, and more generally about the relationship between the personal and the social realm, the private and the public. It suggests some explanations as to who becomes an intellectual and why, or what kind of needs may be met by the role and attitudes associated with being an intellectual. Unfortunately Johnson did not reflect on the influence of the broader social setting, on the process of recruitment for the intellectual role, on how the social-political environment might encourage or discourage the development of attributes and attitudes considered to be central to being an intellectual. He did not ask whether or not intellectuals were, cross-culturally speaking, similar or not, in some essential respects. Instead, he seemed to take for granted that they all suffered from some fundamental deformation of the psyche. Whether or not this is the case, the setting in which they live and work has a great deal to do with how they act and the characteristics they display.

It is beyond dispute that the free exchange of ideas—characteristic of democratic or pluralistic society—is a precondition for a flourishing public intellectual life. It is worth pointing out once more (because it is sometimes overlooked, or perhaps taken for granted in the West) that intellectuals can partake of their distinctive activities only under an unusual combination of circumstances: there must be a critical mass, a sufficient number to generate a critical discourse; they need a tolerant political culture that guarantees free expression and some degree of institutional protection and autonomy; they must also be able to make a living compatible with some freedom from draining routines that allows time and energy for critical reflection and unorthodox thinking.

Not only the public activities but also certain shared personal characteristics of intellectuals can be linked to their social environment, including some that are not especially appealing and were singled out by Johnson. Paradoxically, these unattractive traits may be stimulated by living in free, open, rich, and pluralistic societies which ensure free inquiry and exchange of ideas but are incapable of providing people with a sense of meaning, purpose, or sustaining community. These societies generate anomie as Durkheim so persuasively proposed. His notions of mental health, in the broadest sense, may have relevance to the matters here discussed, especially the characteristic discontent and restlessness of intellectuals in the West.

Durkheim perceived modern individualistic Western societies as those in which

the standard according to which needs were regulated can no longer remain the same . . . the scale is upset . . . the social forces thus freed have not regained equilibrium. . . . The limits are unknown between the possible and the impossible, what is just and what is unjust, legitimate claims and hopes and those which are immoderate. Consequently there is no restraint on aspiration. . . . Appetites, not being controlled by public opinion become disoriented, no longer recognize the limits proper to them.[2]

Elsewhere he commented on behavior "in large part freed from the moderating action of regulation," on individuals who suffer from "the malady of infinite aspiration," societies in which "unregulated emotions are adjusted neither to one another nor to the conditions they are supposed to meet," where "appetites have become freed of any limiting authority," and people spend much of their lives "divorced from any moral influence."[3] As Steven Lukes summed it up "Durkheim saw human nature as essentially in need of limits and discipline" and human beings as possessed of "potentially limitless and insatiable desires." Durkheim held that "we must contract our horizon, choose a definite task and immerse ourselves in it completely, instead of trying to make ourselves a sort of creative masterpiece"[4]—an observation that unexpectedly echoes the satirical comments of Tom Wolfe on the narcissistic individualism sweeping American society since the 1960s.[5] Durkheim anticipated the kind of individualism that is today rampant in much of the West and foremost in American society and that has had a huge influence on intellectuals and their public behavior.

Durkheim's forebodings were well-founded concerning societies that impose little discipline and structure on personal lives and allow a wide lattitude of choice but provide few guiding values as to how these choices are to be made. These (Western) societies also make it easier for intellectuals to avoid abrasive but edifying contract with reality or certain kinds of realities, as they are usually spared any serious deprivation, political or economic. Moreover these wealthy, tolerant, and individualistic societies, especially the American, allow expectations to rise endlessly but cannot gratify them except materially. (And of course the fulfillment of material expectations is inherently unstable; they are also highly elastic especially when combined with the pursuit of social status.)

Thus Western intellectuals have increasingly become people with a chronically unappeased appetite for meaning, justice, and moral truths, constantly on the lookout for plausible belief systems but incapable of finding them, or adhering to them over long periods of time. This quest and its recurring frustration defines much of their outlook and smoldering discontent as they gravitate to and struggle with the role of the secular moralist, whatever their training and ways of making a living. Many of them also feel called upon to display public virtue on every possible occasion, or what George Will called, "conspicuous compassion" and an associated, somewhat idiosyncratic advocacy of selected victim groups.

By contrast, communist systems (not unlike traditional societies) may be characterized in part in Durkheims words as those in which "each in his sphere vaguely realizes the extreme limits set to his ambitions and aspires to nothing beyond. At least if he respects regulations and is docile to collective authority . . . he feels that it is not well to ask more."[6] This, at any rate, was the case until the recent upheavals and changes in several of them.

In communist societies economic and political deprivations prevail. Life is regimented, choices limited, state power is barely restrained, the authorities make sure that only one point of view can be publicly heard on matters political, cultural or ideological; intellectuals are either persecuted dissidents or party functionaries, or possibly apolitical specialists, but under no circumstances are they unfettered social critics. Survival requires either cynical role playing and pretense of loyalty, or abandoning the public realm altogether. Intellectuals are powerless, or the power they retain rests on official favor. But in these circumstances they expect little from the social order or the authorities, least of all that they make their lives meaningful or provide them with a sense of purpose; in fact their loss of freedom is the result of the determination of the authorities to structure life for the citizen, to provide him with approved community and force his behavior into the correct patterns.

Such differences between pluralistic and communist systems suggest that the quality of alienation (or estrangement) felt and displayed by intellectuals will also be different, as will other attributes of the two groups. These differences are likely to persist into the period when communist systems are being transformed into pluralistic ones as has been the case in Eastern Europe.

The observations regarding intellectuals in the East which follow have not been inspired by the latest developments in Eastern Europe (including the Soviet Union) but rather by seeking to grasp the more persistent historical elements in the characteristic situation of intellectuals in both types of societies and to explore the more stable patterns in the relationship they maintain between the private and public realm.

II

The social and political roles and characteristics of intellectuals in communist systems are far more sharply differentiated than those of their counterparts in the West. Intellectuals in communist societies may be divided into three distinct groups: (1) the "true intellectuals"—independent, critical, autonomous, nonconformist dissenters, such as Andrei Sakharov in the Soviet Union, Vaclav Havel in Czechoslovakia, Miklos Haraszti in Hungary, Milovan Djilas in Yugoslavia and their numerous imprisoned, exiled or unemployed collagues. (I am well aware of the changing fortunes or several of these figures); (2) functionary intellectuals—full-time party employees specializing in agit-prop activities broadly defined. They include full-time officials, journalists, educators, establishment writers, and social scientists dealing with ideas and social, cultural, political matters from the official point of view; (3) specialized highly skilled mental workers who are neither dissenters nor functionaries but apolitical experts, specialists (in the sciences, industry, planning).

The relationship between intellectuals and communist systems has a complicated and stormy history both in regard to intellectuals who have lived under such systems and those who "related" to them from a safe distance. The further away the intellectuals from communist systems, the more agreeable has been the relationship, the more benign the attitudes on both sides. By the same token, the longer the communist system has been in existence the more strained the relationship becomes between the system and the resident intellectuals.

Given the long-standing commitment of communist systems to the utilization of intellectuals for political ends, it is of great interest to ask what impact such systems and their policies have had on intellectuals and what influence, in turn, intellectuals may have had on these political systems and how they might effect—especially at this historical juncture—their possible transformation. Indeed, in the countries of Eastern Europe, no longer communist—Czechoslovakia, Hungary, Poland, etc.—intellectuals reentered politics dramatically, sometimes landing at the highest echelons of power like Vaclav Havel in Czechoslovakia and Arpad Goncz in Hungary, both of them writers and current presidents of the republic.

In the following my main focus is not the emerging, still fluid position of intellectuals in some of the former communist countries but the historic relationship that preceded the recent dramatic turn of events. What we may conclude about this relationship—and about the role of intellectuals in the persistence or change of communist states—depends in large measure on our understanding of who these intellectuals are. My own view of this matter (spelled out in earlier writings) is that intellectuals have been and should continue to be perceived primarily as

> social critics and value-formulating elites . . . both producers and interpreters of ideas, but ideas of a more general—social, cultural or political—nature. Intellectuals can be legitimizers or servants of the status quo, but more often than not, they are critics, especially when they have a choice. . . . They don't have much of a choice when the alternative to being a legitimizer is the certitude of punitive sanctions [imposed by the state] which may range from the loss of jobs to exile and imprisonment. When such risks are to be faced, one cannot expect intellectuals to embrace, in significant numbers, the social-critical role. . . . They are people who used to be called philosophers . . . they do what philosophers were supposed to do: reflect, mediate, or pontificate in private and public on a more or less full-time basis on the great issues of life and death, society and the individual, things timely and timeless.[7]

As already noted, it is only in relatively free and open societies, that is, in the West, that intellectuals can publicly identify themselves as social critics, or boast of being (respectable) "troublemakers." In societies where they get into trouble—if they try to make trouble—they take a more subdued attitude. By contract the recent death of

Abbie Hoffman unleashed torrents of celebratory obituaries in the United States which praised him precisely for being a "trouble-maker."[8] If so he managed to avoid *serious* trouble.

Part of the problem of the type of "troublemaking" Hoffman and many of his Western colleagues were engaged in was its frivolous character. It was rather appropriate that Hoffman entitled one of his books *Revolution for the Hell Of It*. In it he wrote, "Do what you want. . . . Extend your boundaries. Break the rules. Protest is anything you can get away with. . . . We are a gang of theatrical cheerleaders."[9] Perhaps when the costs of social criticism and protest are greater (as is the case in communist states) the causes are more carefully and seriously chosen: the prospect of real suffering deflates the propensity for clowning and "theatrical cheerleading"—one of the important differences between intellectuals as social critics in the West and East. It may be that the virtually unlimited freedom of criticism (in the West) tends to trivialize its pursuit and may have some impact on the behavior and possibly the character of those engaged in criticism under these conditions.

The character of the Western, and especially the American mass media further contributes to the phenomenon here emphasized: the trivialization of social criticism; it is the most bizarre and photogenic forms of criticism and protest that will attract the greatest amount of media attention which, in turn, often stimulates the type of "theatrical cheerleading" and clowning Hoffman excelled in. Of course another debatable matter is whether or not a person like Hoffman should be considered an intellectual. He certainly was a social critic and activist, but his credentials as an intellectual are open to question. He may best qualify for the category of the quasi-intellectual: a person with some post-secondary, higher education (in the humanities or social sciences), who is disposed to reject his society, and is ready to express (sometimes act upon) his critical impulses, but has modest intellectuals attainments, rarely making a living out of his preoccupation with ideas or special skills having to do with the use of ideas.

Another important difference between the social critical roles and motives of intellectuals in the West and East is that in the West, it seems, the major source of the protest and criticism and the underlying moral indignation, is a sensation the of emptiness or meaninglessness of life—a disposition alluded to earlier in connection with Durkheim's observations. Many Western social critics are troubled by the burdens of life in secular, consumer societies and continue to nurture dreams of "fundamental change," of "a future yet unrealized" as Norman Birnbaum had in his reassessment and reaffirmation of what he called the "spiritualizing politics" of the New Left of the 1960s.[10]

In the East intellectuals are less likely to complain of meaninglessness and do not expect society to make their life "meaningful"; they have become (with good reason) allergic to the attempts of political authorities to provide them with a sense of purpose. Unlike their American colleagues they are also far more likely to take for granted either the meaningfulness or meaninglessness of life and are less disposed to agonize over either possibility. They are more disposed to protest tangible grievances, observable injustices, indignities, and deprivations. Of course, Western intellectuals also protest such injustices, but I believe that they are more strongly driven by their anger and resentment toward a social system where anything goes and nothing matters (in the words, I believe, of Philip Roth) and which provides little sense of purpose or community. They also have more reason to bemoan the contrast between material wealth and comfort and spiritual deprivations and discomfort.

The observations of Czeslaw Milosz (made over three decades ago in his classic *The Captive Mind*) remain pertinent to this day: "Western intellectuals suffer from a special variety of taedium vitae. . . . Everything they think and feel evaporates like steam in an open expanse. Freedom is a burden to them. No conclusions they arrive at are binding."[11]

III

The literature on intellectuals in communist systems is not extensive. Presumably the relative scarcity of such writings is connected with the widespread assumption that there were hardly any "real" intellectuals left in such countries and those surviving could not function as intellectuals; they were forced to abandon what is central to the traditional conception of the intellectual, namely, autonomy and the critical role and were hardly encouraged to dissect the taken-for-granted verities of their society.

According to some social critics in the West, it is no less difficult for Western intellectuals to maintain their autonomy and have an impact on their societies. George Kennan wrote recently that the intelligentsia in the United States represented a stratum of society for whom "the dominant political forces of the country have little understanding or regard. Its voice is normally silenced or outshouted by the commercial media. It is probably condemned to remain indefinitely, like the Russian intelligentsia of the 19th century, a helpless spectator of the disturbing course of its nation's life."[12] (It is tempting to detect a personal note in these observations.)

As I see it, intellectuals have been highly influential in American public life during the past quarter century or more, and the "dominant political forces" paid a good deal of attention to them. I think Kennan's estimate of their (low) influence rests on his high expectation as to how much influence they should have.

Recent changes in communist societies require a more differentiated view of the role of intellectuals in such systems. Some of them have ceased to be communist altogether, others are in the process of changing while others remain rigidly intolerant of the free circulation of ideas. In one group, where public intellectual life has resumed and the freedom of expression is largely restored, we find the former Soviet bloc nations of Eastern Europe and Nicaragua; freedom of expression has also greatly expanded in the Soviet Union. On the other hand, such happy developments have failed to unfold in the rest of what might still be called the communist world: Albania, Angola, Cuba, Ethiopia, North Korea, and Vietnam. In China, a modest degree of free expression came to an end after the massacres, arrests, and executions of the summer of 1989.

"True intellectuals" of the earlier generations became largely extinct in communist states of long standing such as the Soviet Union. The ranks of intellectuals in communist systems have also been thinned out by emigration or exile. (Though their ranks seem to have been miraculously replenished Eastern Europe and the Soviet Union during the last decade). Intellectuals were mercilessly harassed and repressed in China under Mao; in Cuba they can still earn long prison sentences for possessing or circulating unauthorized manuscripts. ("A typical case" reported The *New York Times* recently, "is that of Ariel Hidalgo, given an eight-year sentence for 'enemy propaganda' after secret police found a personal manuscript in which he assailed what he saw as a new ruling class. He was first confined to a mental hospital, then jailed for a year in 'the rectangle of death,' the notorious punishment wing of the Havana prison. There he spent weeks naked in a bedless cell."[13] Cuban totalitarianism survives intact at the time of this writing (late 1990) and with it the continued repression of free expression and mistreatment of independent intellectuals.[14]

In Cambodia under Pol Pot the lethal persecution of intellectuals (or anybody suspected of being one) reached such grotesque extremes that people wearing eyeglasses (suggesting the experience of higher education) were in special danger. Ironically these policies were designed by a group of intellectuals—beneficiaries of university education in France—who were the leaders of the Khmer Rouge.

Historically speaking intellectuals in communist states had two basic choices. They could maintain a critical and independent position and face the attendant risks and threats (ranging from loss of life to loss of employment)—or they could abandon the intellectual's calling as earlier understood and offer their services to the Party. During the 1960s and 1970s in some communist countries intellectuals could opt for the (moderately) critical role without facing serious retribution; the authorities in Hungary, Poland and, to some extent the Soviet Union, allowed such intellectuals to maintain a precarious and marginal existence making a living from Western royalties or part-time jobs; or the nonconforming minority was permitted to eke out a meager existence from menial, laboring jobs as distinguished writers did in Czechoslovakia or dissident scientists (including those applying for an exit visa) in the Soviet Union, becoming janitors or laboratory technicians. In China during the Cultural Revolution the handling of manure was an activity especially favored by the authorities for those aspiring to the role of independent and critical intellectual (often even for those who did not have such aspirations). Since June 1989, intellectual life in China has once more become silenced—an example of the precariousness of such freedoms in countries lacking in the institutional safeguards of free expression.

For intellectuals less concerned with preserving their traditional attributes and roles and not anxious to take seemingly quixotic positions there was the other option: to become functionaries, mental technicians assisting the ruling Party and the State. According to L. G. Churchward writing in the early 1970s "most Soviet intellectuals . . . are prepared to work within the Communist political system, to observe its rules and to respect its restraints." He described "The basic role of the Soviet intelligentsia 'as providing' high-level specialists for all branches of human endeavor, including government and administration." Moreover, "Soviet intellectuals play an important role in the general process of political legitimation." In his opinion, "a clear distinction cannot be drawn between intellectuals and the apparatchiki."[15] He was obviously not talking about what Sidney Monas, following in the earlier tradition, defined as "a spiritual brotherhood bearing a special burden of conscience"[16] but rather of what I had referred to earlier as the "functionary intellectuals." For a small number of them the transformation from independent social critic into revolutionary activist and later into party functionary was voluntary. As Merle Goldman wrote, in China they "shared his [Mao's] committment to a Marxism-Leninism suffused with faith in the power of the will and the revolutionary consciousness to remold reality."[17] In Eastern Europe, according to Vladimir Tismaneanu, committed party-intellectuals "were perfectly equipped to understand the duplicity of the system and thus turn into its most ardent critics. At the same time they were emotionally involved in the adventure of power and could not find the resources to break with the mesmerising ideological totems."[18]

If one finds the political role of the functionary intellectual compatible with the original notion of what an intellectual is then it can be asserted that intellectuals played an important part in running communist states even in the days of Stalin and Mao. The functionary intellectuals provided indispensable services to these systems as planners, propagandists, educators, and media specialists.

It should be added that the categories proposed earlier are not immutable and impermeable; some intellectuals moved from the conforming-supporting role to the dissenting-critical one (or vice versa) as did for example George Lukacs and many of his lesser known compatriots. The formerly loyal (pro-regime) writers grouped around the weekly *Irodalmi Ujsaq* (*Literary Gazette*) in Hungary became the leading voices of political opposition before and during the 1956 Revolution. Early in their careers many of them were independent social critics (of the pre-communist society) who became supporters of the communist system in the late 1940s but in the end turned once more into dissenters no longer capable of rationalizing and tolerating the discrepancies between "theory and practice."

Most intellectuals in communist states belonged either to the functionary or the apolitical-expert category; the third group, the openly nonconformist, was usually small, given the risks and hardships associated with the display of critical attitudes.

IV

Throughout the 1980s in much of the Soviet empire the number of nonconformist intellectuals has greatly increased while that of the legitimizers has shrunk. Such changes reflected the greater official tolerance of nonconformity, associated with broader political-ideological shifts taking place as the will to and grip on power of the ruling elites in these countries weakened.

It is safe to say that while the political attitudes—and especially their overt expression—of intellectuals in communist countries is greatly influenced by prevailing political conditions, in the West these attitudes are more stable and firmly established. In Western societies most academic and literary intellectuals belong to or sympathize with some sort of an adversary culture or posture. Western intellectuals, especially those in the public eye, almost reflexively take an adversarial, critical position in the face of what they perceive to be the prevailing values, institutions, and injustices of their society. In the West, such a critical stance has been increasingly compatible with secure and well-paid employment, (mostly provided by universities), with opportunities for publishing, and otherwise disseminating publicly one's ideas.

Intellectuals in communist societies (both intact and transitional) also differ from their Western counterparts in that they are capable (with few exceptions) of engaging in social criticism without relying on a Marxist conceptual framework or some residual premise of Marxism; in fact, most of them have little use for Marxism of any variety, neither as a tool of social criticism and analysis, nor as a sustaining world view or secular religion, its most popular use as Leszek Kolakowski emphasized. What Raymond Aron used to call "the opium of intellectuals" in the West (and parts of the Third World) has failed to animate (or narcotize) intellectuals in communist societies including those officially engaged in the approved application, dissemination, or renovation of Marxism and Leninism. Nowhere has the disaffection with Marxism (both as a theory and discredited practice) been more profound than in the societies where it was used as a source of legitimacy and guide to social reconstruction.

To be sure the attractions of Marxism for many Western intellectuals have more to do with their unhappiness with modernity and capitalism than with the subtantive propositions of Marxism as a theory of society and history. The obligatory, somewhat romantic anti-capitalism of these Western intellectuals stands in contrast to the attraction, mild sympathy, or indifference (as the case may be) Eastern intellectuals evince toward capitalism. They did not develop the disposition to identify and confuse the ills of the modern world with capitalism, as have so many of their Western colleagues for whom capitalism has become a metaphor for the discontents of life in a secular world.

E. P. Thompson, the English historian and peace-movement leader personifies some of these attitudes. In his polemic with Kolakowski he insisted that no matter how bad socialist societies are, he was duty-bound to cling to his anticapitalism: "For no matter how hideous the alternative may seem [i.e., existing socialist systems] no word of mine will wittingly be added to the comforts of that old bitch . . . consumer capitalism. . . . I know that the beast [capitalism] is not changed: it is held in the fragile but well-tempered chains of our own watchfulness and actions."[19] In other words if capitalism has become less vicious though basically unchanged it is due to the vigilance and watchfulness of its critics—a curious overestimation of the power of ideas to come from even a latter-day Marxist.

Marxism in the remaining communist states survives only as official doctrine and fails to stimulate or motivate intellectuals—a state of affairs that was also characteristic of communist systems before their recent transformations. Moreover intellectuals in these countries—again, unlike their Western counterparts, were not determined to venerate the *ideals* of Marxian socialism while resolutely averting their eyes from the realities of existing socialist systems which have been using these ideals as alleged guideposts for their practices.

The remarks of a Hungarian writer Istvan Eorsi, on the "virtues" of "existing socialist systems" illustrate the outlook of Eastern intellectuals who have drawn lessons from witnessing the attempted implementation of these theories:

> "Existing" . . . is a very broad category that can provide loopholes for all sorts of things. It is for this reason that [George] Lukacs could maintain that the worst form of socialism is superior to the best form of capitalism because if socialism exists in any form then it is—from the standpoint of world history and the philosophy of history, from the standpoint of universal progress though not from that of the concrete, empirically existing individual—a higher level of development in the history of mankind. This worldview in the case of Lukacs too had its origin in the fact that the great philosopher, protecting his whole life, was reluctant to focus his great analytical powers on the question: what is it, after all that exists? Because undoubtedly something did exist in these countries and if we chose to call it "socialism" then in one jump we found ourselves at a higher rung of human evolution.[20]

While intellectuals in communist societies (no matter which of the three categories they belong to) do not care much about the ideas of Marx and Lenin they recognize that these political systems are deeply concerned with ideas and they allow intellectuals, under appropriate conditions of compliance, to occupy positions of power and influence. This state of affairs is directly linked to the major paradox in the relationship of intellectuals and communist systems, namely that such systems take ideas seriously and treat them like weapons (which is one reason why they attract many intellectuals at first.) Hence these states initially make good use of the support and skill of intellectuals, who are impressed by being taken seriously, but end up regimenting and repressing them, and depriving them of their distinctive intellectual calling, that of autonomous social critic and interpreter of ideas.

Thus on the one hand Marxist-Leninist systems place great emphasis on the role of ideas, on the other they take a highly instrumental and manipulative approach toward them.

In the final analysis the relationship between intellectuals and communist systems is determined by the fact that communist systems are both profoundly anti-intellectual and simultaneously preoccupied with ideas, obsessed with finding theoretical, ideological justification and legitimation for all their policies. Such an ambivalence about the importance of ideas (and intellectuals) derives from the basic action and power-orientation of these systems and movements. Ideas are worthless unless they help to attain political ends, unless they can be used in the struggle to gain and keep (and maximize) power. Hence Lenin's contempt for the typical Russian intellectuals, perceived as unfocused talkers incapable of politically productive action; and hence his determination to build a party of professional revolutionaries, composed of newly toughened intellectuals who were to provide a disciplined vanguard and leadership.

Comprehensive censorship, the thorough refashioning of educational institutions, state monopoly over the media of mass communication and open insistence on at least overt ideological conformity of the entire population—these were the major institutional expressions of the official concern with ideas in "existing socialist systems."

V

The role of intellectuals in communist systems thus used to rest on the importance these systems assigned to ideas. Although ideas were highly rated tools of control, legitimation, and guidance, the longer these systems were in power the less dynamic they became even as manipulators of ideas. It appears that the political use of ideas in communist states declines over time and with it the part played by the functionary intellectuals.

There are at least two reasons for this development. One is the unwitting immunization of the population against the official ideas and ideologies, the pervasive boredom, and reflexive rejection their endless repetition elicits. Another reason is the corresponding recognition on the part of the authorities that the compulsive regurgitation of ideas plays a decreasing role in inspiring and mobilizing the population and in legitimizing the political order which often demonstrated its staying power by crushing outbreaks of dissatisfaction. It also seems that in the final analysis not even the ruling elites find much inspiration or practical guidance in the doctrinal heritage except perhaps a residual assurance that they should stay in power, no matter what.

Vaclav Havel's comments on this state of affairs in Czechoslovakia (before the changes of 1989) apply to other established communist systems as well which endured for decades and some that still exist:

Seldom in recent times has a regime cared so little for the real attitudes of out-wardly loyal citizens or for the sincerity of their statements. . . . No one tries to convince the penitent that he was in error or acted wrongly, but simply . . . that he must repent in order to save himself. . . . Think what you like in private, as long as you agree in public . . . suppress your interest in truth and silence your conscience—and the doors will be wide open to you. . . .

The contrast between the revolutionary teachings about the new man and the new morality and the shoddy concept of life as consumer bliss raises the question of why the authorities actually cling so frantically to their ideology. Clearly, only be-cause their ideology . . . assures them the appearance of legitimacy, continuity, and consistency, and acts as a screen of prestige for their pragmatic practice. . . . From the bowels of that infinite mountain of ideological rhetoric . . . which . . . the public, for the most part, scarcely notices, there emerges one specific and meaningful message, one realistic piece of advice: "Avoid politics if you can; leave it to us! Just do what we tell you, don't try to have deep thoughts, and don't poke your nose into things that don't concern you! Shut up, do your work, look after yourself—and you will be all right!"[21]

This passage describes the communist version of "repressive toler-ance," a concept which—while not helpful for grasping the character of Western societies (where its originator, Herbert Marcuse intended it to apply)—has come to provide a measure of understanding of the policies some communist systems have followed in recent times.

VI

Could intellectuals make a substantial and enduring contribution to the transformation of communist systems? In some they already have. In others, harshly repressive states such as Cuba, Ethiopia, North Korea or post-Tiananmen Square China, such possibilities are extremely limited; there are few known dissenters at liberty to or-ganize or make their views publicly known.

The case of Eastern Europe shows that in more permissive com-munist systems where they could engage in some public criticism and organization—as for instance in pre-1989 Poland and Hungary—intel-lectuals can promote change by gradually undermining the legitimacy of these governments and articulating widely felt discontents. It is likely that they contributed to the decline of self-assurance and the grip on power of the rulers who were not altogether indifferent to their opinions. While nonconformist intellectuals came to be deeply involved with the recent transformation of communist societies, earlier on such intellectuals had little or limited visibility and support among the working classes as Aleksa Djilas among other, observed.[22] In the Soviet Union in particular they were regarded with apprehension not only by the authorities but also many of their fellow citizens who feared change, any change, and who may still be hostile or ambivalent toward intellectuals. The latter certainly benefitted more from glasnost than the masses had, and both are still awaiting the fruits of perestroika.

Whether or not they become eventually a significant force for change, life under communism is a formative and traumatic experience for intellectuals. Many do not survive it, either as intellectuals or otherwise. Harsh as it is for nonconforming intellectuals to live under communist systems, the experience confers upon them some unforeseen and unintended blessings. If for some it was corrupting, for others it is purifying; above all, the experience discourages self-indulgence and the mistaking of personal problems for collective grievances. Living with genuine threats to one's life, freedom, or material well-being is quite different from living in seamless political security and material well-being in a society that fails to make one's life meaningful—as is the case of most Western intellectuals. Living in the proximity of genuine dangers, such as those noted above, is also different from contemplating such dangers from a distance and sympathizing with those, again, from a distance, upon whom such disasters may befall.

If many intellectuals in the East chose to abandon the intellectual calling by working for the authorities, they did so under severe and genuine pressure. By contract, many of their Western counterparts in recent times embraced, without any such pressure, obscurantist ideologies and assorted authoritarian movements and even rationalized infringements on free speech on behalf of what they regarded higher values. They had done so gratuitously and spontaneously, as a matter of poor judgment, misplaced idealism, submission to political-intellectual fads or in the wrongheaded pursuit of some new personal or group identity. (Identity problems are a burden Eastern intellectuals do not carry, unlike many of their American counterparts.)

For the truly critical intellectuals living under communism, the "escape from freedom" and the numerous varieties of anti-intellectualism which has swept Western intellectual and academic life since the 1960s held no attraction. They could not imagine, for example, how the word "Western" or "Eurocentric" could become a pejorative term, or why the classics and major ideas of Western culture and civilization should be treated with suspicion or contempt as they are by many academic intellectuals in the United States today who champion "multicultural studies" and seek to reduce what they consider the pernicious influence of Western culture. Intellectuals in the East, and especially Eastern Europe and the Soviet Union, aspire to become fully integrated into Europe, (by which they mean Western Europe) and to reclaim their Western cultural heritage. For them "the West" and "Western" are words with a radiantly positive content, often approached with reverence. Intellectuals in communist systems, whichever their incarnation, never shared the enthusiasm of their Western colleagues for the Third World, or rather, the myth of the Third World.

For all these reasons it may be that intellectuals in the East will be in a better position to appreciate and offer a new home for the Western ideals of liberalism, which for many of their Western colleagues have become stale and uninspiring. I am of course referring to the older ideals of liberalism and not to the post-1960 varieties of left-of-center liberalism which increasingly replaced the earlier version in the West, and especially in the United States, where ideas traditionally associated with liberalism have undergone considerable change. Liberalism, as Edward Shils among others noted, has become increasingly "collectivist" unlike its original version which stressed individual rights, limited state intervention, and negative freedoms. Adversarial intellectuals in the West invested liberalism with a new meaning: a left-of-center world view that favors social engineering, a greater redistributive role by the state, and sympathy for selected victim groups. This liberalism is compatible with collective guilt and the associated reverse discrimination to compensate for past injustices. Often it has been accompanied by an attitude of giving every benefit of the doubt to Third World dictatorships which employed an egalitarian, progressive rhetoric.

Anthony Hartley, an English writer noted the contrasting attitudes toward liberalism between Western and Eastern intellectuals:

In the West what is called "liberalism" has too often been associated with the soul-searchings and indecision of a cultured elite. A lack of self-confidence, the inability to say boo to the goose—these are patterns of behavior that the word 'liberal' brings to mind. In Eastern Europe things are different. Those who have fought for the more robust liberalism of Mill and Tocqueville have said boo to kites and vultures . . . we take them seriously. Can we expect from Eastern Europe a renewal of political sincerity that will find its echo in the West?[23]

It would be somewhat ironic if intellectuals in communist societies (or what used to be communist societies) would end up not only as the loyal guardians of Western political values and cultural traditions but also in a better position than their Western colleagues to influence constructively public affairs in their societies. To be sure, such contributions may be hindered by the long-standing exclusion from power and effective participation in politics.

Most importantly intellectuals in communist and formerly communist states have fewer illusions about the perfectibility of the social world and human beings than their Western counterparts; they are also freer of an oppressive sense of meaninglessness that often translates into the current forms of political alienation in the West and they are less likely to confuse and conflate the personal and the social realm. Above all, intellectuals in the East are immune to the seductions of political utopias and the temptations of secular religion; this may enable them to pursue an attainable agenda of human improvement and liberation, something that no longer animates many of their Western counterparts.

Notes

1. Paul Johnson, *Intellectuals*, New York: Harper and Row, 1988.
2. Emile Durkheim, *Suicide*, New York: Free Press, 1951, pp. 252–53.
3. Quoted in Steven Lukes, *Essays in Social Theory*, New York: Columbia University Press, 1977, p. 80.
4. Lukes, op. cit., pp. 83, 88.
5. Tom Wolfe, *Mauve Gloves and Madmen, Clutter and Vine*, New York: Bantam, 1977, pp. 111–47.
6. Durkheim, op. cit., pp. 250, 254.
7. Paul Hollander, "American Intellectuals: Producers and Consumers of Social Criticism," In Alain G. Gagnon. *Intellectuals in Liberal Democracies*, New York: Prager, 1987, pp. 68–69.
8. Sidney Schanberg. "Cousin Reveals Portrait of Abbie Hoffman," [Times-Post News Service], *Daily Hampshire Gazette*, 21 April, 1989.

9. Abbie Hoffman, *Revolution for the Hell Of It*, New York: Dial Press, 1968, p. 157.
10. Norman Birnbaum, "Hope's End or Hope's Beginning? 1968—And After." *Salmagundi*, Winter, 1989, pp. 150, 152.
11. Czeslaw Milosz, *The Captive Mind*, New York: Vintage Books, 1955, p. 75.
12. George Kennan, "Sketches from a Life," *Atlantic Monthly*, April 1989, p. 62.
13. Editorial, *New York Times*, 4 April, 1988.
14. For an up to date summary see *Human Rights in Cuba: Special Report*, Washington DC: Cuban American Foundation, 1990, pp. 36.
15. L.G. Churchward, *The Soviet Intelligentsia*, London: Routledge, 1973, pp. 128, 90, 105, 123.
16. Quoted in Churchward, op. cit., p. 135.
17. Merle Goldman, *China's Intellectuals: Advise and Dissent*, Cambridge: Harvard University Press, 1981. p. 2.
18. Vladimir Tismaneanu, *The Poverty of Utopia: The Crisis of Marxist Ideology in Eastern Europe*, London: Routledge, 1988, p. 111–112.
19. E. P. Thompson, *The Poverty of Theory and Other Essays*, New York: Monthly Review Press, 1978, p. 392.
20. Istvan Eorsi, "Urugyeim" (My pretexts), *Beszelo*, Budapest, no. 12., 1985.
21. Vaclav Havel, "Letter to Dr. Gustav Husak," In J. Vladislav, ed., *Vaclav Havel or Living In Truth*, London: Faber, 1987, pp. 8–9, 14.
22. Aleksa Djilas, "Yugoslav Dissent and the Future of Communism," Paper presented at the Conference on the Future of Communist States, New York, October 1987.
23. Anthony Hartley, "Between East and West," *Encounter*, February 1989, p. 77.

Index